The Twentieth Century American

Being a Comparative Study of the Peoples
of the Two Great Anglo-Saxon Nations

Harry Perry Robinson

Alpha Editions

This edition published in 2024

ISBN : 9789362513960

Design and Setting By
Alpha Editions
www.alphaedis.com
Email - info@alphaedis.com

As per information held with us this book is in Public Domain.
This book is a reproduction of an important historical work. Alpha Editions uses the best technology to reproduce historical work in the same manner it was first published to preserve its original nature. Any marks or number seen are left intentionally to preserve its true form.

Contents

PREFATORY NOTE .... - 1 -
THE TWENTIETH CENTURY AMERICAN .... - 2 -
CHAPTER I .... - 4 -
CHAPTER II .... - 22 -
CHAPTER III .... - 37 -
CHAPTER IV .... - 58 -
CHAPTER V .... - 68 -
CHAPTER VI .... - 88 -
CHAPTER VII .... - 101 -
CHAPTER VIII .... - 116 -
CHAPTER IX .... - 136 -
CHAPTER X .... - 156 -
CHAPTER XI .... - 170 -
CHAPTER XII .... - 183 -
CHAPTER XIII .... - 206 -
CHAPTER XIV .... - 220 -
CHAPTER XV .... - 241 -
CHAPTER XVI .... - 253 -
APPENDIX .... - 266 -

PREFATORY NOTE

There are already many books about America; but the majority of these have been written by Englishmen after so brief an acquaintance with the country that it is doubtful whether they contribute much to English knowledge of the subject.

My reason for adding another volume to the list is the hope of being able to do something to promote a better understanding between the peoples, having as an excuse the fact that I have lived in the United States for nearly twenty years, under conditions which have given rather exceptional opportunities of intimacy with the people of various parts of the country socially, in business, and in politics. Wherever my judgment is wrong it is not from lack of abundant chance to learn the truth.

Except in one instance—very early in the book—I have avoided the use of statistics, in spite of frequent temptation to refer to them to fortify arguments which must without them appear to be merely the expression of an individual opinion.

H. P. R.

February, 1908.

THE TWENTIETH CENTURY AMERICAN

"If I can say anything to show that my name is really Makepeace, and to increase the source of love between the two countries, then please, God, I will."—W. M. Thackeray, in Letters to an American Family.

"Certainly there is nothing like England, and there never has been anything like England in the world. Her wonderful history, her wonderful literature, her beautiful architecture, the historic and poetic associations which cluster about every street and river and mountain and valley, her vigorous life, the sweetness and beauty of her women, the superb manhood of her men, her Navy, her gracious hospitality, and her lofty pride—although some single race of men may have excelled her in some single particular—make up a combination never equalled in the world."—The late United States Senator Hoar, in An Autobiography of Seventy Years.

"The result of the organisation of the American colonies into a state, and of the bringing together of the diverse communities contained in these colonies, was the creation not merely of a new nation, but of a new temperament. How far this temperament was to arise from a change of climate, and how far from a new political organisation, no one could then foresee, nor is its origin yet fully analysed; but the fact itself is now coming to be more and more recognised. It may be that Nature said at about that time: 'Thus far the English is my best race; but we have had Englishmen enough; now for another turning of the globe, and for a further novelty. We need something with a little more buoyancy than the Englishman; let us lighten the structure, even at some peril in the process. Put in one drop more of nervous fluid and make the American.' With that drop, a new range of promise opened on the human race, and a lighter, finer, more highly organised type of mankind was born."—Thomas Wentworth Higginson, Atlantic Monthly, 1886.

"The foreign observer in America is at once struck by the fact that the average of intelligence, as that intelligence manifests itself in the spirit of inquiry, in the interest taken in a great variety of things, and in alertness of judgment, is much higher among the masses in the United States than anywhere else. This is certainly not owing to any superiority of the public school system in this country—or, if such superiority exists, not to that alone—but rather to the fact that in the United States the individual is constantly brought into interested contact with a greater variety of things and is admitted to active participation in the exercise of functions which in other countries are left to the care of a superior authority. I have frequently been struck by the remarkable expansion of the horizon effected by a few years of American life, in the minds of immigrants who had come from somewhat benighted regions, and by the mental enterprise and keen discernment with which they took hold of problems to which, in their comparatively torpid condition in their native countries, they had never given thought. It is true that in the large cities with congested population, self-government as an educator does not always bring the most desirable results, partly owing to the circumstance that government, in its various branches, is there further removed from the individual, so that he comes into contact with it and exercises his influence upon it only through various, and sometimes questionable, intermediary agencies which frequently exert a very demoralising influence."—Carl Schurz's Memoirs, II, 79.

"Anglo-Saxon Superiority! Although we do not all acknowledge it, we all have to bear it, and we all dread it; the apprehension, the suspicion, and sometimes the hatred provoked by l'Anglais proclaim the fact loudly enough. We cannot go one step in the world without coming across the Anglo-Saxon.... He rules America by Canada and the United States; Africa by Egypt and the Cape; Asia by India and Burmah; Australasia by Australia and New Zealand; Europe and the whole world, by his trade and industries and by his policy."—M. Edmond Demolins in Anglo-Saxon Superiority "À quoi tient la Supériorité des Anglo-Saxons?"

"It may be asking too much, but if statesmanship could kindly arrange it, I confess I should like to see, before I die, a war in which Britain and the United States in a just quarrel might tackle the world. After that we should have no more difficulty about America. For if the Americans never forget an injury, they ever remember a service."—The late G. W. Steevens in The Land of the Dollar.

CHAPTER I

AN ANGLO-AMERICAN ALLIANCE

The Avoidance of Entangling Alliances—What the Injunction Meant—What it Cannot Mean To-day—The Interests of the United States, no less than those of England, Demand an Alliance—But Larger Interests than those of the Two Peoples are Involved—American Responsiveness to Ideals—The Greatest Ideal of All, Universal Peace: the Practicability of its Attainment—America's Responsibility—Misconceptions of the British Empire—Germany's Position—American Susceptibilities.

The American nation, for all that it is young and lacks reverence, still worships the maxims and rules of conduct laid down by the Fathers of the Republic; and among those rules of conduct, there is none the wisdom of which is more generally accepted by the people than that which enjoins the avoidance of "entangling alliances" with foreign Powers. But not only has the United States changed much in late years, but the world in its political relations and sentiments has changed also and the place of the United States has changed in it. That sacred instrument, the Constitution itself, holds chiefly by virtue of what is new in it. Whatever is unaltered, or is not interpreted in a sense quite other than the framers intended, is to-day comparatively unimportant. It must be so. It would be impossible that any code or constitution drawn up to meet the needs of the original States, in the phase of civilisation and amid the social conditions which then prevailed, could be suited to the national life of a Great Power in the twentieth century. In internal affairs, there is hardly a function of Government, scarcely a relation between the different branches of the Government itself, or between the Government and any of the several States, or between the Government and the people, which is not unlike what the framers of the Constitution intended or what they imagined that it would be.

But it is in external affairs that the nation must find, indeed has found, the old rules most inadequate. The policy of non-association which was desirable, even essential, to the young, weak state, whose only prospect of safety lay in a preservation of that isolation which her geographical position made possible to her, is and must be impracticable in a World-Power. Within the last decade, the United States has stepped out from her solitude to take the place which rightfully belongs to her among the great peoples. By the acquirement of her colonial dependencies, still more by the inevitable exigencies of her commerce, she has chosen (as she had no other choice) to make herself an interested party in the affairs of all parts of the world. All the conditions that made the old policy best for her have vanished.

A child is rightly forbidden by his nurse to make acquaintance with other children in the street; but this child has grown to manhood and gone out into the world to seek—and has found—his fortune. The old policy of isolation has been cast aside, till nothing remains of it but a few old formulæ which have no virtue—not even significance—now that all the conditions to which they applied are gone. The United States has been compelled to make alliances (some, as when she co-operated with the other Powers in China, of the most "entangling" kind), and still the old phrase holds its spell on the popular mind.

The injunction was originally intended to prevent the young Republic from being drawn into the wars with which Europe at the time was rent, by taking sides with any one party against any other. It was levelled not against alliances, but against entanglements. It was framed, and wisely framed, to secure to the United States the peace and isolation necessary to her development. The isolation is no longer either possible or desirable, but peace remains both. The nation would in fact be living more closely up to the spirit of the injunction by entering into an alliance which would secure peace and make entanglements impossible, than she is when she leaves herself and the world exposed to the constant menace of war, merely for the sake of seeming to comply with the letter of a maxim which is now meaningless. If Washington were alive to-day, it does not seem to me possible to doubt that he would favour a new English treaty, even though he might have more difficulty in compelling Congress to accept his views than he had once before.

As the case stands, the United States may easily become involved in war with any one of the Great Powers, no matter how pacific or benevolent her intentions may be. There are at least three Powers with which a trivial incident might precipitate a conflict at almost any time; while the possibilities of friction which might develop into open hostilities with some one of the lesser states are almost innumerable. It is beside the question to say that the United States need have no fear of the result: indeed that very fact contributes largely to the danger. It is ever the man who can fight, and knows it, who gets into trouble. Every American who has lived much in the farther West knows that he who would keep clear of difficulties had best not carry a revolver. In its very self-confidence—a self-confidence amply justified by its strength—the American people is, measured by the standards of other nations, an eminently bellicose people—much more bellicose than it supposes.

Great Britain's alliance with Japan has with reasonable certainty, so far as danger of conflict between any two of the Great Powers is concerned, secured the peace of Asia for some time to come. The understanding between Great Britain and France goes some way towards assuring the peace of Europe, of which the imminent *rapprochement* with Russia (which all thinking Englishmen desire[8-1]) will constitute a further guarantee. But an alliance between Great Britain and the United States would secure the peace of the world. There is but one European Power now which could embark on a war with either Great Britain or the United States with any shadow of justification for hopefulness as to the result; and no combination of Powers could deceive itself into believing that it could make head against the two combined or would dare to disturb the peace between themselves when the two allies bade them be still.

In the days of her youth,—which lasted up to the closing decade of the nineteenth century,—provided that she did not thrust herself needlessly into the quarrels of Europe, her mere geographical position sufficed to secure to America the peace which she required. The Atlantic Ocean, her own mountain chains and wildernesses, these were bulwarks enough. She has, by pressure of her own destiny, been compelled to come out from behind these safeguards to rub shoulders every day with all the world. If she still desires peace, she will be more likely to realise that desire by seeking other shields. Nor must any American reader misunderstand me, for I believe that I estimate the fighting power of the United States more highly than most native-born Americans. She needs no help in playing her part in the world; but no amount of self-confidence, no ability to fight, if once the fight be on, will serve to protect her from having quarrels thrust upon her—not necessarily in wilfulness by any individual antagonist but by mere force of circumstance. Considered from the standpoint of her own expediency, an alliance with Great Britain would give to the United States an absolute guarantee that for as many years as she pleased she would be free to devote all her energies to the development of her own resources and the increase of her commerce.

But there are other considerations far larger than that of her own expediency. This is no question of the selfish interests either of the United States or of Great Britain. There is no people more responsive than the American to high ideals. Englishmen often find it hard to believe that an American is not talking mere fustian when he gives honest expression to his sentiments; but from the foundation of the Republic certain large ideas—Liberty, Freedom of Conscience, Equality—have somehow been made to seem very real things to the American mind. Whether the Englishman does not in his heart prize just as dearly as the American the things which these words signify, is another matter; it is not the Englishman's habit to formulate them even to himself, much less to talk about them to others. Most Englishmen have large sympathy with Captain Gamble who, bewailing the unrest in Canada at the outbreak of the Revolutionary War, complained that the Colonials talked too much about "that damned absurd word Liberty."[10-1]

It is rarely that an English political campaign is fought for a principle or for an abstract idea, and equally rarely that in America the watchword on one side or the other is not some such high-sounding phrase as Englishmen rather shrink from using. It is true that behind that phrase may be clustered a cowering crowd of petty individual interests; the fact remains that it is the phrase itself—the large Idea—on which orators and party managers rely to secure their hold on the imaginations of the mass of the people. It does not necessarily imply any superior morality on the part of the Americans; but is an accident of the different conditions prevailing in the two countries.

British politics are infinitely more complex than American, and foreign affairs play a much larger part in public controversies. The people of the United States have been throughout their history able to confine their attention almost wholly to their home affairs, and in those home affairs, the mere vastness of the country, with the diverse and conflicting interests of the various parts, has made it as a rule impossible to frame any appeal to the minds of the voters as a whole except in terms of some abstract idea. An appeal to the self-interests of the people in the aggregate in any matter of domestic policy is almost unformulable, because the interest of each section conflicts with the interest of others; whence it has necessarily followed that the American people has grown accustomed to be led by large phrases—disciplined to follow the flag of an ideal.

Not all the early colonists who emigrated, even to New England, went solely for conscience' sake. Under the cloak of the lofty principle for which the Revolutionary War was fought there were, again, concealed all manner of personal ambitions, sectional jealousies, and partisan intrigues. It was in truth (as more than one American historian has pointed out) a party strife and not a war of peoples. The precipitating cause of the Civil War was not the desire to abolish slavery, but the bitterness aroused by the political considerations of the advantage given to one party or the other by the establishment or non-establishment of slavery in a new territory. The motive which impelled the United States to make war on Spain was not, as most Europeans believe, any desire for an extension of territory, any more than it was, as some Americans would say, a yearning to avenge the blowing up of the *Maine*; it was the necessity of putting an end to the disturbed state of affairs in Cuba, which was a constant source of annoyance, as well as of trouble and expense, to the United States Government. If a neighbour makes a disturbance before your house and brings his family quarrels to your doorstep, you must after a time ask him to stop; and when, after a sufficient number of askings, he fails to comply with your request, it is justifiable to use force to make him. That was America's justification—the real ground on which she went to war with Spain. But the thing which actually inflamed the mind of the American people was the belief that the Spanish treatment of Cuba was brutal and barbarous. It was an indignation no less fine than that which set England in a blaze in the days of the Bulgarian atrocities. The war may been a war of expediency on the part of the Government; it was a Crusade in the eyes of the people. Thus it may be easy to show that at each crisis in its history there was something besides the nobility of a Cause or the grandeur of a Principle which impelled the American nation on the course which it took, but it has always been love of the Cause or devotion to the Principle which has swayed the masses of the people.

And this people now has it in its power to do an infinitely finer thing than ever it did when it established Liberty of Conscience, or founded a republic on broader foundations than had been laid before, or abolished slavery within its borders, or when it won Cuba's independence of what it believed to be an inhuman tyranny. I believe that it has it in its power to do no less a thing than to abolish war for ever—to give to the peoples of the earth the blessing of Perpetual Peace. The question for it to ask itself is whether it can, with any shadow of justification, refuse to take this step and withhold this boon from humanity.

If it does refuse and wars continue—if, within the coming decade, war should break out, whether actually involving the United States itself or not, more bloody and destructive than any that the world has seen—and if then the facts should be presented to posterity for judgment,—will the American people be held guiltless? It is improbable that the case ever could be so presented, for there is none to put the United States on trial, none to draw an indictment, none to prosecute. The world has not turned to the United States to ask that it be saved; no one has arisen to point at the United States and say, "Thou art the one to do this thing." The historians of another generation will have no depositions before them on which to base a verdict. But if the facts are as stated and the United States knows them to be so, does the lack of common knowledge of them make her responsibility any the less? It remains that the nation has the power to do this, and it alone among nations.

The first idea of most Americans, when a hard and fast alliance with Great Britain is suggested to them, usually formulates itself in the statement that they have no wish to be made into a cat's-paw for pulling England's chestnuts out of the fire. America has no desire to be drawn into England's quarrels. Until less than ten years ago, there was justification for the point of view; for while England seemed to be ever on the brink of war, the United States lived peacefully in her far-off Valley of Avilion. But the map of the world has changed, and while the United States has left her seclusion and come out to play her part in the world-politics, England has been buttressing herself with friendships, until it is at least arguable whether the United States is not the more exposed to danger of the two. But it is no question now of being dragged into other people's quarrels; but of making all quarrelling impossible.

Again, the American will say that the United States needs no allies. She can hold her own; let Great Britain do the same. And again I say that it is no question now of whether either Power can hold its own against the world or not. Great Britain, Americans should understand, has no more fear for herself than has the United States. England "does not seek alliances: she grants them." There is not only no single European Power, but there is no probable combination of European Powers, which England does not in her heart serenely believe herself quite competent to deal with. British pride has grown no less in the last three hundred years:

"Come the four corners of the World in armsAnd we shall shock them."

Americans should disabuse themselves finally of the idea that if England desires an alliance with the United States it is because she has any fear that she may need help against any other enemy. Englishmen are too well satisfied with themselves for that (with precisely the same kind of self-satisfaction as the United States suffers from), and much too confident that, in whatever may arise, it will be the other fellow who will need help. But if England has no misgiving as to her ability to take care of herself when trouble comes, she is far from being ashamed to say that she would infinitely prefer that trouble should not come, either to her or to another, and she would join—oh, so gladly!—with the United States (as for a partial attainment of the same end she has already joined with France on the one hand and with Japan on the other) to make sure that it should never come. Has the United States any right to refuse to enter into such an alliance—an alliance which would not be entangling, but which would make entanglements impossible?

At Christmas time in 1906, the following suggestion was made in the London correspondence of an American paper[15:1]:

"The new ideals which mankind has set before itself, the infinitely larger enlightenment and education of the masses, the desperate struggle which every civilised people is waging against all forms of social suffering and vice within itself, the mere complexity of modern commerce with its all-absorbing interest—these things all cry aloud for peace. War does not belong to this phase of civilisation. Least of all can it have any appeal to the two peoples in whom the spirit of the Twentieth Century is most manifest. Of all peoples, Great Britain and the United States have most cause to desire peace.

"There should be a Christmas message sent from the White House which should run something like this:

> "To His Majesty King Edward the Seventh:
>
> "To your majesty, to her majesty the Queen, and to the people of the British empire, I desire to express the best wishes of myself and of the people of the United States. At the same time, I wish to assure your majesty that you will have both the sympathy and the practical support of the American people in such action as it may seem right to you and to the British people to take in the direction of securing to the nations of the world that peace of which your majesty has always shown yourself so earnest an advocate.
>
> "(Signed), Theodore Roosevelt.
>
> "Some such an answer as this would be returned:
>
> "To His Excellency the President of the United States:
>
> "In acknowledging with gratitude the expression of good wishes to ourselves, to her majesty the Queen, and to the people of the British empire of yourself and the population of the United States, I desire most cordially to reciprocate the sentiments of good will. Even more cordially and gratefully, I acknowledge the assurance of sympathy and support of the great American people in action directed to securing peace to the nations of the world. It will be my immediate care to propose such a course of joint action between us as may secure that blessing to all peoples in the course of the coming year.
>
> "(Signed), Edward.
>
> "Does anybody doubt that, if the two nations bent themselves to the task in earnest, universal peace could be so secured to all the peoples of the earth in the course of the coming year? And if it is in truth in their power to do this thing, how can either conceivably convince itself that it is not its duty?
>
> "And what a Christmas the world would have in 1907!"

Does any one doubt it? Does any one doubt that, if the two peoples were in earnest, though the thing might not be brought about in one year, it is far from improbable that it could be achieved in two years or three? Since the paragraphs which I have quoted were published, a year has passed and for a large part of that year the Conference has been in session at The Hague; and of the results of that Conference it is not easy for either an Englishman or an American to speak with patience. Does any one doubt that if the two Governments had set themselves determinedly, from the beginning of the *pourparlers*, to reach the one definite goal those results might have been very different?

During the last few years, the two Powers, each acting in her own way, have done more to establish peace on earth than has been done by all the other Powers in all time; and I most earnestly believe that it only needs that they should say with one voice that there shall be no more wars and there will be none. Nor am I ignoring the complexities of the situation; but I believe that all the details, the first step once taken, would settle themselves with unexpected facility through the medium of international tribunals. Of course this will be called visionary: but whosoever is tempted so to call it, let him read history in the records of contemporary writers and see how visionary all great forward movements in the progress of the world have seemed until the time came when the thing was to be accomplished. What we are now discussing seems visionary because of its unfamiliarity. It has the formidableness of the unknown. The impossible, once accomplished, looks simple enough in retrospect. The fact is that never before has there been a time when boundaries all over the world have been so nearly established—when there were so few points outstanding likely to embroil any two of the Great Powers in conflict—so few national ambitions struggling for appeasement. It is easy not to realise this unless one studies the field in detail: easy to fail to see how near is the attainment of universal peace.

The Councils of the Powers have in the past been so hampered by the traditions of a tortuous diplomacy, so tossed and perturbed within by the cross-currents of intrigue, that they have shown themselves almost childishly incapable of arriving at clear-cut decisions. Old policies, old formulæ, old jealousies, old dynastic influences still hold control of the majority of the chancelleries of Continental Europe, and these things it is that have made questions simple in themselves seem complex and incapable of solution. But there is nothing to be settled involving larger territorial interests or more beset with delicacies than many questions with which the Supreme Court of the United States has had to deal—none so large as to seem formidable to his Majesty's Privy Council or to the House of Lords. And under the guidance of Great Britain and the United States acting in unison, assured in advance of the sympathy of France and Japan and of whatever other Powers would welcome the new order of things, a Hague committee or other international tribunal could be made a businesslike organisation working directly for results,—as directly as the board of directors of any commercial corporation. And it is with those who consider this impracticable that the onus lies of pointing out the direction from which insuperable resistance is to be expected,—from which particular Powers in Europe, in Asia, or in Central or South America.

The ultimate domination of the world by the Anglo-Saxon (let us call him so) seems to be reasonably assured; and no less assured is it that at some time wars will cease. The question for both Englishmen and Americans to ask themselves is whether, recognising the responsibility that already rests upon it, the Anglo-Saxon race dare or can for conscience' sake—or still more, whether one branch of it when the other be willing to push on, dare or can for conscience' sake—hang back and postpone the advent of the Universal Peace, which it is in its power to bring about to-day, no matter what the motives of jealousy, of self-interest, or of self-distrust may be that restrain it.

It has been assumed in all that has been said that the onus of refusal rests solely on the United States; as indeed it does. Great Britain, it will be objected, has asked for no alliance. Nor has she. Great Britain does not put herself in the position of suing for a friendship which may be denied; and is there any doubt that if Great Britain had at any time asked openly for such an alliance she would have been refused? Would she not be bluntly refused to-day? Great men on either side—but never, be it noted, an Englishman except for the purpose of agreeing with an American who has already spoken—have said many times that a formal alliance is not desirable: that things are going well enough as they are and that it is best to wait. Things are never going well enough, so long as they might go better. And these men who say it speak only with an eye to the interests of the two countries, not considering the greater stake of the happiness of the world at large; and even so (I say it with deference) they know in their own minds that if indeed the thing should become suddenly feasible, neither they nor any thinking man, with the good of humanity at heart, would dare to raise a voice against it or would dream of doing other than rejoice. It is only because it has seemed impossible that it has been best to do without it; and it is impossible only because the people of the United States have not yet realised the responsibilities of the new position which they hold in the councils of the world, but are still bound by the prejudices of the days of little things, still slaves—they of all people!—to an old and outworn formula. They have not yet comprehended that within their arm's reach there lies an achievement greater than has ever been given to a nation to accomplish, and that they have but to take one step forward to enter on a destiny greater than anything foreshadowed even in the promise of their own wonderful history.

And when those who would be their coadjutors are willing and waiting and beckoning them on, have they any right to hold back? Is it anything other than moral cowardice if they do?

I wish that each individual American would give one hour's unprejudiced study to the British Empire,—would sit down with a map of the world before him and, summoning to his assistance such knowledge of history as he has and bearing in mind the conditions of his own country, endeavour to arrive at some idea of what it is that Englishmen have done in the world, what are the present circumstances of the Empire, what its aims and ambitions. I do not think that the ordinarily educated and intelligent American knows how ignorant he is of the nation which has played so large a part in the history of his own country and of which he talks so often and with so little restraint. The ignorance of Englishmen of America is another matter which will be referred to in its place. For the present, what is to be desired is that the American should get some elementary grasp of the character of Great Britain and her dependencies as a whole.

In the first place it is worth pointing out that the Empire is as much bigger than the United States as the United States is bigger than the British Isles. I am not now talking of mere geographical dimensions, but of the political schemes of the two nations. Americans commonly speak of theirs as a young country—as the youngest of the Great Powers,—but in every true sense the British Empire is vastly younger. The United States has an established form of government which has been the same for a hundred years and, all good Americans hope, will remain unchanged for centuries to come. The British Empire is still groping inchoate: it is all makeshift and endeavour. It is in about that stage of growth in which the United States found herself when her transcontinental railways were still unbuilt, when she had not yet digested Texas or California, and the greater part of the West remained unsettled and unsurveyed.

If the American will look to the north, he will see Canada in approximately the phase in her material progress which the United States had reached in, let us say, 1880 to 1885. Australia and New Zealand are somewhat further behind; South Africa further still. Behind that again are the various scattered portions of the Over-Sea Dominions in divers states of political pupilhood. In some there are not even yet the foundations on which a Constitutional or commercial structure can be built. And while each unit has to be led or encouraged along the path of individual development, beyond all is the great vision which every imperially-thinking Englishman sets before himself—the vision of a Federation of all the parts—a Federation not unlike that which the United States has enjoyed for over a hundred years (save that Englishmen hope that there will always be a monarchy at the centre) but which, as has been said, is almost incomparably larger in conception than was the Union of the States and requires correspondingly greater labour in its accomplishment.

If the American will now consider the conditions of the growth of his own country, he will recognise that the only thing which made that growth possible was the fact that the people was undistracted by foreign complications. The one great need of the nation was Peace. It was to attain this that the policy of non-entanglement was formulated. Without it, the people could not have devoted its energies with a single mind to the gigantic task of its own development.

But the task before the British Empire is more gigantic; the need of peace more urgent. It is more urgent, not merely in proportion to the additional magnitude and complexity of the task to be done, but is thrice multiplied by the conditions of the modern world. The British Empire must needs achieve its industrial consolidation in the teeth of a commercial competition a thousand times fiercer than anything which America knew in her young days. The United States grew to greatness in a secluded nursery. Great Britain must bring up her children in the streets and on the high seas, under the eyes and exposed to the seductions of the peoples of all the world.

The American is a reasoning being. A much larger portion of the American people is habituated to reason for itself—to think independently—to form and to abide by its individual judgment—than of any other people in the world. No political fact is more familiar to the American people than the immense advantage which it derived, during the period of its internal development, from its enjoyment of external peace. Will not the American people, then, reasoning from analogy, believe that, under more compelling conditions, England also earnestly desires external peace?

I can almost hear the retort leaping to the lips of the American reader who holds the traditional view of the British Empire. "It is all very well for you to talk of peace now!" I hear him say. "Now that the world is pretty well divided up and you have grabbed the greater part of it. You haven't talked much of peace in the past." And here we are confronted at once with the fundamental misconception of the British Empire and the British character which has worked deplorable harm in the American national sentiment towards England.

First, it is worth remarking that with the exception of the Crimean War (which even the most prejudiced American will not regard as a war of aggression or as a thing for which England should be blamed) Great Britain has not been engaged in hostilities with any European Power since the days of Napoleon. Nor can it be contended that England's share in the Napoleonic wars was of England's seeking. Since then, if she has avoided hostilities it has not been for lack of opportunity. The people which, with Britain's intricate complexity of interests, amid all the turmoils and jealousies of Europe, has kept the peace for a century can scarcely have been seeking war.

And again the American will say: "That's all right; I am not talking of Europe. You've been fighting all over the world all the time. There has never been a year when you have not been licking some little tin-pot king and freezing on to his possessions."

Americans are rather proud—justly proud—of the way in which their power has spread from within the narrow limits of the original thirteen States till it has dominated half a continent. It has, indeed, been a splendid piece of work. But what the American is loth to acknowledge is that that growth was as truly a colonising movement—a process of imperial expansion—as has been the growth of the British Empire. Of late years, American historical writers have been preaching this fact; but the American people has not grasped it. Moreover there were tin-pot kings already ruling America. Sioux, Nez Percé, or Cree—Zulu, Ashanti, or Burmese: the names do not matter. And when the expansive energy of the American people reached the oceans, it could no more stop than it could stop at the Mississippi. Hawaii, the Philippines, and Puerto Rico were as inevitable as Louisiana and Texas. And the acquisition of the two last-named was precisely as imperial a process as the acquisition of the others. It is only the leap over-seas that, quite illogically, gives the latter, to American eyes, a different seeming. It matters not whether you vault a boundary pillar on the plain, a river, a mountain barrier, or seven thousand miles of sea-water. The process is the same. Nor in any of the cases was the forward movement other than commendable and inevitable. It was the necessary manifestation of the unrestrainable centrifugal impulse of the Anglo-Saxon.

The impulse which sent the first English colonists to North America sent them also to Australia, to India and the uttermost parts of the earth. The same impulse drove the American colonists westward, northward, southward, in whatever direction they met no restraining force equal to their own expansive energy. It drove them to the Pacific, to the Rio Grande, to the Sault Ste. Marie; and it has driven them over oceans into the Arctic Circle, to the shores of Asia, down the Caribbean. And as it drove them it drove also those Englishmen who were left at home and they too spread on all lines of least resistance. But no American (I have never met one, though I must have talked on the subject to hundreds) will agree that the dispersal of the Englishmen left at home was as legitimate, as necessary, and every whit as peaceful as the dispersal of those Englishmen who went first and made their new home in America.

With the acquisition of over-sea dominions of their own, many Americans are coming to comprehend something of the powerlessness of a great people in the grip of its destiny. They are also beginning to understand that the ruling and civilising of savage and alien peoples is not either all comfort or all profit. If Americans were given the option to-day to take more Philippines, would they take them? Great Britain has been familiar with *her* Philippines for half a century and more. Does America suppose that she also did not learn her lesson? Will not Americans understand with what utter reluctance she has been compelled again and again to take more? Some day Americans will come to believe that England no more desired to annex Burmah than the United States deliberately planned to take the Philippines; that Englishmen were as content to leave the Transvaal and the Orange Free State alone as ever Americans were to be without Hawaii or Puerto Rico. Egypt was forced upon Great Britain precisely as Cuba is being foisted on America to-day— and every Englishman hopes that the United States will be able to do as much for the Cubans as Great Britain has done for the Egyptians.

Great Britain would always vastly prefer—has always vastly preferred—to keep a friendly independent state upon her borders rather than be compelled to take over the burden of administration. The former involves less labour and more profit; it retains moreover a barrier between the British boundaries and those of any potentially hostile Power upon the other side. England has shown this in India itself and in Afghanistan. She tried to show it in South Africa. She has shown it in Thibet. More conclusively than anywhere perhaps she has shown it in the Federated Malay States—of which probably but few Americans know even the name, but where more, it may be, than anywhere are Englishmen working out their ambition—

"To make the world a better placeWhere'er the English go."

It might happen that, under a weak and incompetent successor to President Diaz, Mexico would relapse into the conditions of half a century ago and the situation along the border be rendered intolerable to Americans. Sooner or later the United States would be compelled to protest and, protests being unheeded, to interfere. The incompetence of the Mexican Government continuing, America would be obliged to establish a protectorate, if not over the whole country, at least over that portion the orderly behaviour of which was necessary to her own peace. Thereafter annexation might follow. Now, at no stage of this process would Englishmen, looking on, accuse the United States of greediness, of bullying, or of deliberately planning to gratify an earth-hunger. They, from experience, understand. But when the same thing occurs on the British frontiers in Asia or South Africa, Americans make no effort to understand. "England is up to the same old game," they say. "One more morsel down the lion's throat."

I am well aware of the depth of the prejudice against which I am arguing. The majority of Americans are so accustomed to consider their own expansion across the continent, and beyond, as one of the finest episodes in the march of human progress (as it is) and the growth of the British Empire as a mere succession of wanton and brutal outrages on helpless and benighted peoples, that the immediate impulse of the vast majority of American readers will be to treat a comparison between the two with ridicule. Minnesota Massacres and the Indian Mutiny—Cetewayo and Sitting Bull—

Aguinaldo and the Mahdi—Egypt and Cuba; the time will come when Americans will understand. It is a pity that prejudice should blind them now.

And if the American reader will refer to the map, which presumably lies open before him, he might consider in what part of the world it is that England is now bent on a policy of aggression—where it is that collision with any Power threatens. In Asia? England's course in regard to Afghanistan and Thibet surely shows that she is content with her present boundaries, while her alliance with Japan and the *rapprochement* with Russia at which she aims should be evidences enough of her desire for peace! In Africa? Where is it that spheres of influence are not delimited? That there will be disturbances, ferments, which will have to be suppressed at one time and another at various points within the British sphere is likely—as likely as it was that similar disturbances would occur in the United States so long as any considerable number of Indians went loose unblanketed,—but what room is left for anything approaching serious war? With the problem of the mixture of races and the necessity of building up the structure of a state, does not England before all things need peace both in the south and north? In America? In Australia? With whom? That perils may arise at almost any point—in mid-ocean even, far away from any land—of course we recognise; but Americans can hardly fail to see, with the map before them, that England cannot seek them, but must earnestly desire to avoid them as she has avoided them with any European Power for this last century. To borrow a happy phrase, Great Britain is in truth a "Saturated Power." She has been compelled to shoulder burdens which she would feign have avoided, to assume obligations which were not of her creating and which she fulfils with reluctance. And she can assume no more, or, if she must, will do it only with the utmost unwillingness. What she needs is peace.

And now one must go as delicately as is compatible with making one's meaning clear.

There is one Power in Europe whose ambitions are a menace to the peace of the world—one only. I do not think that Americans as a rule understand this, but it is true and there can be no harm in saying so, for neither in her press nor in the mouths of her statesmen are those ambitions denied by that Power herself. Indeed they are insisted on to the taxpayer as the reason why she needs so powerful an army and a fleet. It is not suggested that Germany's ambitions are other than legitimate and inevitable: it would be difficult for either Englishman or American to say that with grace. I am not arguing against Germany; I am arguing for Peace.

Germany says frankly enough that she is cooped up within boundaries which are intolerable—that she is an "imprisoned Power." She argues, still with perfect frankness, that it was a mere accident that, to her misfortune, she came into being as a great Power too late to be able to get her proper share of the earth's surface, wherein her people might expand and put forth their surplus energy. The time when there was earth's surface to choose was already gone. But that fact has in no way lessened the need of expansion or destroyed the energy. She must burst her prison walls, she says. It would have been better could she have flowed out quietly into unoccupied land—as the United States has done and as Great Britain has done—but that being impossible, she must flow where she can. And ringed around her are other Powers, great or small, which bar her way. Therefore she needs the army and the fleet. It is logical and it is candid.

It is evident that the Franco-Russian Alliance makes the bursting of her banks difficult in what might seem to be the most natural direction. The Anglo-French *entente* and the Anglo-Japanese Alliance—perhaps even more Germany's own partnership in the Triple Alliance with Italy and Austria—also constitute obstacles which at least necessitate something more of an army and more of a fleet than might otherwise have been sufficient for her purpose. But those barriers are not in the long run going to avert the fulfilment of—or at least the endeavour to fulfil—that purpose.

There is only one instrumentality, humanly speaking,—one Power,—which can ultimately prevent Germany from using that army and that fleet for the ends for which they are being created; and that instrumentality happens to be the United States. It is difficult to see how Germany can make any break for freedom without coming in conflict not only with one of the Great Powers but with a combination of two or more. It is improbable that she will attempt the enterprise without at least the benevolent neutrality of the United States. Assurances of positive sympathy would probably go a long way towards encouraging her to the hazard. But if the United States should range herself definitely on the side of peace the venture would become preposterous.

I am not arguing against Germany; I am arguing for Peace. Least of all am I arguing for an American alliance for England in the event of Germany's dash for liberty taking an untoward direction. England needs no help. What does need help is Peace—the Peace of Europe—the Peace of the World.

There is no talk now of stifling Germany's ambitions: of standing in the way of her legitimate aspirations. It may be that under other conditions, under a different form of government, or even under another individual ruler, those aspirations and ambitions would not appear to the German people so vital as they do now. They certainly do not appear so to an outsider; and the German people is far from being of one mind on the subject. But assuming the majority of Germans to know their own business best, and granting it to be essential that the people should have some larger sphere, under their own flag, in which to attain to their proper growth, if they were compelled to drop war as the means for obtaining that larger sphere out of their calculations, it would not mean that those ambitions and aspirations would have to go unsatisfied. Violence is not the only means of obtaining what one wants.

There was a time when, as between individuals, if one man desired a thing which his neighbour possessed he went with a club and took it; but civilised society has abandoned physical force as a medium for the exchange of commodities and has substituted barter. If physical force were once discountenanced among nations, any nation which needed a thing badly enough could always get it. Everybody who had facilities for sale would be glad to sell, if the price was sufficiently high. It is not unlikely that, in an age of compulsory peace, Germany would be able to acquire all that she desires at a less price than the expenditure of blood and treasure which would be necessary in a war. It would almost certainly cost her less than the price of war added to the capitalised annual burden of the up-keep of her army and navy.[32:1]

But the real cost of war does not fall upon the individual nation. And for the last time let me say that I am not arguing against Germany: I am arguing for Peace. It has been necessary to discuss Germany's position because she is at the moment the only factor in the situation which makes for war. All other Powers are satisfied, or could be satisfied, with their present boundaries. Outside of the German Empire, the whole civilised world earnestly desires peace. It may be that Great Britain, acting in concert with France, Russia, and Japan, will in the near future be able to take a longer step towards securing that peace for the world than seems at present credible. But England's natural coadjutor is the United States. The United States has but to take one step and the thing is done. It is a *rôle* which ought to appeal to the American people. It is certainly one for the assumption of which all posterity would bless the name of America.

Critics will, of course, ridicule this offhand dismissing in a few sentences of the largest of world problems. Each one of several propositions which I have advanced breaks rudely ground where angels might fear to tread; each one ought to be put forth cautiously with much preamble and historical introduction, to be circuitously argued through several hundred pages; but that cannot be done here because those propositions are not the main topic of this book. At the same time they must be stated, however baldly, because they represent the basis on which my plea for any immediate Anglo-American co-operation in the cause of peace must rest.

I am also fully conscious of the hostility which almost everything that I say will provoke from one or another section of the American people, but I am not addressing the irreconcilables of any foreign element of the population of the United States. I am talking to the reasoning, intelligent mass of the two peoples as a whole. The subject of an Anglo-American alliance is one of which it is the fashion to hush up any attempt at the discussion in public. It must be spoken of in whispers. It is better—so the argument runs—to let American good-will to England grow of itself; an effort to hasten it will but hurt American susceptibilities.

In the first place this idea rests largely on an exaggerated estimate of the power of the Irish politician, a power which happily is coming every day to be more nearly a thing of the past,—"tending," as Carlyle says, "visibly not to be." In the second place, I believe that I understand American susceptibilities; and they will not be hurt by any one who shows that he does understand. What the American resents bitterly is the arrogant and superficial criticism of the foreigner who sums up the characteristics and destiny of the nation after a few weeks of observation. Moreover, Americans do not as a rule like whispering or the attempt to come at things by by-paths—in which they much resemble the English. When they want a thing they commonly ask for it—distinctly. When they think a thing ought to be done they prefer to say so—unequivocally. They have not much love for the circuitousnesses of diplomacy; and if England desires American co-operation in what is a great and noble cause she had much better ask for it—bluntly.

Personally I wish that forty million Englishmen would stand up and shout the request all at once.

FOOTNOTES:

[8:1] Since this was written, the Anglo-Russian agreement has been arrived at.

[10:1] Justin H. Smith, *Our Struggle for the Fourteenth Colony*, Putnams, 1907.

[15:1] *The Bellman*, Minneapolis, Dec. 22, 1906.

[32:1] A point which there is no space to dwell upon here but which I would commend to the more leisurely consideration of readers—especially American readers—is that under a *régime* of physical force there can in fact be hardly any transfer of commodities at all. What a man has, he holds, whether his need of it be greater than another's, or whether he needs it not at all. There is no inducement to part with it and pride compels him to hold; so that only the strongest can come by the possession of anything that he desires. If the dollar were substituted for the club in the dealings of nations, the transfer of commodities would forthwith become simplified, and such incidents as the purchase of Alaska and the cession of Heligoland, instead of standing as isolated examples of international accommodation, would become customary. To take an example which will bring the matter home at once, many imperialist Englishmen on visiting the West Indies have become convinced that certain of England's possessions in those regions could with advantage to all parties be transferred to the United States. But so long as the military idea reigns—so long as an island must be regarded primarily as an outpost, a possible naval base, a strategic point—so long will the obstacles to such a transfer remain. As soon as war was put outside the range of possibilities, commercial principles would begin to operate and those territories, however much or little they might be worth, would be acquired by the United States. The same thing would happen in all parts of the world. Possessions, instead of being held by those who could hold them, would tend to pass to those who needed them or to whom they logically belonged by geographical relation, and neither Germany's legitimate aspirations nor those of any other country would need to go unsatisfied.

CHAPTER II

THE DIFFERENCE IN POINT OF VIEW

The Anglo-Saxon Family Likeness—How Frenchmen and Germans View it—Englishmen, Americans, and "Foreigners"—An Echo of the War of 1812—An Anglo-American Conflict Unthinkable—American Feeling for England—The Venezuelan Incident—The Pilgrims and Some Secret History—Why Americans still Hate England—Great Britain's Nearness to the United States Geographically—Commercially—Historically—England's Foreign Ill-wishers in America.

The one thing chiefly needed to make both Englishmen and Americans desire an alliance is that they should come to know each other better. They would then be astonished to find not only how much they liked each other, but how closely each was already in sympathy with the other's ways of life and thought and how inconsiderable were the differences between them. Some one (I thought it was Mr. Freeman, but I cannot find the passage in his writings) has said that it would be a good way of judging an Englishman's knowledge of the world to notice whether, on first visiting America, he was most struck by the differences between the two peoples or by their resemblances. When an intelligent American has travelled for any time on the Continent of Europe, in contact with peoples who are truly "foreign" to him, he feels on arriving in London almost as if he were at home again. The more an Englishman moves among other peoples, the more he is impressed, on reaching the United States, with his kinship to those among whom he finds himself. Nor is it in either case wholly, or even chiefly, a matter of a common speech.

"Jonathan," says Max O'Rell, "is but John Bull expanded—John Bull with plenty of elbow room." And the same thing is said again and again in different phraseology by various Continental writers. It is said most impressively by those who do not put it into words at all, as by Professor Münsterberg[36:1] who is apparently not familiar with England, but shows no lack of willingness to dislike her. There is therefore no intentional comparison between the two peoples, but the writer's point of view has absorbing interest to an Englishman who knows both countries. More than once he remarks with admiration or astonishment on traits of the American character or institutions in the United States which the Englishman would necessarily take for granted, because they are precisely the same as those to which he has been accustomed at home. Writing for a German public, the Professor draws morals from American life which delight an English reader by their naïve and elementary superfluousness. In all unconsciousness, Professor Münsterberg has written a most valuable essay on the essential kinship of the British and American peoples as contrasted with his own.

Two brothers will commonly be aware only of the differences between them—the unlikeness of their features, the dissimilarities in their tastes or capabilities,—yet the world at large may have difficulty in distinguishing them apart. While they are conscious only of their individual differences, to the neighbours all else disappears in the family resemblance. So it is that Max O'Rell sees how like the American is to the Englishman more clearly than Mark Twain: Professor Münsterberg has involuntarily traced the features of the one in the lineaments of the other with a surer hand than Matthew Arnold or Mr. Bryce.

When, in his remarkable book, M. Demolins uses the term Anglo-Saxon, he speaks indifferently at one time of Englishmen and at another of Americans. The peoples are to him one and indistinguishable. Their greatness is a common greatness based on qualities which are the inheritance of their Anglo-Saxon origin. Chief among these qualities, the foundation-stone of their greatness, is the devotion to what we will follow him in calling the "Particularistic" form of society,—a society, that is, in which the individual predominates over the community, and not the community over the individual; a society which aims at "establishing each child in its full independence." This is, a Frenchman sees, eminently characteristic of the English and the Americans, in contrast with other peoples, with those which hold a republican form of government no less than those which live under an autocracy. And it is peculiarly Saxon in its origin,—not derived from the Celt or Norman or Dane. These latter belonged (as do the peoples sprung from, or allied to, them to-day) to that class of people which places the community above the individual, which looks instinctively to the State or the government for initiative. The Saxons alone (a people of earnest individual workers, agriculturalists and craftsmen) relied always on the initiative and impulse of the individual—what M. Demolins calls "the law of intense personal labour"—and it was by virtue of this quality that they eventually won social supremacy over the other races in Britain. It is by virtue of the same quality that the Americans have been enabled to subdue their continent and build up the fabric of the United States. It is this quality, says the French writer almost brutally, which makes the German and Latin races to-day stand to *L'Anglais* in about the same relation as the Oriental and the Redskin stand to the European. And when M. Demolins speaks of *L'Anglais*, he means the American as much as the "Englishman of Britain." It is a convenient term and, so essentially one are they in his eyes, there is no need to distinguish between the peoples. Mr. William Archer's remark is worth quoting, that "It is amazing how unessential has been the change produced in the Anglo-

Saxon type and temperament [in America] by the influences of climate or the admixtures of foreign blood."[38:1]

When individual Englishmen and Americans are thrown together in strange parts of the world, they seldom fail to foregather as members of one race. There may be four traders living isolated in some remote port; but though the Russian may speak English with less "accent" than the American and though the German may have lived for some years in New York, it is not to the society of the German or the Russian that the American or the Englishman instinctively turns for companionship. The two former have but the common terms of speech; the Englishman and the American use also common terms of thought and feeling.

The people who know this best are the officers and men of the British and American navies, who are accustomed to find themselves thrown with the sailors of all nations in all sorts of waters; and wherever they are thus thrown together, the men who sail under the Stars and Stripes and those who fly the Union Jack are friends. I have talked with a good many British sailors (not officers) and it is good to hear the tone of respect in which they speak of the American navy, as compared with certain others.

The opportunities for similar companionship among the men of the armies of the two nations are fewer, but when the allied forces entered China the comradeship which arose between the American and British troops, to the exclusion of all others, is notorious. Every night after mess, British officers sought the American lines and *vice versa*. The Americans have the credit of having invented that rigorous development of martial law, by which, as soon as British officers came within their lines, sentries were posted with orders not to let them pass out again unless accompanied by an American officer. Thus the guests could not escape from hospitality till such hour as their hosts pleased.

Some ten years ago military representatives of various nations were present by invitation at certain manœuvres of the Indian army, and one night, when an official entertainment was impending, the United States officers were guests at the mess of a British regiment. Dinner being over, the colonel pushed his chair back and, turning to the American on his right, said in all innocence:

"Well, come along! It's time to go and help to receive these d———d foreigners."

An incident less obviously *à propos*, but which seems to me to strike very truly the common chord of kinship of character between the races, was told me by a well-known American painter of naval and military subjects. He was the guest of the Forty-fourth (Essex) at, I think, Gibraltar, when in the course of dinner the British officer on his right broke a silence with the casual remark:

"I wonder whether we shall ever have another smack at you fellows."

The American was not unnaturally surprised.

"Why? Do you want it?" he asked.

"No; we should hate to fight you of course, but then, you know, the Forty-fourth was at New Orleans."

It appealed to the American—not merely the pride in the regiment that still smarted under the blow of ninety years ago, but still more the feeling towards himself, as an American, that prompted the Englishman to speak in terms which he knew that he would never have dreamed of using under similar circumstances to the representative of any "foreign" nation. The Englishman had no fear that the American would misunderstand. It appealed to the latter so much that after his return to the United States, being called upon to speak at some entertainment or function at West Point, when, besides the cadets, there were many officers of the United States Army in the room, he told the story. Instantly, as he finished, a simultaneous cry from several places in the hall called for "Three cheers for the Forty-fourth!" There was no Englishman in the company, but, as he told me the story, never had he heard so instantaneous, so crashing a response to any call, as then when the whole room leaped to its feet and cheered the old enemies who had not forgotten.[41:1]

It is not my wish here to discuss even the possibility of war between Great Britain and the United States. The thing is too horrible to be considered as even the remotest of contingencies—the "Unpardonable War," indeed, as Mr. James Barnes has called it. None the less, there is always greater danger of such a war than any Englishman imagines or than many Americans would like to confess. However true it may be that it takes two to make a quarrel, it is none the less true that if one party be bent upon quarrelling it is always possible for him to go to lengths of irritation and insult which must ultimately provoke the most peaceful and reluctant of antagonists. However pacific and reluctant to fight Great Britain might be at the outset, she is not conspicuously lacking in national pride or in sensitiveness to encroachments on the national honour.

Mr. Freeman makes the shrewd remark that "the American feels a greater distinction between himself and the Englishman of Britain than the Englishman of Britain feels between himself and the American," which remains entirely true to-day, in spite of the seemingly paradoxical fact that the American knows more of English history and English politics than the Englishman knows of the politics and history of the United States. This by no means implies that the American knows more of the English character than the Englishman knows of his. On the contrary, the Americans have seen infinitely less of the world than Englishmen, and however many of the bare facts of English history and English politics they may know, they are strangely ignorant of the atmosphere to which those facts belong, and have never learned how much more foreign to them other foreign nations are. The individual American will take the individual Englishman into his friendship—will even accept him as a sort of a relative—but as a political entity Great Britain is almost as much a foreign nation as any.

The casual Englishman visiting the United States for but a short time will probably not discover this fact. He only knows that he is cordially received himself—even more cordially, he feels, than he deserves—and most probably those persons, especially the ladies, whom he meets will assure him that they are "devoted" to England. He may not have time to discover that that devotion is not universal. Only after a while, in all probability, will the fact as stated by Mr. Freeman dawn upon him, and he will somehow be aware that with all the charming hospitality that he receives he is in some way treated as more of a foreigner than he is conscious of being. It is necessary that he should have some extended residence in the country—unless his visit happens to coincide with such an incident as the Venezuelan controversy or the outbreak of the Boer War—before things group themselves in at all their right perspective before his eyes. The intensity of the feeling displayed at the time of the Venezuelan incident came as a shock to Englishmen at home; but those who had lived for any length of time in America (west of New York) were not surprised. It is probable that the greater number of the American people at that time wished for war, and believed that it was nothing but cowardice on the part of Great Britain—her constitutional dislike of fighting anybody of her own size, as a number of the papers pleasantly phrased it—that prevented their wish from being gratified.

The concluding paragraphs of ex-President Cleveland's treatise on this subject are illuminating. In 1895, as I have said, a majority of the American people unquestionably wished to fight; but that numerical majority included perhaps a minority of the native-born Americans, a small minority certainly of the richer or more well-to-do among them, and an almost infinitesimal proportion of the best educated of the native-born. This is what Mr. Cleveland says:

"Those among us who most loudly reprehended and bewailed our vigorous assertion of the Monroe Doctrine were the timid ones who feared personal financial loss, or those engaged in speculation and stock-gambling, in buying much beyond their ability to pay, and generally in living by their wits [*sic*]. The patriotism of such people traverses exclusively the pocket nerve. . . . But these things are as nothing when weighed against the sublime patriotism and devotion to their nation's honour exhibited by the great mass of our countrymen—the plain people of the land. . . . Not for a moment did their Government know the lack of their strong and stalwart support. . . . It [the incident] has given us a better place in the respect and consideration of the people of all nations, and especially of Great Britain; it has again confirmed our confidence in the overwhelming prevalence among our citizens of disinterested devotion to our nation's honour; and last, but by no means least, it has taught us where to look in the ranks of our countrymen for the best patriotism."[44.1]

Mr. Cleveland, now that he is no longer in active politics, holds, as he deserves, a secure place in the affections of the American people. But at the time when this treatise was published, he was a not impossible nominee of the Democratic party for another term as President; and the "plain people of the land" have a surprising number of votes. Mr. Cleveland knows his own people and knows that with a large portion of them war with England would in 1895 have been popular. It is significant also that he still thought it worth while to insist upon this fact at the time when this treatise was given to the world in a volume; and that was as late as 1904, very shortly before the Democratic party selected its nominee for the Presidential contest of that year. It is possible that if Mr. Cleveland had been that nominee instead of Justice Parker, one of the leading features of his campaign would have been a vigorous insistence on the Monroe Doctrine, as interpreted by himself, with especial reference to Great Britain.

Englishmen are inclined (so far as they think about the matter at all) to flatter themselves that the ill-feeling which blazed so suddenly into flame twelve years ago was more or less effectually quenched by Great Britain's assistance to the United States at the time of the Spanish War. Those Englishmen who watched the course of opinion in America at the time of the Boer War must have had some misgivings. It is evident that so good a judge as Mr. Cleveland believed, as late as 1904, that hostility to Great Britain was still a policy which would commend itself to the "plain people of the land."

It is true that the war fever in 1895 was stronger in the West than in the Eastern States. A traveller crossing the United States at that time would have found the idea of hostilities with England being treated as something of a joke in cultivated circles in New York, but among the people in general to the West of Buffalo and Pittsburg it was terrible earnest. A curious point, moreover, which I think I have never seen stated in England, is that many good men in the Democratic Party at that time stood by President Cleveland, though sincerely friendly to Great Britain; the truth being that they did not believe that war with England was seriously to be apprehended, while another Power was at the moment seeking to obtain a foothold in South America, for whose benefit a "vigorous assertion of the Monroe Doctrine" was much to be desired. The thunders of the famous message indeed were, in the minds of many excellent Americans in the East, directed not against Great Britain but against Germany.

None the less it should be noted that it was in the hope of influencing the voters in a local election in New York that Mr. Hearst, as recently as in November, 1907, thought it worth while to appeal to the "traditional hatred" of Great Britain. However little else Mr. Hearst may have to commend him, he cannot be said to be out of touch with the sentiments of the more ignorant masses of the people of New York. That he failed did not signify that he was mistaken as to the extent or intensity of the prejudice to which he appealed, but only that the cry was raised too late and too obviously as an electioneering trick in a campaign which was already lost.

In spite of what happened during the Spanish War, in spite of every effort that England has made to convince America of her friendliness, in spite of the improvement which has taken place in the feelings of (what, without offence, I venture to call) the upper classes in America towards Great Britain, the fact still remains that, with a large portion of the people, war with England would be popular.

That is, perhaps, to state the case somewhat brutally. Let me rather say that, if any pretext should arise, the minds of the masses of the American people could more easily be inflamed to the point of desiring war with England than they could to the point of desiring war with any other nation. It is bitter to have to say it—horrible to think it. I know also that many Americans will not agree with me; but I do not think that among them will be many of those whose business it is, either as politicians or as journalists, to be in touch with the sentiments of the people.

Let me not be suspected of failing to attach sufficient importance to those public expressions of international amity which we hear so frequently, couched in such charming phraseology, at the dinners given by the Pilgrims, either in London or New York, and on similar occasions. The Pilgrims are doing excellent work, as also are other similar societies in less conspicuous ways. The fact has, I believe, never been published, but can be told now without indiscretion, that a movement was on foot some twelve years ago for the organisation of an Anglo-American League, on a scale much more ambitious than that of the Pilgrims or any other of the existing societies. Certain members of the British Ministry of the time had been approached and had welcomed the movement with cordiality, and the active support of a number of men of corresponding public repute in various parts of the United States had been similarly enlisted. It was expected (though I think the official request had not been made) that the Prince of Wales (now his Majesty King Edward VII.) would be the President of the English branch of the

League, while ex-President Harrison was to have acted in a similar capacity in America. By a grim pleasantry of Fate, the letter from England conveying final and official information of the approval of the aforesaid Ministers, and arranging for the publication of the first formal overture from the United States (for the movement was to be made to appear to emanate therefrom) arrived in America on the very day of the appearance—and readers will remember how totally unexpected the appearance was—of Mr. Cleveland's Venezuelan message. What would have been the effect upon the crisis which then ensued if the organisation of the League had been but a few weeks further advanced, is an interesting subject for speculation. That, after a year or two of preparation, the movement should have been beaten by so totally unforeseen a complication at, as it were, the very winning post, was a little absurd. Thereafter, the right moment for proceeding with the organisation on the same lines never again presented itself.

Englishmen must not make the mistake of attaching the same value to the nice things which are said by prominent Americans on public or semi-public occasions as they attach to similar utterances by Englishmen. It is not, of course, intended to imply that the American speakers are not individually sincere; but no American can act as the spokesman for his people in such a matter with the same authority as can be assumed by a properly qualified Englishman. One of the chief manifestations of the characteristic national lack of the sentiment of reverence is the disregard which the American masses entertain for the opinions of their "leading" men, whether in public life or not. The English people is accustomed, within certain limits, to repose confidence in its leaders and to suffer them in truth to lead; so that a small handful of men can within limits speak for the English people. They can voice the public sentiments, or, when they speak, the people will modify its sentiments to accord with their utterances. There is no man or set of men who can similarly speak for the American people; and no one is better aware of that fact than the American, however honoured by his countrymen, when he gives expression in London to the cordiality of his own feelings for Great Britain and expresses guardedly his conviction that a recurrence of trouble between the peoples will never again be possible. For one thing, public opinion is not centralised in America as it is in England. If not *tot homines*, at least *tot civitates*; and each State, each class and community, instinctively objects to any one presuming to speak for it (a prejudice based presumably on political tradition) except its own locally elected representative, and even he must be specifically instructed *ad hoc*.

Only the good-humoured common-sense of British diplomacy prevented war at the time of the Venezuelan incident; and it may be that the same influence would be strong enough to prevent it again. But it is desirable that Englishmen should understand that just as they were astounded at the bitterness against them which manifested itself then, so they might be no less astounded again. It is, of course, difficult for Englishmen to believe. It must necessarily be hard to believe that one is hated by a person whom one likes. It happens to be just as difficult for the mass of Americans (again I should like to say the lower mass) to believe that Englishmen as a whole really like them. In 1895, the American masses believed that England's attitude was the result of cowardice, pure and simple. Knowing their own feeling towards Great Britain, they neither could nor would believe that she was then influenced by a sincere and almost brotherly good-will—that, without one shadow of fear, Englishmen refused to consider war with the United States as possible because it had never occurred to them that the United States was other than a friendly nation—barely by one degree of kinship farther removed than one of Great Britain's larger colonies.

And this is the first great obstacle that stands in the way of a proper understanding between the peoples—not merely the fact that the American nation is so far from having any affection for Great Britain, but the fact that the two peoples regard each other so differently that neither understands, or is other than reluctant to believe in, the attitude of the other. For the benefit of the English reader, rather than the American, it may be well to explain this at some length.

The essential fact is that America, New York or Washington, has been in the past, and still is in only a slightly less degree, much farther from London than London is from New York or Washington. This is true historically and commercially—and geographically, in everything except the mere matter of miles. The American for generations looked at the world through London, whereas when the Englishman turned his vision to New York almost the whole world intervened.

Geographically, the nearest soil to the United States is British soil. Along the whole northern border of the country lies the Dominion of Canada, without, for a distance of some two thousand miles, any visible line of demarcation, so that the American may walk upon the prairie and not know at what moment his foot passes from his own soil to the soil of Great Britain. One of the chief lines of railway from New York to Chicago passes for half its length over Canadian ground; the effect being precisely as if the Englishman to go from London to Birmingham were to run for half the distance over a corner of France. A large proportion of the produce of the wheat-fields of the North-western States, of Minnesota and the two Dakotas, finds its way to New York over the Canadian Pacific Railway and from New York is shipped, probably in British bottoms, to Liverpool. When the American sails outward from New York or other eastern port, if he goes north he arrives only at Newfoundland or Nova Scotia; if he puts out to southward, the first land that he finds is the Bermudas. If he makes for Europe, it is generally at Liverpool or Southampton that he disembarks. On his very threshold in all directions, lies land over which floats the Union Jack and the same flag flies over half the vessels in the harbours of his own coasts.

It is difficult for the Englishman to understand how near Great Britain has always been to the citizen of the United States, for to the Englishman himself the United States is a distant region, which he does not visit unless of set purpose he makes up his mind to go there. He must undertake a special journey, and a long one, lying apart from his ordinary routes of travel. The American cannot, save with difficulty and by circuitous routes, escape from striking British soil whenever he leaves his home. It confronts him on all sides and bars his way to all the world. Is it to be wondered at that he thinks of Englishmen otherwise than as Englishmen think of him?

Yet this mere matter of geographical proximity is trivial compared to the nearness of Great Britain in other ways.

Commercially—and it must be remembered how large a part matters of commerce play in the life and thoughts of the people of the United States—until recently America traded with the world almost entirely through Great Britain. It is not the produce of the Western wheat-fields only that is carried abroad in British bottoms, but the great bulk of the commerce of the United States must even now find its way to the outer world in ships which carry the Union Jack, and in doing so must pay the toll of its freight charges to Great Britain. If a New York manufacturer sells goods to South America itself, the chances are that those goods will be shipped to Liverpool and reshipped to their destination—each time in British vessels—and the payment therefor will be made by exchange on London, whereby the British banker profits only in less degree than the British ship-owner. In financial matters, New York has had contact with the outer world practically only through London. Until recently, no great corporate enterprise could be floated in America without the assistance of English capital, so that for years the "British Bondholder," who, by the interest which he drew (or often did not draw) upon his bonds, was supposed to be sucking the life-blood out of the American people, has been, until the trusts arose, the favourite bogey with which the American demagogue has played upon the feelings of his audiences. Now, happily, with more wealth at home, animosity has been diverted to the native trusts.

It is true that of late years the United States has been striking out to win a world-commerce of her own; that by way of the Pacific she is building up a trade free, in part at least, from British domination; that she is making earnest efforts to develop her mercantile marine, so that her own commerce may in some fair measure be carried under her own flag; that New York is fast becoming a financial centre powerful enough to be able to disregard the dictation—and promising ere long to be a rival—of London; that during the last decade, America has been relieving England of vast quantities of her bonds and shares, heretofore held in London, and that the wealth of her people has increased so rapidly that she can find within herself the capital for her industries and (except in times like the recent panic) need no longer go abroad to beg. It is also true that of recent years England has become not a little uneasy at the growing volume of American trade, even within the borders of the British Isles themselves; but this newly developed uneasiness in British minds, however well grounded, can bear no comparison to the feeling of antagonism towards England—an antagonism compounded of mingled respect and resentment—which Americans of the older generation have had borne in upon them from youth up. To Englishmen, the growing commercial power of the United States is a new phenomenon, not yet altogether recognised and only half-understood; for they have been for so long accustomed to consider themselves the rulers of the sea-borne trade of the world that it is with difficulty that they comprehend that their supremacy can be seriously threatened. To the American, on the other hand, British commercial supremacy has, at least since 1862, been an incontrovertible and disheartening fact. The huge bulk of British commerce and British wealth has loomed so large as to shut out his view of all the world; it has hemmed him in on all sides, obstructed him, towered over him. And all the while, as he grew richer, he has seen that Great Britain only profited the more, by interest on his bonds, by her freight charges, by her profit on exchange. How is it possible that under such conditions the American can think about or feel towards England as the Englishman has thought about and felt towards him?

Yet even now not one half has been told. We have seen that the geographical proximity of Great Britain and the overshadowing bulk of British commerce could not fail—neither separately could fail—to create in American minds an attitude towards England different from the natural attitude of Englishmen towards the United States; but both these influences together, powerful though each may be, are almost unimportant compared to the factor which most of all colours, and must colour, the American's view of Great Britain,—and that is the influence of the history of his own country.

The history of the United States as an independent nation goes back no more than one hundred and thirty years, a space to be spanned by two human lives; so that events of even her very earliest years are still recent history and the sentiments evoked by those events have not yet had time to die. In the days of the childhood of fathers of men still living (the thing is possible, so recent is it) the nation was born out of the throes of a desperate struggle with Great Britain—a struggle which left the name "British" a word of loathing and contempt to American ears. American history proper begins with hatred of England: nor has there been anything in the course of that history, until the present decade, calculated to tend to modify that hatred in any material degree.

During the nineteenth century, the United States, except for the war with Spain at its close, had little contact with foreign Powers. She lived isolated, concentrating all her energies on the developing of her own resources and the work of civilising a continent. Foreign complications scarcely came within the range of her vision. The Mexican War was hardly a foreign war. The only war with another nation in the whole course of the century was that with Great Britain in 1812. Reference has already been made to the English ignorance of the War of 1812; but to the American it was the chief event in the foreign politics of his country during the first century and a quarter of its existence, and the Englishman's ignorance thereof moves him either to irritation or to amusement according to his temperament. In the American Civil War, British sympathy with the South was unhappily exaggerated in American eyes by the *Alabama* incident. The North speedily forgave the South; but it has not yet entirely forgiven Great Britain.

The other chief events of American history have nearly all, directly or indirectly, tended to keep Great Britain before the minds of the people as the one foreign Power with whom armed conflict was an ever-present possibility. The cession of her North American territory on the part of France only served to accentuate England's position as the sole rival of the United States upon the continent. Alaska was purchased from Russia; but Russia has long ago been almost forgotten in the transaction while it was with Great Britain that the troublesome question of the Alaskan boundary arose. And through all the years there have been recurring at intervals, not too far apart, various minor causes of friction between the two peoples,—in the Newfoundland fisheries question on the east and the seal fisheries on the west, with innumerable difficulties arising out of the common frontier line on the north or out of British relations (as in the case of Venezuela) with South American peoples.

If an Englishman were asked what had been the chief events in the external affairs of England during the nineteenth century he would say: the Napoleonic wars, the Crimean War, the Indian Mutiny, the China, Ashanti, Afghan, Zulu, Soudan, Burmese, and Boer wars, the occupation of Egypt, the general expansion of the Empire in Africa—and what not else besides. He would not mention the United States. To the American the history of his country has chiefly to do with Great Britain.

Just as geographically British territory surrounds and abuts on the United States on almost every side; just as commercially Great Britain has always hemmed in, dominated, and overshadowed the United States, so, historically, Great Britain has been the one and constant enemy, actual or potential, and her power a continual menace. How is it possible that the American should think of England as the Englishman thinks of the United States?

There have, moreover, been constantly at work in America forces the chief object of which has been to keep alive hostility to Great Britain. Of native Americans who trace their family back to colonial days, there are still some among the older generation in whom the old hatred of the Revolutionary War yet burns so strongly that they would not, when at work on the old family farm in, let us say, Vermont, be very seriously surprised on some fine morning to see a party of red-coated Hessians come round the angle of the hill. There are those living whose chief pastime as boys was to fight imaginary battles with the loathed British in and out among the old farm-buildings—buildings which yet bear upon them, perhaps, the marks of real British bullets fired in the real war.[57.1] And those boys, moving West as they came to manhood, carried the same spirit, the same inherited dislike of the name "British," into the cities of the Mississippi Valley, across the prairies and over the mountains to the Pacific slope. But it is not the real American—except one here and there on the old New England homestead—who talks much of his anti-British feeling. It is the imported American who has refused to allow the old hostility to die but has kept pouring contumely on the British name and insisted on the incorporation of an "anti-British" plank in his party platform to catch the votes of the citizens of his own nationality at each succeeding election.

Englishmen are generally aware of the importance in American politics of the Irish vote. It is probable, indeed, that, particularly as far as the conditions of the last few years are concerned, the importance of that vote has been magnified to the English mind. In certain localities, and more particularly in a few of the larger cities, it is still, of course, an important factor by its mere numbers; but even in the cities in which the Irish vote is still most in evidence at elections, the influx during the past decade from all parts of Europe of immigrants who in the course of the five-years term become voters has, of necessity, lessened its relative importance.

In New York City, for instance, through which pass annually some nineteen twentieths of all the immigrants coming into the country, the foreign elements other than Irish—German, Italian (mainly from the less educated portions of the Peninsula), Hungarian, Polish, Russian, Hebrew, Roumanian, etc.,—now far outnumber the Irish. In New York, indeed, the Germans are alone more numerous; but the Irish have always shown a larger interest in, and a greater capacity for, political action, so that they still retain an influence out of all proportion to their voting number. On the other hand the Irish, or their leaders, have maintained so corrupt a standard of political action (so that a large proportion of the evils from which the affairs of certain of the larger American cities suffer to-day may be justly charged to their methods and influence) that it is uncertain whether their abuse of Great Britain does not, in the minds of certain, and those not the worst, classes of the people react rather to create good-will towards England than to increase hostility.

The power of the Irish vote as an anti-British force, then, is undoubtedly overrated in England; but it must be borne in mind that some of the other foreign elements in the population which on many questions may act as a counterpoise to the Irish are not themselves conspicuously friendly to England. If we hear too much of the Irish in America, we hear perhaps too little of some of the other peoples. And the point which I would impress on the English reader is that he cannot expect the American to feel towards England as he himself feels towards the United States. The American people came in the first instance justly by its hatred of the name "British," and there have not since been at work any forces sufficiently powerful to obliterate that hatred, while there have been some operating to keep it alive.

FOOTNOTES:

[36:1] *The Americans,* by Hugo Münsterberg, 1905.

[38:1] *America To-day,* by William Archer (1900). Mr. Archer's study of the American people is in my opinion the most sympathetic and comprehending which has been written by an Englishman.

[41:1] The battle of New Orleans, in the War of 1812, is not one of those incidents in English history which Englishmen generally insist on remembering, and it may be as well to explain to English readers that it was on that occasion that an inferior force of American riflemen (a "backwoods rabble" a British officer called them before the engagement) repulsed a British attack, from behind improvised earthworks, with a loss to the attacking force of 3300 killed and wounded, and at a cost to themselves of 13 wounded and 8 killed—or 21 casualties in all. Of the Forty-fourth (Essex) Regiment 816 men went into action, and after less than thirty minutes 134 were able to line up. The Ninety-third (Sutherland) Highlanders suffered even more severely. Of 1008 officers and men only 132 came out unhurt. The battle was fought after peace had been concluded, so that the lives were thrown away to no purpose. The British had to deliver a direct frontal attack over level ground, penned in by a lake on one side and a swamp on the other. It was the same lesson, in even bloodier characters, as was taught on several occasions in South Africa.

[44:1] *Presidential Problems,* by Grover Cleveland, p. 281 (New York, 1904).

[57:1] I had written this before reading Senator Hoar's Reminiscences in which, in speaking of his own youth, he tells how "Every boy imagined himself a soldier and his highest conception of glory was to 'lick the British'" (*An Autobiography of Seventy Years*).

CHAPTER III

TWO SIDES OF THE AMERICAN CHARACTER

Europe's Undervaluation of America's Fighting Power—The Americans as Sailors—The Nation's Greatest Asset—Self-reliance of the People—The Making of a Doctor—And of a Surveyor—Society in the Rough—New York and the Country—An Anglo-Saxon Trait—America's Unpreparedness—American Consuls and Diplomats—A Homogeneous People—The Value of a Common Speech—America more Anglo-Saxon than Britain—Mr. Wells and the Future in America.

One circumstance ought in itself to convince Americans that cowardice or fear has no share in the greater outspokenness of England's good-will during these later years, namely that when Great Britain showed her sympathy with the United States at the time of the Spanish War, Englishmen largely believed that they were giving that sympathy to the weaker Power,[60:1]—weaker, that is as far as organised fighting strength, immediately available, was concerned. It is a century or two since Englishmen did Spain the compliment of being afraid of her. How then, in 1895, could they have had any fear of the United States?

Few Europeans, indeed, have any conception of the fighting power of the United States, for it is not large on paper. Nor is an Englishman likely to make special allowance for the fighting efficiency of either the ships or the men, for the reason that, in spite of experiences which might have bred misgivings (English memory for such matters is short), it remains to him unthinkable that, in the last resort, any men or still less any ships will prove—man for man and gun for gun—better than his own. He might be glad to concede that 25,000 American troops are the equivalent of 50,000 Germans or 100,000 Cossacks, or that two American men of war should be counted as the equivalent of three Italian. He makes no such concession when it comes to a comparison with British troops or British ships. What then can there be in the fighting strength of the United States, for all the figures that she has to show, to breed in him a suggestion of fear?

This is a statement which will irritate many a patriotic American, who will say that it is the same old British superciliousness. But it should not irritate; and if the American understood the Englishman better and the spirit which inspires him, he would like it. The Englishman prefers not to regard the American troops or ships as potentially hostile, and Great Britain has sufficient to do in measuring the strength of her possible enemies. As for the people of the United States, he opines that they know their own business. They are best able to judge how many ships and how many men under arms will serve their purpose. England would, indeed, be glad to see the United

States with a few more ships than she has, but—it is none of England's business. Englishmen can only wish her luck and hope that she is making no mistake in her calculations and go on about their own affairs, which are pressing enough. At the same time if the United States should prove to have miscalculated and should ever need . . .—well, England has a ship or two herself.

It would be a gain for the world if Americans would only understand!

The Englishman of the present generation knows practically nothing of the Americans as a maritime nation; and again let me say that this arises not from superciliousness or any intentional neglect, but merely from the fact that the matter is one beyond his horizon. He is so familiar with the fact that Britain rules the waves that he has no notion that whenever opportunity of comparison has offered the Americans have generally shown themselves (if there has been anything to choose) the better sailors of the two. Every English reader will probably read that sentence again to see if he has not misunderstood it. The truth is that Englishmen have forgotten the incidents of the Revolutionary War almost as completely as they have forgotten those of the War of 1812; Paul Jones is as meaningless a name to them as Andrew Jackson. While it is true that American historians have given the American people, up to the present generation, an unfortunately exaggerated idea of the heroism of the patriot forces and have held the British troops up to all manner of unmerited odium, it is also true that English historians, while the less partial of the two, have perhaps been over-careful not to err in the same direction. Not until the last twenty years—hardly until the last four or five—have there been accessible to the public of the two countries the materials for forming a just judgment on the incidents of the war. It must be confessed that there is at least nothing in the evidence to permit the Englishman to think that a hundred years ago the home-bred Briton could either sail or fight his ships better than the Colonial. Nor has the Englishman as a rule any idea that in the middle of the nineteenth century the American commercial flag was rapidly ousting the British flag from the seas. Even with a knowledge of the facts, it is still hard for us to-day to comprehend.

So amazing was the growth of the mercantile marine of the young republic—such qualities did the Americans show as shipbuilders, as sailors, and as merchants—that in 1860, the American mercantile marine was greater in tonnage and number of vessels than that of all other nations of the world combined, except Great Britain, and almost equal to that of Great Britain herself. These were of course the days of glory of the American clipper. It appeared then inevitable that in a few years the Stars and Stripes—a flag but little more than half a century old—would be the first commercial flag of the world; and but for the outbreak of the Civil War, it is at least probable that by now Englishmen would have grown accustomed to recognising that not they but another people were the real lords of the ocean's commerce. When the Civil War broke out, the tonnage of American registered vessels was something over five and one-half millions; and when the war closed it was practically non-existent. The North was able to draw from its merchant service for the purposes of war no fewer than six hundred vessels of an aggregate tonnage of over a million and carrying seventy thousand men. Those ships and men went a long way towards turning the tide of victory to the North; but when peace was made the American commercial flag had disappeared from the seas.

It would be out of place here to go into a statement of the causes which co-operated with the substitution of iron for wood in shipbuilding to make it hard at first for America to regain her lost position, or into a discussion of the incomprehensible apathy (incomprehensible if one did not know the ways of American legislation) which successive Congresses have shown in the matter.

A year or so back, the nation seemed to have made up its mind in earnest to take hold of the problem of the restoration of its commercial marine; but the defeat in the early part of 1907 of the Ship Subsidies Bill left the situation much where it was when President Grant, President Harrison, and President McKinley, in turn, attempted to arouse Congress to the necessity of action; except that with the passage of time conditions only become worse and reform necessarily more difficult. The Ship Subsidies Bill was defeated largely by the votes of the representatives of the Mississippi Valley and the Middle Western States, and to an outsider the opposition of those regions looked very much like a manifestation of selfishness and lack of patriotism, on the part of the inland population jealous of the seaboard States. In the East, various reasons were given at the time for the failure of the measure. I happened myself to be travelling then through the States of the Mississippi Valley, and I discussed the situation with people whom I met, and particularly with politicians. The explanations which I received fell into one of two categories. Some said: "It is true that the Mississippi Valley and the West have little direct interest in our shipbuilding industry, but none the less we should like to see our merchant marine encouraged and built up. The trouble is that we have from experience acquired a profound distrust of a certain 'gang' in the Senate [and here would often follow the names of certain four or five well-known Senators, chiefly from the East], and the mere fact that these Senators were backing this particular bill was enough to convince us Westerners that it included a 'steal.'"

Others took this ground: "The Mississippi Valley and the West believe in the general principle of Protection, but we think that our legislation has carried this principle far enough. We should now prefer to see a little easing off. We do not believe that the right way to develop our commercial marine is, first by our tariff laws to make it impossible for us to build or operate ships in competition with other countries and then to be obliged, in order to equalise things, to have recourse to bounties. What we want is a modification of our law which will help us, in the first instance, to build and to run the ships at a reasonable price. When a bill to that effect comes along, the Mississippi Valley will be found all right."

Not a few of the voters in the East, also cordially interested in any plan that seemed to them promising and equitable for building up the American commercial marine, took the ground that it was an absurdity to build up barriers against foreign trade by enacting a tariff bill, such as the Dingley measure, with higher duties than the country had ever known, and then to attempt to overcome that barrier by means of bounty measures, which must themselves constitute a fresh form of taxation on the general public.

The mass of the people, in fact, are in sympathy with the movement to encourage American shipping, but, for sectional or other reasons, a large proportion of them objected to the particular form in which the end was sought to be reached in the last Congress. So long as the voice and opinion of Mr. Roosevelt have any weight, it is not to be expected that the subject is going to be allowed to drop; and with his strength of will and determination of character it is at least not improbable that, where successive Presidents before him have failed, he will, whether still in the Presidential chair or not, ultimately succeed, and that not the smallest of the reasons for gratitude to him which future generations of Americans will recognise will be that he helped to recreate the nation's merchant marine. At present, less than nine percent of the American foreign commerce is carried in American bottoms, a situation which is not only sufficiently humiliating to a people who but a short while ago hoped to dominate the carrying trade of all countries but also, what perhaps hurts the Americans almost as much as the injury to their pride, absurdly wasteful and unbusinesslike. English shipping circles may take the prospect of efforts being made by the United States to recover some measure of its lost prestige seriously or not: but it would be inadvisable to admit as a factor in their calculations any theory as to the inability of the Americans either to build ships or sail them as well as the best. With the growth of an American merchant marine—if a growth comes—will come also the obvious need of a larger navy; and other nations might do well to remember that Americans have never yet shown any inability to fight their ships, any more than they have to build or sail them.

In basing any estimate of the fighting strength of the United States on the figures of her army or navy as they look on paper, the people of other nations—Englishmen no less than any—leave out of sight, because they have no standard for measuring, that remarkable attribute of the American character, which is the greatest of the national assets, the combination of self-reliance and resourceful ingenuity which seems to make the individual American equal to almost any fortune. It is remarkable, but not beyond explanation. It is an essentially Anglo-Saxon trait. The British have always possessed it in a degree, if inferior to the present day American, at least in excess of other peoples. The history of the Empire bears witness to it on every page and it is in truth one of the most fundamentally English things in the American character. But the conditions of their life have developed it in Americans beyond any need which the Englishman has felt. The latter, living at home amid the established institutions of a society which moves on its way evenly and without friction regardless of any effort or action on his part, has had no occasion for those qualities on which the American's success, his life, have commonly depended from day to day amid the changing emergencies of a frontier life. The American of any generation previous to that which is now growing up has seldom known what it meant to choose a profession or a vocation in life; but must needs do the work that came to him, and, without apprenticeship or training, turn to whatever craft has offered.

The notion that every American is, without any special training, by mere gift of birthright, competent to any task that may be set him, is commonly said to have come in with Andrew Jackson; and President Eliot, of Harvard, has dubbed it a "vulgar conceit."[68:1] It is undoubtedly a dangerous doctrine to become established as a tenet of national belief and least of all men can the head of a great institution for the training of the nation's youth afford to encourage it. None the less, when the American character is compared with that of any European people, it has, if not justification, at least considerable excuse.

Once into a new mining camp in the West there drove in the same "stage-coach" two young men who became friends on the journey. Each was out to seek his fortune and each hoped to find it in the new community. Each had his belongings in a "valise" and in each "valise" among those belongings was a "shingle," or name-plate, bearing each the name of its respective owner followed by the words "Attorney at Law." The young men compared their shingles and considered. The small camp would not need two lawyers, even if it would provide a living for one. So they "matched" coins (the American equivalent of tossing up) to see which of the two should erase "Attorney at Law" from his sign and substitute "Doctor of Medicine." Which is history; as also is the following:

In another mining camp, some twenty-three years ago, there was at first no surveyor. Men paced off the boundaries of their claims and went to work as fancy inclined them, and in the town which began to grow up houses were built at random regardless of any street-line and with no finnicking considerations of a building frontage. So a young fellow whose claim was unpromising sent out to civilisation for a set of instruments (he had never seen a transit or a level before) and began business as a surveyor. He used to come to me secretly that I might figure out for him the cubic contents of a ditch or the superficial area of a wall. He could barely write and knew no arithmetic at all; but he worked most of the night as well as all the day, and when the town took to itself a form of organised government he was appointed official surveyor and within a few weeks thereafter was made surveyor to the county. I doubt not that G—— T—— is rich and prosperous to-day.

On a certain wharf, no matter where, lounged half a dozen seamen when to them came the owner of a vessel. It was in the days of '49 when anything that could be made to float was being put into commission in the California trade, and men who could navigate were scarce.

"Can any of you men" said the newcomer "take a boat out for me to San Francisco?"

"I'll do it, sir" said one stepping forward.

"Thunder, Bill!" exclaimed a comrade in an undertone, "you don't know nothing about navigating."

"Shut your mouth," said Bill. "Maybe I don't know nothing now, but you bet I will by the time I get to 'Frisco."

The same spirit guides almost every young American who drifts West to tackle hopefully whatever job the gods may send. The cases wherein he has any destiny marked out for him or any especial preference as to the lines on which his future career shall run (except that he may hope ultimately to be President of the United States) are comparatively few. In ten years, he may be a grocer or a banker or a dry-goods merchant or a real-estate man or a lawyer. Whatever he is, more likely than not ten years later he will be something else.

"What is your trade?" is the first question which an Englishman asks of an applicant for employment; and the answer will probably be truthful and certainly unimaginative.

"What can you do?" the American enquires under the same circumstances. "'Most anything. What have you got to do?" is commonly the reply.

It is an extraordinarily impressive experience for an Englishman to go out from the old-established well-formulated ways of the club-life and street-life of London, to assist in—not merely to watch but to co-operate in—the organisation of society in the wilderness: to see a town grow up—indeed, so far as his clumsy ability in the handling of an ax will permit, to help to build it; to join the handful of men, bearded, roughly clad, and unlettered most of them, proceeding deliberately to the fashioning of the framework of government, the election of town officers, the appointment of a sheriff, and the necessary provisions, rough but not inadequate, for dealing with the grosser forms of crime. Quickly thereafter, in the case which I have especially in mind, came the formation of the county government and, simultaneously therewith, the opportunity (automatically and by mere right of the number of the population) to elect a representative to the Territorial Legislature. In the first year, however, this last privilege had to be pretermitted. The Territorial laws required that any member must have been resident in the district from which he came for not less than six months prior to his election and must be able to read and write; and, as cruel chance would have it, among the first prospectors to find their way into the new diggings in the preceding winter, who alone could comply with the required term of residence, not one could write his name. Had but one been able to do it ever so crudely—could one but have made a reasonable pretence of an ability to stumble through the opening paragraphs of the Constitution of the United States,—that man would inevitably and unanimously have been elected a full-blown Legislator. As it was, the new district was perforce compelled to go without representation in the Territorial Capital.

"But," it will be objected, and by no one more quickly than by the American of the Eastern States, "All Americans do not go through these experiences. How many New Yorkers have helped to organise a new mining town?" Not many, certainly; and that is one of the reasons why New York is, perhaps, the least representative section of all the United States. But though the American of to-day may not have had to do these things, his father and his grandfather had to. The necessity has long ago left New York, but Illinois was not far removed from the circumstances of frontier life when Abraham Lincoln was a youth; and the men who laid the foundations of Minneapolis, and Kansas City, and Omaha, and Duluth, are still alive. The frontiersman is latent in every American.

For the benefit of many Englishmen who think that they have been to the United States, when as a matter of fact they have only been to New York, it may be as well to explain why New York City is the least typically American of all parts of the country. There are some who go back as far as Revolutionary days for the explanation, and point out that even then New York was more loyalist than patriot; one might go even farther back and show that New York always had a conspicuously large non-Anglo-Saxon element. But there is no need to go back even to the Revolution. In the century that has passed since then, the essential characteristics of the American character have been the products of the work which the people had to do in the subduing of the wilderness and of the isolation of the country—of its segregation from contact with the outside world. New York has been the one point in America farthest removed from the wilderness and most in touch with Europe, and it has been there that the chief forces which have moulded the American character have been least operative. The things in a New Yorker which are most characteristic of his New-Yorkship are least characteristically American, and among these is a much greater friendliness towards Great Britain than is to be found elsewhere except in one or two towns of specialised traits. This is not in any way to depreciate the position of New York as the greatest and most influential city in the United States, as well as (whatever may have been the relative standing of it and Boston up to twenty years ago) the literary and artistic centre of the country; and I do not know that any city of the world has a sight more impressive in its way than upper-middle New York—that is to say, than Fifth Avenue from Madison Square to the Park. But the English visitor who acquires his ideas of American sentiments from what he hears in New York dining-rooms or in Wall Street offices, is likely to go far astray. There is an instructive, if hackneyed, story of the little girl whose father boasted that she had travelled all over the United States. "Dear me!" said the recipient of the information, "she has travelled a great deal for one of her age!" "Yes, sir! all over the United States—all, except east of Chicago."

In the course of a long term of residence in the United States, this adaptability, this readiness to turn to whatever seems at the time to offer the best "opening" (which is so conspicuously a national trait but is not especially noticeable in the typical New Yorker) becomes so familiar that it ceases to be worth comment. I have seen among my own friends journalists become hotel managers, advertising solicitors turn to "real estate agents," merchants translated straight into responsible positions in the executive departments of railway companies, and railway men become merchants and bankers, editors change into engineers and engineers into editors, and lawyers into anything from ambassadors to hotel clerks. I am not now speaking in praise of these conditions or of the results in individual cases. The point to be noticed is that the people among whom these conditions prevail must in the long run develop into a people of extraordinary resourcefulness and versatility. And in the individual cases, the results are not nearly as deplorable as an Englishman might suppose or as they would be if the raw material consisted of home-staying Englishmen.

The trait however is, as has been said, essentially an Anglo-Saxon trait—an English trait—and the colonial Englishman develops the same qualities in a not incomparable degree. The Canadian and the New Zealander acquire a like unconquerable soul, but the Englishman at home is not much impressed thereby, chiefly for the reason that he is almost as ignorant of the Canadian and the New Zealander as he is of the American, and with the same benevolent ignorance.

In the individual citizen of the United States, he recognises the quality in a vague way. "Yankee ingenuity" is familiar to him and he is interested in, and amused at, the imperturbability with which the individual American—and especially the individual American woman—confronts and rises at least equal to whatever new and unheard of conditions he (or she) may find himself (or herself) placed among in England. But just as the American will not from the likability and kindliness of individual Englishmen draw any general inference as to the likability and kindliness of the nation, so the Englishman or other European rarely gives to these occasional attributes, which he sees reproduced again and again in particular Americans, their proper value as the manifestations of a national trait of the first importance, a trait which makes the people unquestionably formidable as competitors in peace and would make them correspondingly formidable as antagonists in war. The trait is, as I have said, perhaps the most precious of all the American national assets.

Great Britain has recently had abundant evidence of the difficulty of turning out all the paraphernalia of victory ready made and is now making earnest effort to guard against the necessity of attempting it again. But the rules which apply to European peoples do not apply, with anything like equal force, to America. England in the South African war found by no means despicable fighting material almost ready made in her colonial troops; and that same material, certainly not inferior, America can supply in almost unlimited quantities. From the West and portions of the South, the United States can at any time draw immense numbers of men who, in the training of their frontier life, their ability to ride and shoot, their habituation to privations of every kind, possess all those qualities which made the Boers formidable, with the better moral fibre of the Anglo-Saxon to back them.

But this quality of resourcefulness and self-reliance is not a mere matter of the moral or physical qualities of the individual. Its spirit permeates the nation as a unit. The machinery of the government will always move in emergencies more quickly than that of any European country; and unpreparedness becomes a vastly less serious matter. The standing army of the United States, in spite of the events of the last few years, remains little more than a Federal police force; and with no mercantile marine to protect and no colonies, there has been till lately no need of an American navy. But the European who measures the unpreparedness of the nation in the terms of the unpreparedness of his own, or any other European, country, not taking into account the colonial character of the population, the alertness and audacity of the national mind, the resourcefulness and confident self-reliance of the people, is likely to fall into error.

The reverse of the medal is, perhaps, more familiar to Europeans, under the form of what has generally been called the characteristic American lack of the sentiment of reverence. The lack is indubitably there—is necessarily there; for what the Englishman does not commonly understand is that that lack is not a positive quality in itself. It is but the reflection, as it were, or complement, of the national self-reliance. How should the American in his new country, with his "Particularist" spirit, his insistence on the independence and sovereignty of the individual, seem to Europeans other than lacking in reverence?

It is true that now, by mere passage of years, there are monuments in the United States which are beginning to gather the dignity and respect which naturally attach to age. The American of the present day has great veneration for the wisdom of the Fathers of the Republic, much love for the old buildings which are associated with the birth of the nation. Even the events of the Civil War are beginning to put on something of the majesty of antiquity, but there are still alive too many of the combatants in that war—who are obviously but commonplace men—for the figures of any but some three or four of the greatest of the actors to have yet assumed anything like heroic proportions. For the rest, what is there in the country which the living American has not made himself, or which his fathers did not make? The fabric of society is of too new a weaving, he knows too well the trick of it, for it to be wonderful in his eyes.

Lack of reverence is only a symptom of the American's strength—not admirable in itself, yet, as the index to something admirable, not, perhaps, altogether to be scorned. Nor must it be supposed that the lack of reverence implies any want of idealism, or any poverty of imagination, any absence of love or desire of the good and beautiful. The American is idealist and imaginative beyond the Englishman.

The American national character is, indeed, a finer thing than the European generally supposes. The latter sees only occasional facets and angles, offshoots and outgrowths, some of them not desirable but even grotesque in themselves, while those elements which unify and harmonise the whole are likely to escape him. The blunders of American diplomats—the *gaucheries* and ignorances of American consular representatives—these are familiar subjects to Europeans; on them many a travelling Englishman has based his rather contemptuous opinion of the culture of the American people as a whole. But it is unsafe to argue from the inferiority of the representative to the inferiority of the thing represented.

If two fruit-growers have adjoining orchards and, for the purpose of making a display at an agricultural show, one spends months of careful nourishing, training, and pruning of certain trees wherefrom he selects with care the finest of his fruit, while the other without preparation goes out haphazard to his orchard and reaches for the first fruit that he sees, it is probable that, judging by their exhibits, the public will get an erroneous idea of the characters of the orchards as a whole. And this is precisely the difference between the representatives whom the United States sends abroad and those sent to be displayed beside them by other nations.

There is no recognised diplomatic service in the United States, no school for the training of consular representatives, no training or nurturing or pruning of any sort. The fundamental objection of the American people to the creation of any permanent privileged class, has made the thing impossible in the past, while, under the system of party patronage, practically the entire representation of the country abroad—commercial as well as diplomatic—is changed with each change of government. The American cannot count on holding an appointment abroad for more than four years; and while four years is altogether too short a term to be considered a career, it is over-long for a holiday. So in addition to the lack of any trained class from which to draw, even among the untrained the choice is much restricted by the undesirability of the conditions of the service itself.

Though the conditions have improved immensely of late years, the fact remains that the consular service as a whole is not fairly to be compared on equal terms with that of other countries; and the majority of appointments are still made as the reward for minor services to the party in power. Nor are the conditions which govern the appointments to the less important diplomatic posts much different; but Great Britain has abundant cause to be aware that when the place is one which appeals to the ambition of first-class men, first-class men enough are forthcoming; though even Ambassadors to London are generally lacking in any special training or experience up to the time of their appointment.

Sydney Smith's phrase has been often enough quoted—that when a woman makes a public speech, we admire her as we admire a dog that stands upon its hind legs, not because she does it well, but because she does it at all. Congress includes among its members many curious individuals and, as a unit, it does queer things at times. State legislatures are sometimes strange looking bodies of men and on occasions they achieve legislation which moves the country to mirth. The representatives of the nation abroad make blunders which contribute not a little to the gaiety of the world. But the thing to admire is that they do these things at all—that the legislators, whether Federal or State, and the members of the consular service, appointed or elected as they are, and from the classes which they represent, do somehow manage to form legislative bodies which, year in and year out, will bear comparison well enough with other Parliaments, and do in one way and another succeed in giving their country a service abroad which is far from despicable as compared with that of other peoples, nor all devoid of dignity. The fact that results are not immeasurably worse than they are is no small tribute to the adaptability of the American character. There is no other national character which could stand the same test.

In the absence of any especially trained or officially dedicated class, the American people in the mass provides an amazing quantity of not impossible material out of which legislators and consuls may be made—just as it might equally well be made into whatever should happen to be required.

And this fact strikes at the root of a common misapprehension in the minds of foreigners as to the constitution of the American people, a misapprehension which is fostered by what is written by other foreigners after inadequate observation.

Much is thus written of the so-called heterogeneousness of the people of America. The Englishman who visits the United States for a few weeks only, commonly comes away with an idea that the New Yorker is the American people; whereas we have seen why it is that good American authorities maintain that in all the width and depth of the continent there is no aggregation of persons so little representative of the American people as a whole as the inhabitants of New York. After the Englishman has been in the United States for some months or a year or two, he grows bewildered and reaches the conclusion that there is no common American type—nothing but a patchwork of unassimilated units. In which conclusion he is just as mistaken as he was at first. There does exist a clearly defined and homogeneous American type.

Let us suppose that all the negroes had been swept as with some vast net down and away into the Gulf of Mexico; that the Irishmen had been gathered out of the cities and deposited back into the Atlantic; that the Germans had been rounded up towards their fellows in Chicago and Milwaukee and then tipped gently into Lake Michigan, while the Scandinavians, having been assembled in Minnesota, had been edged courteously over the Canadian border;—when all this had been done, there would still remain the great American People. Of this great People there would remain certain local variations—in parts of the South, in New England, on the plains—but each clearly recognisable as a variety only, differing but superficially and in substance possessing well-defined all the generic and specific attributes of the race.

If the entire membership of the Chicago Club were to be transferred bodily to the Manhattan Club-house in New York, and all the members of the Manhattan were simultaneously made to migrate from Fifth Avenue to Michigan Avenue, the club servants, beyond missing some familiar faces, would not find much difference. Could any man, waking from a trance, tell by the men surrounding him whether he was in the Duquesne Club at Pittsburgh or the Minnesota Club in St. Paul? And, if it be urged that the select club-membership represents a small circle of the population only, would the disturbance be much greater if the entire populations of Erie and Minneapolis and Kansas City were to execute a three-cornered "general post" or if Portland, Oregon, and Portland, Maine, swapped inhabitants? How long would it take the inhabitants of any one town to settle down in their new environment and go to work on precisely the same lines as their predecessors whom they dislodged? The novelty would, I think, be even less than if Manchester and Birmingham were miraculously made to execute a similar change in a night.

I do not underrate the magnitude of the problem presented to the people of America by the immense volume of immigration from alien races, and chiefly from the most undesirable strata in those races, of the last few years. On the other hand, I have no shadow of doubt of the ability of the people to cope with the problem and to succeed in assimilating to itself all the elements in this great influx while itself remaining unchanged.

It seems to me that the American himself constantly overestimates the influence on his national character of the immigration of the past. To persons living in New York, especially if, from philanthropic motives or otherwise, they are brought at all into immediate contact with the incoming hordes as they arrive, this stream of immigration may well be a terrifying thing. Those who are in daily touch with it can hardly fail to be oppressed by it, till it gets upon their nerves and breeds nightmares; and to such I have more than once recommended that they would do well to take a holiday of six months; journey through the West, and so come to a realisation of the magnitude of their country and correct their point of view. With every mile that one recedes from Castle Garden, the phenomenon grows less appalling: the cloud which was dense enough to blacken New York harbour makes not a veil to stop one ray of sunlight when shredded out over the Mississippi Valley and the Western plains.

A bucket of sewage (or of Eau de Cologne), however formidable in itself, makes very little difference when tipped into the St. Lawrence River. It is, of course, a portentous fact that some twenty millions of foreigners should have come into the country to settle in the course of half a century; but, after all, the process of assimilation has been constantly and successfully at work throughout those fifty years, and I think the figures will show that in no one year (not even in 1906, when the volume of immigration was the largest and contained the greatest proportion of the distinctly "undesirable" elements), if we set against the totals the number of those aliens returning to their own countries and deduct those who have come from the English-speaking countries, has the influx amounted to three quarters of one per cent of the entire population of the country.

So far, the dilution of the original character of the people by the injection of the foreign elements has been curiously slight, and while recognising that the inflow of the last few years has been more serious, both in quantity and character, than at any previous period, there does not seem to me any reason for questioning the ability of the country to absorb and assimilate it without any impairment of the fundamental qualities of the people. That at certain points near the seaboard, or in places where the newly introduced aliens become congested in masses of industrial workers, they present a local problem of extreme difficulty may be granted, but I think that those who are in contact with these local problems are inclined to exaggerate the general or national danger. The dominating American type will persist, as it persists to-day; the people will remain, in all that is essential, an Anglo-Saxon and a homogeneous people.

In one sense—and that the essential one—the American people is more homogeneous than the English. What individuals among them may have been in the last generation does not matter. The point is here:—When one speaks of the "average Englishman" (as, without regard to grammar, we persist in doing) what he really means is the typical representative of a comparatively small section of the population, from the middle, or upper middle, classes upward. It is the same when one speaks of Frenchmen. When he says "the average Frenchman dresses," or "thinks," or "talks" in such and such a way, he merely means that so does the normal specimen of a class including only a few hundred thousand men, and those city dwellers, dress or think or speak. The figure is excusable because (apart from the fact that an "average" of the entire population would be quite unfindable) the comparatively small class does indeed guide, rule, and, practically, think for, the whole population. So far as foreign countries are concerned, they represent the policy and mode of thought of the nation. The great numerical majority is practically negligible.

The same is true of the people of the United States, but with this difference, that the class represented by the "average"—the class of which, when grouped together, it is possible to find a reasonably typical representative—

includes in the United States a vastly larger proportion of the whole people than is the case in other countries. It would not be possible to find a common mental or moral divisor for the members of Parliament in the aggregate, and an equal number of Norfolk fishermen or Cornish miners. They are not to be stated in common terms. But no such incongruity exists between the members of Congress, Michigan lumbermen, and the men of the Texas plains.

It may be that within the smaller circle in England, the individuals—thanks to the public schools and the universities—are more nearly identical and the type specimen would more closely represent the whole. But as soon as we get outside the circle, much greater divergences appear. The English are *homogeneous* over a small area: the Americans *homogeneous* over a much larger.

"You may go all over the States," said Robert Louis Stevenson (and Americans will, for love of the man, pardon his calling their country "the States") "and—setting aside the actual intrusion and influence of foreigners, negro, French, or Chinese—you shall scarce meet with so marked a difference of accent as in forty miles between Edinburgh and Glasgow, or of dialect as in the hundred miles between Edinburgh and Aberdeen." And Stevenson understates the case. There are differences of speech in America, but at the most they remain so slight that, after all, the resident in one section will rather pride himself on his acuteness in recognising the intonation of the stranger as being that of some other—of the South, it may be, or of New England. An educated Londoner has difficulty in understanding even the London cockney. Suffolk, Cornish, or Lancashire—these are almost foreign tongues to him. The American of the South has at least no difficulty in understanding the New Englander: the New Yorker does not have to make the Californian repeat each sentence that he utters.

And this similarity of tongue—this universal mutual comprehensibility—is a fact of great importance to the nation. It must tend to rapidity of communication—to greater uniformity of thought—to much greater readiness in the people to concentrate as a nation on one idea or one object. How much does England not lose—there is no way of measuring, but the amount must be very great—by the fact that communication of thought is practically impossible between people who are neighbours? How much would it not contribute to the national alertness, to national efficiency, if the local dialects could be swept away and the peasantry and gentry of all England—nay of the British Isles—talk together easily in one tongue? It is impossible not to believe that this ease in the interchange of ideas must in itself contribute greatly to uniformity of thought and character in a people. Possessing it, it is not easy to see how the American people could have failed to become more homogeneous than the English.

But there is a deeper reason for their homogeneousness. The American people is not only an English people; it is much more Anglo-Saxon than the English themselves. We have already seen how the essential quality of both peoples is an Anglo-Saxon quality—what has been called (and the phrase will do as well as any other) their "Particularist" instinct. The Angles and Saxons (with some modification in the former) were tribes of individual workers, sprung from the soil, rooted in it, accustomed always to rely on individual labour and individual impulse rather than on the initiative, the protection, or the assistance of the State or the community. The constitutional history of England is little more than the story of the steps by which the Anglo-Saxon, by the strength which this quality gave him, came to dominate the other races which invaded or settled in Britain and finally worked his way up to and through the Norman crust which, as it were, overlay the country.

In England many institutions are of course Norman. An hereditary aristocracy, the laws of primogeniture and entail—these are Norman. By the help of them the Norman hoped to perpetuate his authority over the Saxon herd; and failed. Magna Charta, Cromwell, the Roundheads, the Puritans, the spirit of nonconformity, most of the limitations of the power of the Throne, the industrial and commercial greatness of Britain—these things are Anglo-Saxon. The American colonists (however many individuals of Norman blood were among them) were Anglo-Saxon; they came from the Anglo-Saxon body of the people and carried with them the Anglo-Saxon spirit. They did not reproduce in their new environment an hereditary aristocracy, a law of primogeniture or of entail. It is probable that no single English colony to-day, if suddenly cut loose from the Empire and left to fashion its form of society anew, would reproduce any one of these things. In the United States the Anglo-Saxon spirit went to work without Norman assistance or (as we choose to view it) Norman encumbrances. The Anglo-Saxon spirit is still working in England—never perhaps has its operation been more powerfully visible than in the trend of thought of the last few years. It is working also in the United States; but, because it there works independently of Norman traditions, it works faster.

In many things—in almost everything, as we shall see—the two peoples are progressing along precisely the same path, a path other than that which other nations are treading. In many things—in almost everything—the United States moves the more rapidly. It seems at first a contradiction in terms to say that the Americans are an English people and then to show that in many individual matters the English people is approximating to American models. It is in truth no contradiction; and the explanation is obvious. Both are impelled by the same spirit, the same motives, the same ambitions; but in England that spirit, those motives and ambitions work against greater resistance.

What looks at first like a peculiar departure on the part of the American people will again and again, on investigation, be found to be only the English spirit shooting ahead faster than it can advance in England. When, in a particular matter, it appears as if England was coming to conform to American precedent, it is, in truth only that, having given the impulse to America, she herself is following with less speed than the younger runner, but with such speed as she can.

If we bear this fact in mind we shall see how it is illustrated, borne out, supported by a score of things that it falls in our way to notice; as it is by many hundred things that lie outside our present province.

We shall have occasion to notice hereafter how in the past the American disposition to dislike England has been fed by the headlong and superficial criticism of American affairs by English "literary" visitors; and it is unfortunate that the latest[88:1] English visitor to write on the United States has hurt American susceptibilities almost as keenly as any of his predecessors. With all its brilliant qualities, few more superficial "studies" of American affairs have been given to the world than that of Mr. H. G. Wells.

Mr. Wells, by his own account, went about the country confronting all comers with the questions, "What are you going to make of your future?" . . . "What is the American Utopia, how much Will is there shaping to attain it?" This, he says, was the conundrum to find an answer to which he crossed the Atlantic, and he is much depressed because he failed in his search. "When one talks to an American of his national purpose he seems a little at a loss"; and when he comes to sum up his conclusions: "What seems to me the most significant and pregnant thing of all is . . . best indicated by saying that the typical American has no 'sense of the State.'"[89:1]

Has Mr. Wells ever gone about England asking Englishmen the same question: "What are you going to make of your future?" How much less "at a loss" does he anticipate that he would find them? Mr. Wells apparently expected to find every American with a card in his vest pocket containing a complete scheme of an American Utopia. He was disappointed because the government at Washington was not inviting bids for roofing in the country and laying the portion north of Mason and Dixon's Line with hot-water pipes.

The quality which Mr. Wells—seeing only its individual manifestations, quite baffled and unable to look beyond the individuals to any vision of the people as a whole (he travelled over a ludicrously small portion of the country)—sums up as a "lack of sense of the State" is in truth the cardinal quality which has made the greatness of the United States—and of England. It is precisely because the peoples rely on individual effort and not on the State that they have become greater than all other peoples. That is their peculiar political excellence—that they are not for ever framing schemes for a paternal all-embracing State, but are content to work each in his own sphere, asserting his own independence and individuality, from the things as they are, little by little towards the things as they ought to be.

If Mr. Wells had prevailed on any typical American to sit down and write what, as he understood it, his people were working to accomplish, the latter would have written something like this:

"We have got the basis of a form of government under which, when perfected, the individual will have larger liberty and better opportunity to assert himself than he has ever had in any country since organised states have existed. We have a people which enjoys to-day more of the material comforts of life than any other people on earth, and the chief political problem with which we are wrestling to-day is to see that that enjoyment is confirmed to them in perpetuity—not taken from them or hampered or limited by any power of an oppressive capitalism. We are spending more money, more energy, more earnest thought on the study of education as a science or art and on the endowment of educational establishments than any other people; as a result we hope that the next generation of Americans, besides being the most materially blessed, will be the most educated and intelligent of peoples. We are doing all we can to weed out dishonesty from our commercial dealings. In the period of our growth there was necessarily some laxity in our business ethics, but we are doing the best we know how to improve that, and we believe that on the whole our methods of doing business are calculated to produce more honest men than those in vogue in other countries. What we hope to make of our future therefore is to produce a nation of individuals freer, better off, and more honest than the world has yet seen. When that people comes it can manage its own government."

Not only are these, I fear, larger national aims than the average Englishman dares to propose to himself, but they are, I venture to say, much more definitely formulated in the "typical American's" mind. If Mr. Wells desires to find a people which considers it the duty of good citizenship to go about to fashion first the roofs and walls, rafters, cornices, and chimney-pots of a governmental structure, relying on the State afterwards to legislate comfort and culture and virtue into the people, he visited the wrong quarter of the globe. In the Latin races he will find the "sense of the State" luxuriantly developed.

Mr. Wells appears infinitely distressed by his failure to find any unified national feeling in the American people—by "the chaotic condition of the American Will"—by "the dispersal of power"—by the fact that "Americans knew of America mainly as the Flag." Which is a most curiously complete demonstration of the inadequacy of his judgment.

If Mr. Wells had seen the United States twenty-five years ago, ten years ago, and five years ago, before his present visit, the one thing that would have most impressed him would have been the amazing growth of the sense of national unity. Mr. Wells looks superficially upon the country as it is to-day and finds society more chaotic, distances larger, sentiment less crystallised than—*mirabile!*—in the older countries of Europe, and is plunged in despair. Had he had any knowledge of America's past conditions by which to measure the momentary phase in which he found the people, he would have known that exactly that thing of which he most deplores the absence is the thing which, in the last thirty years, has grown with more wonderful rapidity than anything else in all this country of wonderful growths.

The mere fact of this development of national feeling is a thing which will necessarily call for attention as we go on; for the present it is enough to say that Mr. Wells could hardly have exposed more calamitously the superficial and cursory quality of his "study" of the country.[92:1]

As a man may not be able to see the forest because of the trees, so Mr. Wells is as one who has stood by a great river's bank for a few minutes and has not seen the river for the flash of the ripples in the sun, the swirl of an eddy here and there, the flotsam swinging by on the current; and he has gone away and prattled of the ripples and the eddy and the floating branch. The great flow of the river down below does not expose itself to the vision of three minutes. He only comes to understand it who lives by the river for awhile, sits down by it and studies it—sees it in flood and drought—swims in it, bathes in it. Then he will forget the ripples and the branches and will come to know something of the steadiness of purpose, the depth and strength of it, its unity and its power. Nothing but a little more experience would enable Mr. Wells to see the national feeling of the American people.

Literature contains few pictures more delightful than that of Mr. Wells, drawn by himself, standing with Mr. Putnam—Herbert Putnam of all people!—in the Congressional Library at Washington and saying (let me quote): "'With all this,' I asked him 'why doesn't the place *think*?' He seemed, discreetly, to consider it did."

Mr. Putnam is fortunately always discreet. Otherwise it would be pleasant to know what *he* thought—of his questioner.

Note.—On the subject of the homogeneousness of the American people, see Appendix A.

FOOTNOTES:

[60:1] As a statement of this nature is always liable to be challenged let me say that it is based on the opinions expressed in conversation by the correspondents of English papers who came to America at that time in an endeavour to reach Cuba. They certainly did not anticipate that the American fleet would be able to stand against the Spanish. And, lest American readers should be in danger of taking offence at this, let it be remembered with how much apprehension the arrival of Admiral Cervera's ships was awaited along the eastern coast and how cheaply excellent seaside houses were to be acquired that year. Events have moved so rapidly since then (above all has the position of the United States in the world changed so much) that it is not easy now to conjure up the circumstances and sentiments of those days. If Americans generally erred as widely as they did in their estimate of the Spanish sea-power as compared with their own, it is not surprising that Englishmen erred perhaps a little more.

[68:1] *History of the United States*, by James Ford Rhodes, vol. vi.

[88:1] Mr. Crosland has written since; but he has fortunately not been taken sufficiently seriously by the American people even to cause them annoyance.

[89:1] *The Future in America*, by H. G. Wells, 1906.

[92:1] The futility of this kind of impressionist criticism is well illustrated by the fact that almost simultaneously with the appearance of Mr. Wells' book, a distinguished Canadian (Mr. Wilfred Campbell) was recording his impressions of a visit to England and said: "The people of Britain leave national and social affairs too much in the hands of such men [professional politicians]. There is a sad lack of the education of the people in the direction of a common patriotism. . . . She must get back to the sane idea that it is only as a nation and through the national ideal that she can help humanity. . . . She has great men in all walks of life; she has still the highest-toned Press in the world; she has . . . the most ideal legislature, she has great universities and churches with the finest and greatest Christian ideals. But none of these influences are used, as they should be, for the general national good. They work separately, or too much as individuals. It is only the leavening of these institutions with a large spirit of the national destiny that will lift Britain . . . out of its present material slough." (*The Outlook*, November 17, 1906.) These words are almost a paraphrase of Mr. Wells' indictment of the United States.

CHAPTER IV

MUTUAL MISUNDERSTANDINGS

America's Bigness—A New Atlantis—The Effect of Expansion on a People—A Family Estranged—Parsnips—An American Woman in England—An Englishman in America—International Caricatures—Shibboleths: dropped H's and a "twang"—Matthew Arnold's Clothes—The Honourable S—— B——.

"John Bull with plenty of elbow-room" was the phrase. It does not necessarily follow that the widest lands breed the finest people; and there is worthless territory enough in the United States to cut up into two or three Englands. Yet no patriotic American would wish one rod, pole, or perch of it away, whether of the Bad Lands, the Florida Swamps, the Alkali Plains of the Southwest, or the most sterile and inaccessible regions of the Rockies. If of no other use, each, merely as an instrument of discipline, has contributed something to the hardening of the fibre of the people; and good and bad together the domain of the United States is very large. Englishmen are aware of the fact, merely as a fact; but they seldom seem to appreciate its full significance.

Let us consider for a minute what would be the effect on the British people if it suddenly came into possession of such an estate. We are not talking now of distant colonies: Australia, Canada, New Zealand, South Africa—these may be equal together to more than another United States, and they are working out their own destiny. The inhabitants of each are a band of British men and women just as were the early inhabitants of the United States and as, essentially, the people of the United States still remain to-day. Each of those bands will follow its own path and work its own miracles—whether greater than that which the people of the United States has wrought or not, only later generations will know. Each of these, though British still and always, is launched on its individual career; and it is not of them that we are speaking now, but of the Englishmen who remain at home, of the present-day population of the British Isles.

What would be the result if suddenly the limits of the British Isles were to be miraculously expanded? What would happen if the floor of the ocean heaved itself up and Great Britain awoke to find the coast of Cornwall and Wales mysteriously reaching westward, the Irish Sea no more than a Hudson River which barely kept the shores of Lancashire and Cumberland from touching Ireland,—an Ireland of which the western coast—the coast of Munster and Connaught—was prolonged a thousand leagues towards the setting sun; while the west coast of the north of Scotland, Ross and Sutherland, had absorbed the Hebrides and stretched unbroken into two thousand miles of plain and mountain range—Britain no longer but Atlantis come again and all British soil? It was to nothing less miraculous that the thirteen original States fell heir. And what would be the effect on the British race?

Coal and iron, silver and gold, rivers full of fish, forest and prairie teeming with game, pasture for millions of cattle, wheat land and corn land, cotton land and orchard for any man who chose to take them;—the wretches struggling and stifling in the London slums having nothing to do but grasp axe and rifle and go out to subdue the wilderness;—farms, not by the half-acre, but by the hundred acres for every one of the unemployed. Is it possible to doubt that the race would be strengthened, not materially only, but in its moral qualities,—that Englishmen in another generation would not only be a wealthier and a more powerful people but a healthier, lustier, nobler? How then are we to suppose that just such a change, such an uplifting, has not come about in that other British people to whom all this has happened, who came into their wonderful birthright four generations ago and for a century and a quarter have been fashioning it to their will and being fashioned by it after the will of Another? By what process of logic, English reader, are you going to convince yourself that this race—your own with larger opportunities—is not the finer race of the two?

I have not, be it observed, expressed the opinion that the American national character is finer than the English; only that it is finer than the European commonly supposes. Nor am I expressing such an opinion now but only setting forth certain elementary considerations for the reader's judgment. When the European sees in the individual American, or in a dozen individual Americans, certain peculiarities, inelegancies, and sometimes even impertinences—call them what you will,—he is too prone to think that these are the essentials of the American character. The essentials of the American character are the essentials of the English character—with elbow-room. "While the outlook of the New Yorker is wider than ours," says Mr. Archer, "his standpoint is the same." In that elbow-room, with that wider outlook, it is likely that new offshoots from the character will have developed—excrescences, not perhaps in themselves always lovely—but if we remember what the trunk is from which they spring, or what it was, we shall probably think better, or less, of those excrescences, while remembering also the likelihood that in the larger room and richer soil the trunk itself may also have expanded and strengthened and solidified.

The English reader might decide for himself what justification there is for supposing that the character of that offset from the British stock which, a century and a quarter ago, was put in possession of this magnificent estate should have deteriorated rather than improved as compared with the character of that portion of the stock which remained rooted in the old soil hemmed in between the ancient boundaries.

There have been, of course, many other influences at work in the moulding of the American character, besides the mere vastness of his continent; but the fact remains that this has been immensely the most powerful of all the factors. English originally, the American is still English in his essentials, modified chiefly by the circumstances of his material environment, the magnificence of his estate, the width of his horizons, the disciplining of his nature by the Titanic struggle with the physical conditions of the wilderness and the necessary development of those qualities of resourcefulness, buoyancy, and self-reliance which the exigencies of that struggle have demanded. Moreover, what is almost the most important item of all, his entire national life has been lived, and that struggle conducted, in practical isolation from all contact with other peoples. Immigrants, indeed, from all of them, the United States has constantly been receiving; but as a nation the American people has been singularly segregated from the rest of the earth, blessedly free from friction with, and dependence on, other countries. As we have seen, it has had no friction with any Power except Great Britain; and with Great Britain itself so little that Englishmen hardly recall that it has occurred.

It may be worth while to stop one minute to rehearse and to re-enforce the points which so far it has been my aim to make.

For their own sakes, anything like conflict between the two nations is not to be dreamed of; but, for the world's sake, an intimate alliance between them in the cause of peace would be the most blessed conceivable thing. There is every justification for such an alliance, not merely in the incalculable benefits that would result, but in the original kinship of the peoples, the permanent and fundamental sympathy of their natures, and their community of ambitions and ways of thought. Unfortunately these reasons for union have been obscured by a century of aloofness, so that to-day neither people fully understands the other and they look, one at the other, from widely different standpoints. By reason chiefly of their isolation, in which they have had little contact with other peoples, the Americans have come to think of Great Britain as little less foreign (and by the accidents of their history as even more hostile) than any other Power. Still acknowledging as an historical fact the original kinship, they, like many a son who has gone out into the world and prospered exceedingly, take pleasure chiefly in contemplating how far they have travelled since they struck out for themselves and how many characteristics they have developed which were not part of the inheritance from the old stock. Dwelling on these they have become blind to the essential family likeness to that old stock which still remains their dominant trait.

Moreover, seeing how during all these years the old folk have let them go their own way, seemingly indifferent to their future, at times, intentionally or not, making that future none the easier of accomplishment, they have come to nurse a resentment against those at home and will not believe that the family still bears them an affectionate good-will quite other than it feels for even the best-liked of the friends who are not of the same descent.

On England's part, she saw the younger ones go out into the world with regret, strove to restrain them unwisely, obstinately, unfairly—and failed. Since then she has been very busy, supremely occupied with her own affairs. The young ones who had gone out into the world in, as seemed to her, such headstrong fashion, for all that she knows now that she was wrong, have been doing well, and she has always been glad to hear it, but—well, they were a long way off. At times she has thought that the young ones were somewhat too pushing—too anxious to get on regardless of her or others' welfare,— and half-heartedly (not all unintentionally, but certainly with no thought of alienating the affection of the others) she has interfered or passively stood in the young folk's way. At last the day came when she was horrified to find that the younger branch—very prosperous and independent now—had not only ceased to regard her as a mother but had come almost to the point of holding her as an enemy. It was at first incredible and she strove as best she could to put matters right and to explain how foreign to her wishes it was and how unnatural it seemed to her that there should be any approach to ill-feeling between them. But she does not convince the other, partly because she herself has in her turn grown out of touch with that other's ideas. At intervals she has met members of the younger branch who have come home to visit and she has discovered all sorts of new tricks of manner, new ways of speech, new points of view that they have picked up in their new surroundings, and, like the members of the younger branch themselves, she sees more of these little things than she does of the character that is behind them. Her vision of the family likeness is blurred by the intrusion of provoking little points of difference. She sees the mannerisms, but the strength of the qualities of which they are manifestations escapes her.

So it comes about that the two are at cross purposes. "We may call this country Daughter," wrote G. W. Steevens, "she does not call us Mother." The elder sincerely desires the affection of the younger—sincerely feels affection herself; but is hampered in making the other realise her sincerity by a constant desire to criticise those little foreign ways that the other has acquired. Just so does a parent obscure her love for a son by deploring the strange manners which he picks up at school; just so is she blinded to his real qualities as a man, because he will insist on giving his time to messing about with machinery instead of settling down properly to study for the Church.

Burke (was it not?) spoke of his love for Ireland as "dearer than could be justified to reason." Englishmen might well have difficulty in justifying to their reason their affection for America; for to hear an Englishman speak of American peculiarities and eccentricities, it would often seem that to love such men would be pure unreason. But these criticisms are no true index to the British national feeling for the Americans as a people. Does a brother not love his sister because he says rude things about her little failings? Americans hear the criticisms and, their own hearts being alienated from Great Britain, cannot believe that Britishers have any affection for them.

I am well aware that I make—and can make—no general statement from which many readers, both in England and America, will not dissent. Englishmen will arise to say that they do not love America; and Americans—many Americans—will vow with their hands on their hearts that they have the greatest affection for Great Britain. Vast numbers of Americans will protest against being called a homogeneous people, and a vast number more against the accusation of being still essentially English; the fact being that it is no easier now than it was in the days of Burke (I am sure of my author this time) to "draw up an indictment against a whole people." A composite photograph is commonly only an indifferent likeness of any of the individuals—least of all will the individual be likely to recognise it as a portrait of himself. But the type-character will stand out clearly—especially to the eyes of others not of the type. Most of the notions of Englishmen about Americans are drawn from the casual contact with individual Americans in England (where from contrast with their surroundings the little peculiarities stand out most conspicuously) or from the hasty "impressions" of visitors who have looked only on the surface—and but a small portion of that. Even, I am aware, after a lifetime spent in studying the two peoples, in pondering on their likenesses and unlikenesses and striving to measure the feeling of each for the other, there is always danger of talking what I will ask to be permitted to call "parsnips."

When I first went to the United States I carried with me a commission from certain highly reputable English papers to incorporate my "impressions" in occasional letters. Among the earliest facts of any moment which I was enabled to communicate to English readers was that the middle classes in America (I was careful to explain what the "middle classes" were in a country where none existed)—that the middle classes, I say, lived almost entirely on parsnips. I had not arrived at this important ethnological fact with any undue haste. I had already lived in the United States for some three months, half of which time had been spent in New York hotels and boarding houses and half in Northern New York and rural New England, where, staying at farms or at the houses of families in the smaller towns to which I bore letters of introduction, I flattered myself that I had probed deep—Oh, ever so deep!—below the surface and had come to understand the people as they lived in their own homes. And my ripened judgment was that the bulk of the well-to-do people of the country supported life chiefly by consumption of parsnips.

Some fifteen years later I was at supper at the Century Club in New York and the small party at our table as we discussed the scalloped oysters (which are one of the pillars of the Century) included a well-known American author and journalist and an even better known and much-loved artist. But why should I not mention their names? They were Montgomery Schuyler and John La Farge. Both had been to Europe that year—La Farge to pay his first visit to Italy, while Schuyler, whether with or without La Farge I forget, had made a somewhat extensive trip through rural England in, I think, a dog-cart. The conversation ran chiefly on their experiences and suddenly Schuyler turned to me with: "Here, you Englishman, why do the middle classes of England live chiefly on parsnips?"

The thing is incredible—except that it happened. Schuyler, no less than I fifteen years before, spoke in the fulness of conviction arising from what he, no less than I, believed to have been wide and adequate experience. The memory of that experience has made me tolerant of the cocksure generalisations with which the Englishman who has visited America, or the American who has been in England, for a few months delights to regale his compatriots on his return. Quite recently a charming American woman who is good enough to count me among her friends, was in London for the first time in her life. She is perhaps as typical a representative of Western American womanhood—distinctively Western—as could be found; very good to look upon, warm-hearted, fearless and earnest in her truth-loving, straightforward life. But in voice, in manner, and in frankness of speech she is peculiarly and essentially Western. She loved England and English people, so she told me at the Carlton on the eve of her return to America,—just loved them, but English women (and I can see her wrinkling her eyebrows at me to give emphasis to what she said) were so *dreadfully* outspoken: they did say such *awful* things! I thought I knew the one Englishwoman from whose conversation she had derived this idea and remembering my own parsnips, I forgave her. She has, since her return, I doubt not, dwelt often to her friends on this amazing frankness of speech in Englishwomen. And if she only knew what twenty Englishwomen thought of her outspokenness!

Not long ago I heard an eminent member of the medical profession in London, who had just returned from a trip to Canada and the United States with representatives of the British Medical Association, telling a ring of interested listeners all about the politics, geography, manners, and customs of the people of America. Among other things he explained that in America there was no such thing known as a *table d' hôte*; all your meals at hotels and restaurants had to be ordered *à la carte*. "I should have thought," he said, "that a good *table d' hôte* at an hotel in New York and other towns would pay. It would be a novelty." It may be well to explain to English readers who do not know America, that fifteen years ago a meal *à la carte* was, and over a large part of the country still is, practically unknown in the United States. The system of buying one's board and lodging in installments is known in America as "the European plan."

If it would not be too long a digression, I would explain how this is a cardinal principle of the American business mind. The disposition of every American is to take over a whole contract *en bloc*, which in England, where every man is a specialist, would be split into twenty different transactions. The American thinks in round numbers: "What will the whole thing come to?" he asks; while the Englishman wants to know the items. This habit permeates American life in every department. It is labour-saving. Few things amuse or irritate the American visitor to England more than the having to pay individually for a number of small conveniences which at home he is accustomed to have "thrown in"; and the first time when he is presented with an English hotel bill (I am not speaking of the modern semi-American hotels in London) with its infinite list of items, is an experience that he never forgets.

All of which is only to explain that the distinguished physician, when he spoke of the absence of *tables d'hôte* in America, was talking parsnips. His experience had been limited to a few hotels and restaurants in New York and one or two other large towns.

If only it were possible to catch in some great "receiver" or "coherer," or some similar instrument, all the things that were said in London in the course of twenty-four hours about the United States by people who had been there, and all the things that were said in New York in the same period about England by people of equal experience, and set them down side by side, it would make entertaining reading. The wonder is, not that we misunderstand each other as much as we do, but that somehow we escape a vast mutual, international contempt.

Several times in the course of my residence in the United States I have had said to me: "What! Are you an Englishman? But you don't drop your H's!"

Which is ridiculous, is it not, English reader? But before you smile at it, permit me to explain that it is no whit worse than when you say:—"What! Are you an American? But you don't speak with an accent!" Or possibly you call it a "twang" or you say "speak through your nose."

You may be dining, English reader, at, let us say, the Carlton or Savoy when a party of Americans comes into the room—Americans of the kind that every one knows for Americans as soon as he sees or hears them. The women are admirably dressed—perhaps a shade too admirably—and the costumes of the men irreproachable. But there is that something of manner, of walk, of voice which draws all eyes to them as they advance to their table, and the room is hushed as they arrange their seats. "Those horrid Americans!" says one of your party and no one protests. But at the next table to you there is seated another party of delightful people—low-voiced, well-mannered, excellently bred in every tone and movement. You wonder dimly if you have not met them somewhere. At all events you would very much like to meet them. They are infinitely more distressed than you at the behaviour of the American party which has just come in—because they are Americans also. And I may add that they will not be in the least flattered, if you should be lucky enough to meet them, by your telling them that you "never would have thought it."

Perhaps, English reader, you have lived long enough in some other country than England to have learned what a loathsome thing the travelling Englishman often appears. Possibly you have been privileged to hear the frank and unofficial opinion of some native of that country—an opinion not intended for your ears, but addressed to a compatriot of the speaker—of English people in general, based upon his experience of those whom he has seen. Such an experience is quite illuminating. I know few things more offensive than the behaviour of a certain class of German when he is in Paris. The noisy, nasal American at the Carlton or Savoy is no more representative of America than the loud-voiced, check-suited Englishman at Delmonico's or the Waldorf-Astoria is the man by whom you wish your nation to be judged. It may be a purposeful provision of a higher Power that the people of all countries should appear unprepossessing when they are abroad, for the fostering in each nation of the spirit of patriotism; for why should any of us be patriots if all the foreigners who came to our shores were as inoffensive as ourselves? The truth is that those who are inoffensive pass unnoticed. It is the occasional caricature—the parody—of the national type that catches our eye; and on him we too often base our judgment of a whole people.

Those Englishmen who only England know are inclined to think that the check-suited fellow countryman is a creation of the French and German comic press. Those who have lived outside of England for some considerable number of years have learned better. The late Senator Hoar in his

Autobiography of Seventy Years has some very shrewd remarks about Matthew Arnold. The Senator had a cordial regard for Matthew Arnold—"a huge liking" he calls his feeling,—and he has this delightful sentence in regard to him: "I do not mean to say that his three lectures on translating Homer are the greatest literary work of our time. But I think, on the whole, that I should rather have the pair of intellectual eyes which can see Homer as he saw him, than any other mental quality I can think of." "But"—and mark this—"Mr. Arnold has never seemed to me fortunate in his judgment about Americans . . . The trouble with Mr. Arnold is that he never travelled in the United States when on this side of the Atlantic. . . . He visited a great City or two, but never made himself acquainted with the American people. He never knew the sources of our power or the spirit of our people."

Senator Hoar, with a generous nature made thrice generous by the mellowness of years, speaking of the man he hugely liked, tempered the truth to a more than paternal mildness. But it is the truth. Matthew Arnold, to put it bluntly, was wrong-headed in his judgment of America and Americans to a degree which one living long in the United States only comes slowly and reluctantly to understand. And if he so erred, how shall all the lesser teachers from whom England gets its knowledge of America keep straight?

But what the American people really objected to in Matthew Arnold was not any blundering things that he said of them, but the fact that he wore on inappropriate occasions in New York a brown checked suit.

And across all the gulf of more than twenty years there looms up in my memory—"looms like some Homer-rock or Troy-tree"—the figure of the Hon. S——y B——l flaunting his mustard coloured suit, gridironed with a four-inch check, across three thousand miles of continent, to the delight of cities, filling prairies with wonder and moving the Rocky Mountains to undisguised mirth. And how could we others explain that he, with his undeniably John-Bull-like breadth of shoulder and ruddy face, was not a fair sample of the British aristocrat? Was he not an Honourable and the son of a Baron and the "real thing" in every way? I have no doubt that there still live in the prairie towns of North Dakota and in the recesses of the mountains of Montana hundreds of men and women, grown old now, who through all the mists of the years still remember that lamentable figure; and to them, though they may have seen and barely noticed ten thousand Englishmen since, the typical Britisher still remains the Hon. S——y B——l.

It is not possible to say how far the influence of one man may extend. I verily believe that twenty years ago those clothes of Matthew Arnold stood for more in America's estimate of England than the *Alabama* incident. Ex-President Cleveland, as we have seen, speaks of the "sublime patriotism and devotion to their nation's honour" of the "plain people of the land" who backed him up when war with Great Britain seemed to be so near. But I wonder in how many breasts the desire for war was inspired not by patriotism but by memory of the Hon. S——y B——l. And when the Englishman thinks of the possibility of war with the United States, with whom is it that he pictures himself as fighting? Some one individual American, whom he has seen in London, drunk perhaps, certainly noisy and offensive. Such a one stands in the mind of many an Englishman who has not travelled as the type of the whole people of the United States.

If it were possible for the two peoples to come to know each other as they really are—if one half of the population of each country could for a season change places with one half of the other, so that all the individuals of both nations would be acquainted with the ways and thoughts of the other, not as the comic artists draw them, nor as they are when they are abroad, but as they live their daily lives at home—then indeed would all thought of difference between the two disappear, and war between them be as impossible as war between Surrey and Kent.

CHAPTER V

THE AMERICAN ATTITUDE TOWARDS WOMEN

The Isolation of the United States—American Ignorance of the World—Sensitiveness to Criticism—Exaggeration of their Own Virtues—The Myth of American Chivalrousness—Whence it Originated—The Climatic Myth—International Marriages—English Manners and American—The View of Womanhood in Youth—Co-education of the Sexes—Conjugal Morality—The Artistic Sense in American Women—Two Stenographers—An Incident of Camp-Life—"Molly-be-damned"—A Nice Way of Travelling—How do they do it?—Women in Public Life—The Conditions which Co-operate—The Anglo-Saxon Spirit again.

It will be roughly true to say that the Englishman's misunderstanding of America is generally the result of misinformation—of "parsnips"—of having had reported to him things which are superficial and untrue; whereas the American's misunderstanding of England is chiefly the result of his absorption in his own affairs and lack of a standard of comparison. The Americans as a people have been until recently, and still are in only a moderately less degree, peculiarly ignorant of other peoples and of the ways of the world.

This has been unfortunate, so far as their judgment of England is concerned, in two ways,—first, as has already been said, because they have had no opportunity of measuring Great Britain against other nations, so that one and all are equally foreign, and second and more positively, in the general misconception in the American mind as to the character and aims of the British Empire and the temper of British rule. From the same authorities, the popular histories and school manuals, as supplied the American people for so long with their ideas of the conduct of the British troops in the Revolutionary War, they also learned of India and the British; and the one fact which every American, twenty years ago, knew about British India was that the English blew Sepoys from the mouths of cannon. Every American youth saw in his school history a picture of the thing being done. It helped to point the moral of British brutalities in the War of Independence and it was beaten into the plastic young minds until an impression was made which was never effaced. Of late years not a few Americans have arisen to tell the people something of the truth about British rule in India—of its uprightness, its beneficence, its tolerance,—but it will be a generation yet before the people as a whole has any approximate conception of the facts.

It was in no way to the discredit of the American people—and enormously to their advantage—that they were for so long ignorant of the world. How should they have been otherwise when separated from that world by three thousand miles of ocean? They had, moreover, in the problems connected with the establishment of their own government, and the expansion of that government across the continent, enough to occupy their thoughts and energies. For a century the people lived self-concentrated, introspective, their minds filled only with thoughts of themselves. If foreign affairs were discussed at all it was in curiously childlike and impracticable terms. The nation grew up a nation of provincials (there is no other word for it), with a provincialism which was somewhat modified, but still provincial, in the cities of the Atlantic coast, and which, after all, had a dignity of its own from the mere fact that it was continent-wide.

The Spanish-American War brought the people suddenly into contact with the things of Europe and widened their horizon. The war itself was only an accident; for the growth of American commerce, the increase of wealth, the uncontainable expansive force of their industrial energy, must have compelled a departure from the old isolation under any circumstances. The quarrel with Spain did but furnish, as it were, a definite taking-off place for the leap which had to be made.[113:1] Since then, foreign politics and foreign affairs have acquired a new interest for Americans. They are no longer topics entirely alien from their every-day life and thoughts. It would still be absurd to pretend that the affairs of Europe (or for that matter of Asia) have anything like the interest for Americans that they have for Europeans, or that the educated American is not as a rule still seriously uninformed on many matters (all except the bare bones of facts and dates) of geography, of ethnology, of world-politics which are elementary matters to the Englishman of corresponding education;[113:2] but with their *début* as a World-Power—above all with the acquisition of their colonial dependencies—Americans have become (I use the phrase in all courtesy) immensely more intelligent in their outlook on the affairs of the world. With a longer experience of the difficulties of colonial government, they will also come to appreciate more nearly at its true value the work which Great Britain has done for humanity.

Americans may retort that their knowledge of Europe was at least no scantier than the Englishman's knowledge of America, and the mistakes of travelling Englishmen in regard to the size, the character, and the constitution of the country have been a fruitful source of American witticism. But why should Englishmen know anything of the United States? The affairs of the United States were, after all, however big, the affairs of the United States and not of any other part of the rest of the world; while the affairs of Europe were the affairs of all the world outside of the United States. Undoubtedly the American could fairly offset the Englishman's ignorance of America against the American's ignorance of England; but what has never failed to strike an Englishman is the American's ignorance of other parts of the world, which might be regarded as common to both. They were not common to both; for, as has been said, since the beginning of her history, which has stretched over some centuries, England has been constantly mixed up with the affairs, not only of Europe, but of the remoter parts of the earth, while the United States for the single century of her history has lived insulated and almost solely intent on her own affairs. So though the American has no adequate retort against the Englishman for his ignorance, he need not defend it. It has been an accident of his geographical situation and needs no more apology than the Rocky Mountains. But, like the Rocky Mountains, it is a fact which has had a distinct influence on his character. It is probably unavoidable that a people—as an individual—which lives a segregated life, with its thoughts turned almost wholly on itself, should come to exaggerate, perhaps its own weaknesses, but certainly its virtues.

The boy who lives secluded from companionship, when he goes out into the world, will find not merely that he is diffident and sensitive about his own defects, real or imaginary, but that he is different from other people. It may take him all his life to learn—perhaps he will never learn—that his emotional and intellectual experiences are no prodigies of sentiment and phœnixes of thought, but the common experiences of half his fellows. It has been such a life of seclusion that the American people lived—though they hardly know it (and perhaps some American readers will resent the statement), because the mere fact of their seclusion has prevented them from seeing how secluded, as compared with other peoples, they have been. It is true that individual Americans of the well-to-do classes travel more (and more intelligently) than any other people except the English; but this, as leavening the nation, is a small off-set against the daily lack of mental contact with foreign affairs at home.

But if this sheltered boy be further occasionally subjected to the inspection and criticism of some one from the outside world—a candid and outspoken elderly relative—he is likely to become, on the one hand, morbidly sensitive about those things which the other finds to blame, and, on the other, no less puffed up with pride in whatever is awarded praise.

Both these tendencies have been acutely developed in the American character—an extraordinary sensitiveness to criticism by outsiders of certain national foibles, and a no less conspicuous belief in the heroic proportions of their good qualities. For surely no people has ever been blessed in its seclusion with such an abundance of criticism of singular candour. The frank brutality with which the travelling Englishman has made his opinions known on any peculiar trait or unusual institution which he has been pleased to think that he has noticed in the United States has been vastly more ill-mannered than anything in the manners of the Americans themselves on which he has animadverted so freely. The thing most comparable to it—most nearly as ill-mannered—is, perhaps, the frank brutality with which the travelling

American expresses himself—and herself—in regard to things in Europe. In it, in fact, we see again another aspect of the same fundamentally English trait,—the insistence on the sovereignty of the individual—and Americans come by it legitimately. Every time that they display it they do but make confession of their original Anglo-Saxon descent and essentially English nature. The Englishman in America has, however, had some excuse for his readiness to criticise, in the interest, the anxiety, with which, at least until recent years, the Americans have invited his opinions. But if that has gone some way to justify his expression of those opinions, it has furnished no sort of excuse for the lack of tact and breeding which he has shown in the process. The American does not commonly wait for the invitation.

"My! But isn't that quaint! Now in America we ..." etc. So speaks an uncultivated American on seeing something that strikes him—or her—as novel in London, not unkindly critical, but anxious to give information about his country—and uninvited. But whereas the Englishman is so accustomed to the abuse and criticism of other peoples that the harmless chatter of the American ripples more or less unheeded by him, the American, less case-hardened in his isolation, hears the Englishman's bluntly worded expression of contempt, and it hurts. It does not hurt nearly as much now as it did twenty years ago; but the harm has largely been done.

The harm would not be so serious but for the American sensitiveness bred of his seclusion,—if that is (at the risk of seeming to repeat myself I must again say) he knew enough of the world to know that he himself has precisely the same critical inclination as the Englishman and that it is a trait inherited from common ancestors. The Anglo-Saxon race acquired early in its life the conviction that it was a trifle better than any other section of the human kind. And it is justified. We—Americans and Englishmen alike—hold that we are better than any other people. That the root-trait has developed somewhat differently in the two portions of the family is an accident.

The Englishman—who, when at home, has himself lived, not entirely secluded, but in a measure shut off from contact with other peoples—by continual going abroad and never-ceasing friction with his neighbours, by perpetual disheartenment with the perplexities of his colonial empire, has become less of a critic than a grumbler; and to do him justice he is, in speech, infinitely more contemptuous of his own government than he is of the American or any other. The American on the contrary remains cheerfully, light-heartedly, garrulously critical. He comes out in the world and gazes on it young-eyed, and he prattles: "My father is bigger than your father, and my sister has longer hair than yours, and my money box is larger than yours." It is neither unkindly meant nor, by Englishmen, very unkindly taken. It is less offensive than the mature, corrosive sullenness of the Englishman; but it is the same thing. "The French foot-guards are dressed in blue and all the marching regiments in white; which has a very foolish appearance. And as for blue regimentals, it is only fit for the blue horse or the Artillery," says the footman in Moore's *Zeluco*.

Similarly, when he has been praised, the lad has plumed himself unduly on the thing that found approval. He would not do it now; for the American people of to-day is, as it were, grown up; but, again, the harm has been done. Americans rarely make the mistake of underestimating the excellence of their virtues. Nor is it their fault, but that of their critics.

The American people labours under delusions about its own character and qualities in several notable particulars. It exaggerates its own energy and spirit of enterprise, its sense of humour and its chivalrousness towards women. That it should be aware that it possesses each of these qualities in a considerable degree would do no harm, for self-esteem is good for a nation; but it believes that it possesses them to the exclusion of the rest of mankind. And that is unfortunate; for it makes the individual American assume the lack of these qualities in the English and thereby decreases his estimate of the English character. I am not endeavouring to reduce the American's good opinion of himself—only to make him think better of the Englishman by assuring him that in each of these particulars there is remarkably little to choose between them. And what excellence he has in each he owes to the fact that he is in the main English in origin.

That Americans should think that they have a higher respect for womanhood than any other people is not surprising; for every other people thinks precisely the same thing. They would be unique among peoples if they thought otherwise. Frenchman, German, Italian, Spaniard, Greek—each and every one who has not had his eyes opened by travel and knowledge of the world believes, with no less sincerity of conviction than the American, that to him alone of all peoples has it been vouchsafed to know how duly to reverence the divine feminine. To the Englishman it seems that the German not seldom treats his wife much as if she were a cow; and he is sometimes distressed at the way in which, for all the pretty things he says to her, the Frenchman, not of the labouring classes only, will allow his wife to work for and wait on him. While the language which an Italian can, on occasions, use towards the partner of his joys is, to English ears, appalling. But each goes on serenely satisfied of his own superiority. You others, you may pay lip-service, yes; but deep down, in the heart of hearts—*we* know. The American has as good a right to this same foible as any other; but what is to be noted is that whereas Englishmen laugh at the pretensions of Continental peoples, they have been willing to accept the chivalry of the American at his own valuation: the fact being that the valuation is not originally American, but was made by the travelling Englishmen of the past who communicated their appraisement to the people at home as well as to the American whom they complimented. Englishmen of the present day have accepted the belief as an inheritance and without question; for it was at least a generation and a half ago that the myth first obtained vogue, and the two facts most commonly adduced in its support by the English visitors who spread it were, first, that women could walk about the streets of New York or any other American city, unattended and at such hours as pleased them, without being insulted; and, second (absurdly enough), the provision of special "ladies' entrances" to hotels, which seem to have enormously impressed several English visitors to the United States who afterwards wrote their "impressions."

For the first of these, it is a mere matter of local custom and police regulation. When it is understood that in certain streets of certain cities, at certain hours of the day, no women walk unattended except such as desire to be insulted, it is probable that other women, who go there in ignorance, will suffer inconvenience. Nor has the difference in local custom any bearing whatever on the respective morality of different localities. These things are arranged differently in different countries; that is all. Moreover, in this particular a great change has come over American cities in late years, nor are all American cities or all English by any means alike.

A similar change has come in the matter of "ladies' entrances" to hotels. If the provision of the separate doors was a sign of peculiar chivalry, are we then to conclude that their disappearance shows that chivalry is decaying? By no means. It only means that the hotels are improving. The truth is that as the typical old-fashioned hotel was built and conducted in America, with the main entrance opening directly from the street into the large paved lobby, where men congregated at all hours of the day to talk politics and to spit, where the porters banged and trundled luggage, and whither, through the door opening to one side, came the clamour of the bar-room, it was out of the question that women should frequent that common entrance. Had a hotel constructed and managed on the same principles been set down in any English town, women would have declined to use it at all, nor would Englishmen have expected their womenfolk to do so. Americans avoided the difficulty by creating the "ladies' entrance." But it was no evidence of superior chivalry on the part of the people that, having devised a place not fit for woman's occupancy and more unpleasant than was to be found in any other part of the world, they provided (albeit rather inadequate) means by which women could avoid visiting it.

Once I saw two young English girls—sweet girls, tall and graceful, with English roses blooming in their cheeks—come down-stairs in the evening, after dinner, as they might have done in any hotel to which they had been accustomed in Europe, to the lobby of the Fifth Avenue Hotel in New York. It was a time of some political excitement and there are enough men living now who remember what the Fifth Avenue Hotel used to be at such seasons twenty years ago. The girls—it was probably their first night on American soil and they could not stand being cooped up in their room upstairs all the evening—made their way to the nearest seat and sat down clinging each to the other's hand. Around them surged perhaps a hundred men, chewing, spitting, smoking, slapping each other on the backs, and laughing coarsely. The girls gazed in wonder and with visibly increasing embarrassment for perhaps five minutes, before they slipped away, the roses in their cheeks doubly carmine and still clinging each to the other's hand.

For the benefit of my companion (whose appearance indicated an Englishman) an American on an adjoining seat held forth to his friends on what he called the "indecency" of the conduct of the girls in coming down to the public hall and the "effrontery" of Englishwomen in general.

In hotels of the modern type there is no need for women to use a separate entrance or to draw their skirts aside and hurry through the public passages. But it is sad if we must conclude that the building of such hotels is an evidence of dying national chivalry.

Every American firmly believes that he individually, as well as each of his countrymen, has by heritage a truer respect for womanhood than the peoples of less happy countries are able to appreciate. But many Americans also believe that every Englishman is rough and brutal to his wife, who does daily all manner of menial offices for him, a belief which is probably akin to the climatic fiction and of Continental origin. In the old days, when there was no United States of America, the peoples of the sunny countries of Southern Europe jibed at the English climate; and with ample justification. English writers have never denied that justification—in comparison with Southern Europe; and volumes could be compiled of extracts from English literature, from Shakespeare downwards, in abuse of British fog and mist and rain. But because Nice and Naples are entitled to give themselves airs, under what patent do Chicago and Pittsburgh claim the same right? Why should Englishmen submit uncomplainingly when Milwaukee and Duluth arrogate to themselves the privilege of sneering at them which was conceded originally and willingly enough to Cannes? Riverside in California, Columbia in South Carolina, Colorado Springs or Old Point Comfort—these, and such as they, may boast, and no one has ground for protest; but it is time to "call for credentials" when Buffalo, New Haven, and St. Paul and the rest propose to come in in the same company. If, in the beginning of things, English writers had had to compare the British climate not with that of Europe but with the northern part of the United States, the references to it in English literature would constitute a hymn of thanksgiving.

As the case stands, however, the people of all parts of the United States alike, in many of which mere existence is a hardship for some months in the year, are firmly convinced that the inhabitants of the British Isles are in comparison with themselves profoundly to be pitied for their deplorable climate; and it is probable that the prevailing idea as to the Englishman's habitual treatment of his wife has much the same origin. It is an inheritance of the Continental belief that John Bull sold his womenfolk at Smithfield. The frequency of international marriages and the continued stream of travel across the Atlantic is, of course, beginning to correct the popular American point of view, but there are still millions of honest and intelligent people in the United States who, when they read that an American girl is going to be married to an Englishman, pity her from their hearts in the belief that, for the sake of a coronet or some such bauble, she is selling herself to become a sort of domestic drudge.

Occasionally also even international marriages turn out unhappily; and whenever that is the case the American people hear of it in luxuriant detail. But of the thousands of happy unions nothing is said. Not many years ago there was a conspicuous case, wherein an American woman, whom the people of the United States loved much as Englishmen loved the Empress Frederick or the Princess Alice, failed to find happiness with an English husband. Of the rights and wrongs of that case, neither I nor the American people in the mass know anything, but it is the generally accepted belief in the United States that the lady's husband was some degrees worse than Bluebeard. I would not venture to hazard a guess at the number of times that I have heard a conversation on this subject clinched with the argument: "Well, now, look at N—— G——!" Against that one instance the stories of a thousand American women who are living happy lives in Europe would not weigh. If they do not confess their unhappiness, indeed, "it is probably only because they are proud, as a free-born American girl should be, and would die rather than to let others know the humiliations to which they are subjected."

"Oh, yes, you Englishmen!" an American woman will say, "your manners are better than our American men's and you are politer to us in little things. But you despise us in your hearts!" It is an argument which, in anything less than a lifetime, there is no way of disproving. American men also, of course, habitually comfort themselves with the same assurance, viz.,—that with less outward show of courtesy, they cherish in their hearts a higher ideal of womanhood than an Englishman can attain to. Precisely at what point this possession of a higher ideal begins to manifest itself in externals does not appear. After twenty years of intimacy in American homes I have failed to find any trace of it.

Let me not be misunderstood! I know scores of beautiful homes in the United States, in many widely sundered cities, where the men are as courteous, as chivalrous, as devoted to their wives—and where the women are as sweet and tender to, and as wholly wrapped up in, their husbands—as in any homes on earth. As I write, the faces of men and women rise before me, from many thousand miles away, whom I admire and love as much as one can admire and love one's fellow-beings. There are these homes I hope and believe—there are noble men and beautiful women finding and making for themselves and each other the highest happiness of which our nature is capable—in every country. But we are not now speaking of the few or of the best individuals, but of averages; and after twenty years of opportunity for observing I have entirely failed to find justification for believing that there is any peculiar inward grace in the American which belies the difference in his outward manner.

This is, of course, only an individual opinion,[126:1] which is necessarily subject to correction by any one who may have had superior opportunities for forming a trustworthy judgment. I contend, however, not as a matter of opinion, but as what seems to me to be a certainty, that whatever may be the inward feeling in regard to the other sex on the part of the men of either nation after they have arrived at mature years, the young Englishman, as he comes to manhood, possesses a much higher ideal of womanhood than is possessed by the young American of corresponding age. And I hold to this positively in spite of the fact that many Americans possessing a large knowledge of transatlantic conditions may very possibly not admit it.

I rejoice to believe that to the majority of English youths of decent bringing up at the age at which they commonly leave the public school to go to the university, womanhood still is a very white and sacred thing, in presence of which a mere man or boy can but be bashful and awkward from very reverence and consciousness of inferiority, even as it surely was a quarter of a century ago and as, at the same time, it as surely was not to the youth of the United States. Again, of course, in both countries there are differences between individuals, differences between sets and cliques; but I am not mistaken about the tone of the English youth of my own day nor am I mistaken about the tone of the American youths, of the corresponding class, with whom I have come in intimate contact in the United States. Their language about, their whole mental attitude towards, woman was during my first years in America an amazement and a shock to me. It has never ceased to be other than repellent.

The greater freedom of contact allowed to the youth of both sexes in the United States, and above all the co-educational institutions (especially those of a higher grade), must of course have some effect, whether for good or ill. It may be that the early-acquired knowledge of the American youth is in the long run salutary; that his image of womanhood is, as is claimed, more "practical," and likely to form a better basis for happiness in life, than the dream and illusion of the English boy; but here we get into a quagmire of mere speculation in which no individual opinion has any virtue whatsoever.

I am well aware also of the serious offence that will be given to innumerable good and earnest people in the United States by what I now say. This is no place to discuss the question of co-education. I am speaking only of one aspect of it, and even if it were to be granted that in that one aspect its results are evil, that evil may very possibly be outweighed many times over by the good which flows from it in other directions. Even in expressing the opinion that there is this one evil result, I am conscious that I shall call down upon myself much indignation and some contempt. It will be said that I have not studied the subject scientifically (which may be true) and that I am not acquainted with what the statistics show (which is less true), and that my observation has been prejudiced and superficial. Let me say however that I have been brought to the conclusions to which I have been forced not by prejudice but against prejudice and when I would have much preferred to feel otherwise. Let me also say that my condemnation is not directed against the elementary public schools so much as against that more select class of co-educational establishments for pupils of less juvenile years. It would, I think, be interesting to know what percentage of the girls at present at a given number of such establishments are the daughters of parents—fathers especially—who were at those same institutions in their youth. It is a subject which—so amazed was I, coming with an English-trained mind, at certain things which were said in incidental conversation—I sought a good many opportunities of enquiring into; with the result that I know that there are some parents who, though they had fifty daughters, would never allow one to go to the institutions at which they themselves spent some years. And this condemnation covers, to my present memory, five separate institutions scattered from the Atlantic Coast to the Mississippi River.

"If you marry an American girl," says *Life*—I quote from memory,—"you may be sure that you will not be the first man she has kissed. If you marry an English one, you may be certain you will not be the last."

Whether this is true, viz., that, granting that the American girl is, before marriage, exposed to more temptation than her English sister, the latter more than makes up for it in the freedom of married life, is another quagmire. No statistics, whether of marriage, of divorce, or of the ratio of increase in population, are of any use as a guide. Each man or woman, who has had any opportunity of judging, will be guided solely by the narrow circle of his or her personal experience; and I know that the man whose opinion on the subject I would most regard holds exactly opposite views to myself—and what my own may be I trust I may be excused from stating. But while on the subject of the relative conjugal morality of the two peoples opinions will differ widely with individual experience, I have never met a shadow of disagreement in competent opinion in regard to the facts about the youth of the two countries. It may be, as I have heard a clever woman say, that the way for a member of her sex to get the greatest enjoyment out of life is to be brought up in America and married in England. If so let us rejoice that so many charming women choose the way which opens to them the possibility of the greatest felicity.

There is, of course, a widespread impression in England that American women as a rule are not womanly. The average American girl acquires when young a self-possession and an ability to converse in company which Englishwomen only, and then not always, acquire much later in life. Therefore the American girl appears, to English eyes, to be "forward," and she is assumed to possess all the vices which go with "forwardness" in an English maiden. Which is entirely unjust. Let us remember that there is hardly a girl growing up in England to-day who would not have been considered forward and ill-mannered to an almost intolerable degree by her great-grandmother. But that the girls of to-day are any the less womanly, in all that is sweet and essential in womanliness, than any generation of their ancestors, I for one do not believe. Nor do I believe that in another generation, when they will perhaps, as a matter of course, possess all the social precocity (as it seems to us) of the American girl of to-day, they will thereby be any the less true and tender women than their mothers.

In particular, are American girls supposed to be so commercially case-hardened that their artistic sensibilities have been destroyed. A notorious American "revivalist" some years ago returned from a much-advertised trip to England and told his American congregations of the sinfulness which he had seen in the Old World. Among other things he had seen, so he said, more tipsy men and women in the streets of London in (I think) a month than he had seen in the streets of his native town of Topeka, Kansas, in some—no matter what—large number of years. Very possibly he was right. But he omitted to say that he had also seen several million more sober ones. A population of 6,000,000 frequently contains more drunkards than one of 30,000. It also contains more metaphysicians. On the same principle it is entirely likely that the American girl, who talks so much, says many more foolish things than the English one who, if she can help it, never talks at all. The American girl is only a girl after all, and because she has acquired a conversational fluency which the Englishwoman will only arrive at twenty years later, it is not just to suppose that she must also have acquired an additional twenty years' maturity of mind.

Most English readers are familiar with the picture of the American girl who flits through Europe seeing nothing in the Parthenon or in Whitehall beyond an inferiority in size and splendour to the last new insurance company's building in New York. She has been a favourite character in fiction, and the name of the artist who first imagined her has long been lost. Perhaps she was Daisy Miller's grandmother. In reality, in spite of that lack of reverence which is undoubtedly a national American characteristic, the average American woman has an almost passionate love for those glories of antiquity which her own country necessarily lacks, such as few Englishwomen are capable of feeling.

"How in our hearts we envy you the mere names of your streets!" said an American woman to me once. It is not easy for an English man or woman to conceive what romance and wonder cluster round the names of Fleet Street and the Mall to the minds of many educated Americans. We, if we are away from them for half a dozen years, long for them in our exile and rejoice in them on our return. The American of sensibility feels that he—and more especially she—has been cut off from them for as many generations and adores them with an ardour proportionately magnified. But he (or she) would not exchange Broadway or Fifth Avenue or Euclid Avenue or the Lake Shore Drive, as the case may be, for all London.

It was once my fortune to show over Westminster Abbey an American woman whose name, by reason of her works—sound practical common-sense works,—has come to be known throughout the United States, and I heard "the wings of the dead centuries beat about her ears." I took her to Poet's Corner. She turned herself slowly about and looked at the names carved on either side of her, and then looked down and saw the names that lay graven beneath her feet; and she dropped sobbing on her knees upon the pavement. Johnson was not kind to the American colonies in his life. Those tears which fell upon his name, where it is cut into the slab of paving, were part of America's revenge.

We all remember Kipling's "type-writer girl" in San Francisco,—"the young lady who in England would be a Person,"—who suddenly quoted at him Théophile Gautier. It is an incident which many Englishmen have read with incredulity, but which has nothing curious in it to the American mind. A stenographer in my own offices subsequently, I have heard, married a rich owner of race-horses and her dinners I understand are delightful. She was an excellent stenographer.

In all frontier communities, where women are few and the primitive instincts have freer play than in more artificial societies, there blossoms a certain rough and ready chivalrousness which sets respect of womanhood above all laws and makes every man a self-constituted champion of the sex. This may be seen in a thousand communities scattered over the farther West; but it is no outgrowth of the American character, for it flourishes in all new societies in all parts of the world, no matter to what nationality the men of those societies belong.

In a certain mining camp, late at night, a man—a man of some means, the son of a banker in a neighbouring town—was walking with a woman. Neither was sober and the woman fell to the ground. The man kicked her and told her to get up. As she did not comply he cursed her and kicked her again. Then chanced to come along one Ferguson, a gambler and a notoriously "bad man," who bade the other stop abusing the woman, whereupon he was promptly told to go to —— and mind his own business. Ferguson replied that if the other touched the woman again he would shoot him. It was at this point that the altercation brought me out of my cabin, for the thing was happening almost where my doorstep (had I had a doorstep) ought to have been. The banker's son paid no heed to the warning, and once more proceeded to kick the woman. Thereupon Ferguson shot him. And, with the weapon which Ferguson carried and his ability as a marksman, when he shot, it might be safely regarded as final.

No attempt was made to punish Ferguson. The deputy sheriff, arriving on the scene, heard his story and mine and those of one or two others who had heard or seen more or less of what passed; and Ferguson was a free man. Nor was there any shadow of a suggestion in camp that justice should take any other course. The fact was established that the dead man had been abusing a woman. Ferguson had only done what any other man in camp must have done under the same circumstances.

And while the banker's son was a person of some standing, there was certainly nothing in her whom he had maltreated, beyond her mere womanhood, to constitute a claim on one grain of respect.

I trust that I am not reflecting on the chivalry of the camp when I record the fact that the name by which the lady was universally known was "Molly-be-damned." The camp, to a man, idolised her.

One of my earliest revelations of the capacity of the American woman was vouchsafed to me in this way:

A party of us, perhaps fifteen in all, had travelled a distance of some two thousand miles to assist at the opening of a new line of railway in the remote Northwest. We duly arrived at the little mountain town at which the junction was to be made between the line running up from the south and that running down from the north, over which we had come. The ceremony of driving the last spike was conducted with due solemnity, after which a "banquet" was given to us by the Mayor and citizens of the small community. After the banquet—which was really a luncheon—we again boarded our train to complete the run to the southern end of the line, a number of the citizens of the town with their wives accompanying us on the jaunt. It chanced to be my privilege to escort to the car, and for the remainder of the journey to sit beside, the wife of the editor of the local paper. She was pretty, charming, and admirably dressed. We talked of many things,—of America and England, of the red Indians, and of books,—when in a pause in the conversation she remarked:

"I think this is such a nice way of travelling, don't you?"

It puzzled me. What did she mean? Was she referring to the fact that we were on a special train composed of private cars, or what? The truth did not at first occur to me—that she was referring to railway travelling as a whole, it being the first time that she had ever been on or seen a train. Explanations followed. She had been brought by her parents, soon after the close of the Civil War, when two or three years old, across the plains in a prairie schooner (the high-topped waggon in which the pioneers used to make their westward pilgrimage), taking some four months for the trip from the old home in, I think, Kentucky. At all events she was a Southerner. Since then during her whole life she had known no surroundings but those of the little mining settlement huddled in among the mountains, her longest trips from home having been for a distance of thirty or forty miles on horseback or on a buckboard. She had lived all her life in log cabins and never known what it meant to have a servant. She read French and Italian, but could not take any interest in German. She sketched and painted, and was incomparably better informed on matters of art than I, though she knew the Masters only, of course, through the medium of prints and engravings. What she most dearly longed to do in all the world was to see a theatre—Irving for choice—and to hear some one of the Italian operas, with the libretti of which, as well as the music, so far as her piano would interpret for her, she was already familiar.

Now at last the railway had come and she was, from that day forward, within some six days' travelling of New York; and her husband had faithfully promised that they should go East together for at least three or four weeks that winter. And as she sat and talked in her soft Southern voice, there in the heart of the wilds which had been all the world to her, she might, so far as a mere man's eyes could judge, have been dropped down in any country house in England to be a conspicuously charming member of any charming house-party.

Familiarity with similar instances, though I think with none more striking, has robbed the miracle, so far as its mere outward manifestation is concerned, of something of its wonder; but the inward marvel of it remains as inexplicable as ever. By what power or instinct do they do it? With nothing of inheritance, so far as can be judged, to justify any aspirations towards the good or beautiful, among the poorest and hardest of surroundings, with none but the most meagre of educational facilities, by what inherent quality is it that the American woman, not now and again only, but in her tens of thousands, rises to such an instinctive comprehension of what is good and worth while in life, that she becomes, not through any external influence, but by mere process of her own development, the equal of those who have spent their lives amid all that is most beautifying and elevating of what the world has to afford? When she takes her place, graciously and composedly, as the mistress of some historic home or amid the surroundings of a Court, we say that it is her "adaptability." But adaptability can do no more than raise one to the level of one's surroundings—not above them. Is it ambition? But whence derived? And by what so tutored and guided that it reaches only for what is good? How is it tempered that she remains all pure womanly at the last?

It may be that the extent to which, especially in the Western States, American women of wealth and position are called upon to bear their share in public work—in the management of art societies, the building of art buildings and public libraries, the endowment and conduct of hospitals, and in educational work of all kinds—gives them such an opportunity of showing the qualities which are in them, as is denied to their English sisters of similar position but who live in older established communities. And there are, of course, women in England who lead lives as beautiful and as beneficent as are lived anywhere upon earth. The miracle is that the American woman—and, again I say, not now and again but in her tens of thousands—becomes what she is out of the environment in which her youth has so often been lived.

It will be necessary later to refer to the larger part played by American women, as compared with English, in the intellectual life of the country,—a matter which itself has, as will be noticed, no little bearing on the question of the merits and demerits of the co-education of the sexes. The best intellectual work, the best literary work, the best artistic work, is still probably done by the men in the United States; but an immensely larger part of that work is done by women than in England, and in ordinary society (outside of the professional literary and artistic circles) it is the women who are generally best informed, as will be seen, on literature and art. To which is to be added the fact that they take a much livelier and more intelligent interest than do the majority of Englishwomen in public affairs, and assume a more considerable share of the work of a public or quasi-public character in educational and similar matters. It might be supposed that this greater prominence of women in the national life of the country was in itself a proof that men deferred more to them and placed them on a higher level; but when analysed it will be found far from being any such proof. Rather is woman's position an evidence of, and a result of, man's neglect. By which it is not intended to imply any discourteous or inconsiderate neglect; but merely that American men have been, and still are, of necessity more busy than Englishmen, more absorbed in their own work, whereby women have been left to live their own lives and thrown on their own resources much more than in England. The mere pre-occupation of the men, moreover, necessarily leaves much work undone which, for the good of society, must be done; and women have seized the opportunity of doing it. They have been especially ready to do so, inasmuch as the spirit of work and of pushfulness is in the atmosphere about them, and they have been educated at the same schools as the men. The contempt of men for idleness, in a stage of society when there was more than enough work for all men to do, necessarily extended to the women. It is not good, in the United States, for any one, woman hardly more than man, to be idle.

Women being compelled to organise their own lives for themselves, they carried into that organisation the spirit of energy and enthusiasm which filled the air of the young and growing communities. Finding work to their hands to do, they have done it—taking, and in the process fitting themselves to take, a much more prominent part in the communal life than is borne by their sisters in England or than those sisters are to-day, in the mass, qualified to assume. Precisely so (as often in English history) do women, in some beleaguered city or desperately pressed outpost, turn soldiers. No share in, or credit for, the result is to be assigned to any peculiar forethought, deference, or chivalrousness on the part of the men, their fellows in the fight. It is to the women that credit belongs.

And while we are thus comparing the position of women in America with their position in England, it is to be noted that so excellent an authority among Frenchmen as M. Paul Cambon, in speaking of the position of women in England, uses precisely the same terms as an Englishman must use when speaking of the conditions in America. Americans have gone a step farther—are a shade more "Feminist"—than the English, impelled, as has been seen, by the peculiar conditions of their growing communities in a new land. But it is only a step and accidental.

Englishmen looking at America are prone to see only that step, whereas what Frenchmen or other Continental Europeans see is that both Englishmen and Americans together have travelled far, and are still travelling fast, on a path quite other than that which is followed by the rest of the peoples. In their view, the single step is insignificant. What is obvious is that in both is working the same Anglo-Saxon trait—the tendency to insist upon the independence of the individual. Feminism—the spirit of feminine progress—is repugnant to the Roman Catholic Church; and we would not look to see it developing strongly in Roman Catholic countries. But, what is more important, it is repugnant to all peoples which set the community or the state or the government before the individual, that is to say to all peoples except the Anglo-Saxon.

We see here again, as we shall see in many things, how powerless have been all other racial elements in the United States to modify the English character of the people. The weight of all those elements must be, and, so far as they have any weight, is directly against the American tendency to feminine predominance. All the Germans, all the Irish, all the Frenchmen, Spaniards, Italians, or other foreigners who are in the United States to-day or have ever come to the United States have not, as Germans, or Irish, or Frenchmen, contributed among them one particle, one smallest impulse, to the position which women hold in the life of the country to-day; rather has it been achieved in defiance of the instincts and ideas of each of those by the English spirit which works irrepressibly in the people. There could hardly be stronger testimony to the dominating quality of that spirit. One may approve of the conditions as they have been evolved; or one may not. One may be Feminist or anti-Feminist. But whether it be for good or evil, the position which women hold in the United States to-day they hold by virtue of the fact that the American people is *Anglais*—an English or Anglo-Saxon people.

And in spite of all the precautions that I have taken to make myself clear and to avoid offence, I feel that some word of explanation, lest I be misunderstood, is still needed. It is not here said that American men do not place woman on a higher plane than any Continental European people. I earnestly believe that both branches of the Anglo-Saxon stock do hold to a higher ideal of womanhood than some (and for all I know to the contrary, than all) of the peoples of Europe. What I am denying is that Americans have any greater reverence for women, any higher chivalrousness, than Englishmen. And this denial I make not with any desire to belittle the chivalry of American men but only in the endeavour to correct the popular American impression about Englishmen, which does not contribute to the promotion of that good-will which ought to exist between the peoples. I am not suggesting that Americans should think less of themselves, only that, with wider knowledge, they would think better of Englishmen.

And, on the subject of co-education, it seems that yet another word is needed, for since this chapter was put into type, it has had the advantage of being read by an American friend whose opinion on any subject must be valuable, and who has given especial attention to educational matters. He thinks it would be judicious that I should make it clearer than I have done that, in what I have said, I am not criticising the American co-educational system in any aspect save one. He writes:

"The essential purpose of the system of co-education which had been adopted, not only in the State universities supported by public funds, but in certain colleges of earlier date, such as Oberlin, in Ohio, and in comparatively recent institutions like Cornell University, of New York, is to secure for the women facilities for training and for intellectual development not less adequate than those provided for the men.

"It was contended that if any provision for higher education for women was to be made, it was only equitable, and in fact essential, that such provision should be of the best. It was not practicable with the resources available in new communities, to double up the machinery for college education, and if the women were not to be put off with instructors of a cheaper and poorer grade and with inadequate collections and laboratories, they must be admitted to a share of the service of the instructors, and in the use of the collections, of the great institutions.

"It is further contended by well-informed people that what they call a natural relation between the sexes, such as comes up in the competitive work of university life, so far from furthering, has the result of lessening the risk of immature sentiment and of undesirable flirtations. By the use of the college system, the advantages of these larger facilities can be secured to women, and have in fact been secured without any sacrifice of the separate life of the women students.

"In Columbia University, for instance (in New York City), the women students belong to Barnard College. This college is one of the seven colleges that constitute Columbia University: but it possesses a separate foundation and a faculty of its own. The women students have the advantage of the university collections and of a large number of the university lectures. The relation between the college and the university is in certain respects similar to that of Newnham and Girton with the University of Cambridge, with the essential difference that Barnard College constitutes, as stated, an integral part of the university, and that the Barnard students are entitled to secure their university degrees from A.B. to Ph.D."

From the above it is by no means certain that on the one point on which I have dwelt, his opinion coincides with mine; and the best explanation thereof that I can offer is that while he knows certain parts of the country and some institutions better than I, I know certain parts of the country and some institutions better than he. And we will "let it go at that."

As for the rest, for the general economic advantages of the co-educational system to the community, I think I am prepared to go as far as almost anyone. I am even inclined to follow Miss M. Carey Thomas, the President of Bryn Mawr College, who attributes the industrial progress of the United States largely to the fact that the men of the country have such well-educated mothers. It seems to me a not unreasonable or extravagant suggestion. I am certainly of the opinion that the conversational fluency and mental alertness of the American woman, as well as in large measure her capacity for bearing her share in the civic labour, are largely the result of the fact that she has in most cases had precisely the same education as her brothers.

At present I believe that something more than one-half (56 per cent.) of the pupils in all the elementary and secondary schools, whether public or private, in the United States are girls; and that the system is permanently established cannot be questioned. What are known as the State universities, that is to say universities which are supported entirely, or almost entirely, by State grants, or by annual taxes ordered through State legislation, have from their first foundation been available for women students as well as for men. The citizens, who, as taxpayers, were contributing the funds required for the foundation and the maintenance of these institutions, took the ground, very naturally, that all who contributed should have the same rights in the educational advantages to be secured. It was impossible from the American point of view to deny to a man whose family circle included only daughters the university education, given at public expense, which was available for the family of sons.

Co-education had its beginning in most parts of the United States in the fact that in the frontier communities there were often not enough boy pupils to support a school nor was there enough money to maintain a separate school for girls; but what began experimentally and as a matter of necessity has long become an integral part of the American social system. So far from losing ground it is continually (and never more rapidly than in recent years) gaining in the Universities as well as in the schools, in private as well as public institutions.

But, as I said in first approaching the subject, the merits or demerits of co-education are not a topic which comes within the scope of this book. It was necessary to refer to it only as it impinged on the general question of the relation of the sexes.

FOOTNOTES:

[113:1] The English reader will find this explained at length in Mr. A. R. Colquhoun's work, *Greater America*.

[113:2] That Americans may understand more clearly what I mean and, so understanding, see that I speak without intention to offend, I quote from the list of "arrangements" in London for the forthcoming week, as given in to-day's London *Times*, those items which have a peculiarly cosmopolitan or extra-British character:

Friday—Pilgrims' Club, dinner to Lord Curzon of Kedleston, ex-Viceroy of India.

Saturday—Lyceum Club, dinner in honour of France to meet the French Ambassador and members of the Embassy, etc.

Sunday—Te Deum for Greek Independence, Greek Church, Moscow Road.

Monday—Royal Geographical Society, Sir Henry MacMahon on "Recent Exploration and Survey in Seistan."

Tuesday—Royal Colonial Institute, dinner and meeting. Royal Asiatic Society, Major Vost on "Kapilavastu." China Association, dinner to Prince Tsai-tse and his colleagues, Mr. R. S. Grundy, C. B., presiding.

Wednesday—Central Asian Society, Mr. A. Hamilton on "The Oxus River." Japan Society, Professor J. Takakusu on "Buddhism as we Find it in Japan."

This, it should be explained, is not a good week, because it is "out of the season," but the list will, I fancy, as it stands suffice to give American readers an idea of the extent to which London is in touch with the interests of all the world—an idea of how, by comparison, it is impossible to speak of New York (and still more of America as a whole) as being other than non-cosmopolitan, or in a not offensive sense, provincial.

[126:1] It is worth remarking that Dr. Emil Reich (whose opinion I quote not because I attach any value to it personally, but in deference to the judgment of those who do) prophesies that the "silent war" between men and women in the United States "will soon become so acute that it will cease to be silent." It is to be borne in mind, of course, that the Doctor's experience in the United States has as yet been but inconsiderable.

CHAPTER VI

ENGLISH HUMOUR AND AMERICAN ART

American Insularity—A Conkling Story—English Humour and American Critics—American Literature and English Critics—The American Novel in England—And American Art—Wanted, an American Exhibition—The Revolution in the American Point of View—"Raining in London"—Domestic and Imported Goods.

It is no uncommon thing to hear an American speak of British insularity—the Englishman's "insular prejudices" or his "insular conceit." On one occasion I took the opportunity of interrupting a man who, I was sure, did not know what "insular" might mean, to ask for an explanation.

"Insular?" he said. "It's the same as insolent—only more so."

Flings at Britain's "insularity" were (like the climatic myth) originally of Continental European origin; and from the Continental European point of view, the phrase, both in fact and metaphor, was justified. England *is* an island. So far as the Continent of Europe is concerned, it is *the* island. And undoubtedly the fact of their insular position, with the isolation which it entailed, has had a marked influence on the national temperament of Englishmen. Ringed about with the silver sea, they had an opportunity to meditate at leisure on their superiority to other peoples, an opportunity which, if not denied, was at least restricted in the case of peoples only separated from neighbours of a different race by an invisible frontier line, a well bridged stream, or a mountain range pierced by abundant passes. Their insularity bred in the English a disposition different from the dispositions of the Continental peoples just as undeniably as it kept them aloof from those peoples geographically.

Vastly more than Great Britain, has the United States been isolated since her birth. England has been cut off from other civilisations by twenty miles of sea; America by three thousand. As a physical fact, the "insularity" of America is immensely more obvious and more nearly complete than that of Britain; and it is no less so as a moral fact. It is true that America's island is a continent; but this superiority in size has only resulted in producing more kinds of insularity than in England. The American character is, in all the moral connotation of the word, pronouncedly more insular than the British.

Like the English, except that they were much more effectively staked off from the rest of the world, the Americans have found the marvel of their own superiority to all mankind a fit and pleasing subject for contemplation. Perhaps there was a time when Englishmen used to go about the world talking of it; but for some generations back, having settled the fact of their greatness entirely to their satisfaction, they have ceased to put it into words, merely accepting it as the mainspring of their conduct in all relations with other peoples, and without, it is to be feared, much regard for those other peoples' feelings. Americans are still in the boasting stage. Mr. Howells has said that every American when he goes abroad goes not as an individual citizen but as an envoy. He walks wrapped in the Stars and Stripes. It is only the insularity of the Britisher magnified many times.

It is as if there were gathered in a room a dozen or so of well-bred persons, talking such small talk as will pass the time and hurt no susceptibilities. It may be that the Englishman in his small talk is unduly dogmatic, but in the main he complies with the usages of the circle and helps the game along. To them enters a newcomer who will hear nothing of what the others have to say—will take no share in the discussion of topics of common interest—but insists on telling the company of his personal achievements. It may be all true; though the others will not believe it. But the accomplishments of the members of the present company are not at the moment the subject of conversation; nor is it a theme under any circumstances which it is good manners to introduce. This is what not a few American people are doing daily up and down through the length and breadth of Europe; and they must pardon Europe if, occasionally, it yawns, or if at times it expresses its opinions of American manners in terms not soothing to American ears.

"The American contribution to the qualities of nations is hurry," says the author of *The Champagne Standard*, and this has enough truth to let it pass as an epigram; but many Americans have a notion that their contribution is neither more nor less than All Progress. With their eyes turned chiefly upon themselves, they have seen beyond a doubt what a splendid, energetic, pushful people they are, and they have talked it all over one with another. Moreover, have not many visitors, though finding much to criticise, complimented them always on their rapidity of thought and action? So they have come to believe that they monopolise those happy attributes and, going abroad, whenever they see—it may be in England, or in Germany—an evidence of energy and force, they say: "Truly the world is becoming Americanised!" Bless their insular hearts! America did not invent the cosmic forces.

When the first suspension bridge was thrown over Niagara, there was a great and tumultuous opening ceremony, such as the Americans love, and many of the great ones of the United States assembled to do honour to the occasion, and among them was Roscoe Conkling. Conkling was one of the most brilliant public men whom America has produced: a man of commanding, even beautiful, presence and of, perhaps, unparalleled vanity. He had been called (by an opponent) a human peacock. After the ceremonies attending the opening of the bridge had been concluded, Conkling, with many others, was at the railway station waiting to depart; but, though others were there, he did not mingle with them, but strutted and plumed himself for their benefit, posing that they might get the full effect of all his majesty.

One of the station porters was so impressed that, stepping up to another who was hurrying by trundling a load of luggage, he jerked his thumb in Conkling's direction and:

"Who's that feller?" he asked. "Is he the man as built the bridge?"

The other studied the great man a moment.

"Thunder! No," said he. "He's the man as made the Falls."

It is curious that with their sense of humour Americans should so persistently force Europeans into the frame of mind of that railway porter. The Englishman, in his assurance of his own greatness, has come to depreciate the magnitude of whatever work he does; nor is it altogether a pose or an affectation. He sees the vastness of the British Empire and the amazing strides which have been made in the last two generations, and wonders how it all came about. He knows how proverbially blundering are British diplomacy and British administration, so he puts it all down to the luck of the nation and goes grumbling contentedly on his way. There is no country in which policies have been so haphazard and unstable, or ways of administration so crude and so empirical, as in the United States. "Go forth, my son," said Oxenstiern, "go forth and see with how little wisdom the world is governed"; and on such a quest, it is doubtful if any civilised country has offered a more promising field for consideration than did the United States from, say, the close of the Civil War to less than a decade ago. All thinking Americans recognise this fact to the full; but whereas the Englishman sees only the blunders that he has made and marvels at the luck that pulled him through, the American generally ignores the luck and is more likely to believe that whatever has been achieved is the result of his peculiar virtues.

I never heard an American ascribe the success of any national undertaking to the national luck. The Englishman on the other hand is for ever speaking of the "luck of the British Army," and the "luck that pulls England through."

And there is one point which I have never seen stated but which is worth the consideration of Americans. It has already been said that it would be of great benefit if the American people knew more of the British Empire as a whole. They have had an advantage in appreciating the magnitude of their own accomplishments in the fact that their work has all to be done at home. They have had the outward signs of their progress constantly before their eyes. It is true that the United States is a large country; but it is continuous. No oceans intervene between New York and Illinois, or between Illinois and Colorado; and the people as a whole is kept well informed of what the people is doing.

The American comes to London and he sees things which he regards with contemptuous amusement much as the Englishman might regard some peculiar old-world institution in a sleepy Dutch community. The great work which is always being done in London is not easy to see; there is so much of Old London (not only in a material sense) that the new does not always leap to the eye. The man who estimates the effective energy of the British people by what he sees in London, makes an analogous mistake to that of the Englishman who judges the sentiments of America by what is told him by his charming friends in New York. The American who would get any notion of British enterprise or British energy must go afield—to the Upper Nile and Equatorial Africa, to divers parts of Asia and Australia. He cannot see the Assouan dam, the Cape to Cairo Railway, the Indian irrigation works, from the Carlton Hotel, any more than a foreigner can measure the destiny of the American people by dining at the Waldorf-Astoria.

This is a point which will bear insisting on. Not long ago an American stood with me and gazed on the work which was being done in the Strand Improvement undertaking, and he said that it was a big thing. "But," he added thoughtfully, "it does not come up to what we have on hand in the Panama Canal." I pointed out that the Panama Canal was not being cut through the heart of New York City and apparently the suggestion was new to him. The American rarely understands that the British Isles are no more—rather less—than the thirteen original states. Canada and India are the British Illinois and Florida, Australia and New Zealand represent the West from Texas to Montana, while South Africa is the British Pacific Slope; just as Egypt may stand for Cuba, and Burma and what-not-else set against Alaska and the Philippines. Many times I have known Americans in England to make jest of the British railways, comparing them in mileage with the transcontinental lines of their own country. But the British Transcontinental lines are thrown from Cairo to the Cape, from Quebec to Vancouver, from Brisbane to Adelaide and Peshawar to Madras. The people of the United States take legitimate pride in the growth of the great institutions of learning which have sprung up all over the West; but there are points of interest of which they take less account, in similar institutions in, say, Sydney and Allahabad.

It is not necessary to say that I do not underestimate the energy of the American character. I have seen too much of the people, am familiar with too many sections of the country, and have watched it all growing before my eyes too fast to do that. But I think that the American exaggerates those qualities in himself at the expense of other peoples, and he would acquire a new kind of respect for Englishmen—the respect which one good workman necessarily feels for another—if he knew more of the British Empire.

A precisely similar exaggeration of his own quality has been bred by similar causes in the American mind in his estimate of his national sense of humour. I am not denying the excellence of American humour, for I have in my library a certain shelf to which I go whenever I feel dull, and for the books on which I can never be sufficiently grateful. The American's exaggeration of his own funniness is not positive but comparative. Just as he is tempted to regard himself as the original patentee of human progress, and the first apostle of efficiency, so he is very ready to believe that he has been given something like a monopoly among peoples of the sense of humour. With a little more humour, he would undoubtedly have been saved from this particular error. Especially are the Americans convinced that there is no humour in Englishmen. Germans and Frenchmen may possess humour of an inferior sort, but not Englishmen. It is my belief that in the American clubs where I find copies of *Fliegende Blätter* and the *Journal Amusant*, these papers are much more read than *Punch*, and in not a few cases, I fear, by men who have but slight understanding of the languages in which they are printed. Indeed, *Punch* is a permanent, hebdomadally-recurrent proof to American readers that Englishmen do not know the meaning of a joke.[153:1] Americans, of course, do not understand more than a small proportion of the pages of *Punch* any more than they would understand those pages if they were printed in Chinese; but because *Punch* is printed in English they think that they do understand it, and because they cannot see the jokes, they conclude that the jokes are not there.

A certain proportion of American witticisms are recondite to English readers for precisely similar reasons, but the American belief is that when an Englishman fails to understand an American joke, it is because he has no sense of humour; when an American cannot understand an English one, it is because the joke is not funny. It is a view of the situation eminently gratifying to Americans; but it is curious that their sense of humour does not save them from it.

Whatever American humour may be, it is not subtle. It has a pushfulness—a certain flamboyant self-assertiveness—which it shares with some other things in the United States; and, however fine the quality of mind required to produce it, a rudimentary appreciative sense will commonly suffice for its apprehension. The chances are, when any foreigner fails to catch the point of an American joke or story, that it is due to something other than a lack of perceptive capability.

What I take to be (with apologies to Mr. Dunne) the greatest individual achievement in humorous writing that has been produced in America in recent years, the Wolfville series of books of Mr. Alfred Henry Lewis, is practically incomprehensible to English readers, not from any lack of capacity on their part, but from the difficulties of the dialect and still more from the strangeness of the atmosphere. In the same way the Tablets of the scribe Azit Tigleth Miphansi must indeed be but ancient Egyptian to Americans. But it would not occur to an Englishman to say, because Americans have not within their reach the necessary data for a comprehension of Mr. Reed, that, therefore, they do not understand a joke. Still less because he himself falls away baffled from the Old Cattleman does the Englishman conclude that the Wolfville books are not funny. He merely deplores his inability to get on terms with his author. The English public indeed is curiously ready to accept whatever is said to be funny and comes from America as being in truth humorous even if largely unintelligible; but few Americans would give credit for the existence of humour in those parts of an English book outside their ken. Yet I think, if it were possible to get the opinion of an impartial jury on the subject, their verdict would be that the number of humorous writers of approximately the first or second class is materially greater in England than in the United States to-day. I am sure that the sense of humour in the average of educated Englishmen is keener, subtler, and eminently more catholic than it is in men of the corresponding class in the United States. The Atlantic Ocean, if the Americans would but believe it, washes pebbles up on the beaches of its eastern shores no less than upon the western.[155:1]

American humour [distinctively American humour, for there are humorous writers in America whose genius shows nothing characteristically American; but among those who are distinctively American I should class nearly all the writers who are best known to-day, Mr. Clemens (Mark Twain), Mr. Dunne, Mr. Lewis, Mr. Lorimer, Mr. Ade]—this distinctively American humour, then, stands in something the same relation to other forms of *spirituellisme* as the work of the poster artist occupies to other forms of pictorial art. Poster designing may demand a very high quality of art, and the American workmen are the Cherets, Grassets, Muchas, of their craft. Few of them do ordinary painting, whether in oil or water colour. Fewer still use the etcher's needle. None that I am aware of attempts miniatures—except Mr. Henry James, who, if Americans may be believed, is not an American, and he has invented a department of art for himself more microscopic in detail than that of any miniaturist. The real American humourist, however small his canvas, strives for the same broad effects.

It is not the quality of posters to be elusive. Their appeal is to the multitude, and it must be instantaneous. It is easily conceivable that a person of an educated artistic sense might stand before a poster and find himself entirely unable to comprehend it, because the thing portrayed might be something altogether outside his experience. His failure would be no indictment either of his perceptivity or of the merit of the work of art.

It is a pity that Americans as a rule do not consider this, for I know few things that would so much increase American respect for Englishmen in the mass as the discovery that the latter were not the ponderous persons they supposed, but even keener-witted than themselves. At the time of the Venezuelan incident, it is probable that more than all the laborious protests of good men on both sides of the ocean, more than all the petitions and the interchange of assurances of good-will between societies in either country, the thing that did most to allay American resentment and bring the American people to its senses was that delightful message sent (was it not?) by the London Stock Exchange to their *confrères* in New York, begging the latter to see that when the British fleet arrived in New York harbour there should be no crowding by excursion steamers. Like Mr. Anstey's dear German professor, who had once laboriously constructed a joke and purposed, when he had ample leisure, to go about to ædificate a second, will Americans please believe that Englishmen too, if given time, can certainly make others?

And need I say again that in each of the things that I have said, whether on the subject of American chivalry, American energy, or American humour, I am not decrying the American's qualities but only striving to increase his respect for Englishmen?

Now let us look at the other side of the picture. Just as undue flattery awoke in the American people an exaggerated notion of their chivalry and their sense of humour, so the reiteration of savage and contemptuous criticism made them depreciate their general literary ability. It goes farther back than the "Who ever reads an American book?" Three quarters of a century earlier the *Edinburgh Review* (I am indebted for the quotation to Mr. Sparks) asked: "Why should Americans write books when a six-weeks' passage brings them in their own tongue our sense, science, and genius in bales and hogsheads? Prairies, steamboats, gristmills are their natural objects for centuries to come."

Franklin's *Autobiography* and Thoreau's *Walden* are only just, within the last few years, beginning to find their way into English popular reprints of the "classics." Few Englishmen would listen with patience to an argument that the contribution to literature of the Concord school was of greater or more permanent value than, let us say, the work of the Lake Poets. So little thought have Englishmen given to the literature of the United States, that they commonly assume any author who wrote in English to be, as a matter of course, an Englishman. It is only the uneducated among the educated classes who do not know that Longfellow was an American—though I have met such,—but among the educated a small percentage only, I imagine, would remember, unless suggestion was made to them, that, for instance, Motley and Bancroft among historians, or Agassiz and Audubon among men of science (even though one was born in Switzerland) were Americans. To the vast majority, of course, such names are names and nothing more, which may not be particularly reprehensible. But while on the one hand a general indifference to American literature as a whole has carried with it a lack of acquaintance with individual writers, that lack of acquaintance with the individuals naturally reacted to confirm disbelief in the existence of any respectable body of American literature. And the chilling and century-long contempt of the English public and of English critics for all American writing produced its result in a national exaggeration in American minds of their own shortcomings. Only within the last ten years have Americans as a whole come to believe that the work of an American writer (excepting only a very small group) can be on a plane with that of Englishmen.

In England the situation has also changed. American novelists now enjoy a vogue in England that would have seemed almost incredible two decades ago. At that time the English public did not look to America for its fiction, while Americans did look to England; and each new book by a well-known English novelist was as certain of its reception in the United States as—perhaps more certain than it was—in England. That has changed. There are not more than half a dozen writers of fiction in England to-day of such authority that whatever they write is of necessity accepted by the American public. Americans turn now first to their own writers—a dozen or a score of them—and only then do they seek the English book, always provided that, no matter whose the name may be that it bears, it has won the approval of their own critics on its merits. They no longer take it for granted that the best work of their own authors is as a matter of course inferior to the work of a well-known Englishman. It may not be many years before the American public will be so much preoccupied with its own literary output—before that output will be so amply sufficient for all its needs—that it will become as contemptuously indifferent to English literature of the day as Englishmen have, in the past, shown themselves to the product of American writers. There is, perhaps, no other field in which the increase of the confidence of the nation in itself is more marked than in the honour which Americans now pay to their own writers.

It is worth noticing that the English appreciation of American literature as yet hardly extends beyond works of fiction. Specialists in various departments of historical research and the natural sciences know what admirable work is being done in the same fields by individual workers in the

United States; but hardly yet has the specialist—still less has the general public—formed any adequate conception of the great mass of that work in those two fields, still less of its quality. Englishmen do not yet take seriously either American research or American scholarship. It would be absurd to count noses to prove that there were more competent historians writing—more scientific investigators searching into the mysteries—in America than in England or vice versa; but this I take to be an undoubted fact, namely, that men of science in more than one field in other countries are beginning to look rather to the United States than to Great Britain for sound and original work.

The English ignorance of American literature extends even more markedly to other departments of productive art.[159:1] The ordinary educated and art-loving Englishman would be sore put to it to name any single American painter or draughtsman, living or dead, except Mr. C. D. Gibson. Whistler and Sargent, of course, are not counted as Americans. There is not a single American sculptor whose name is known to one in a hundred of, again I say, educated and art-loving Englishmen, though I take it to be indisputable that the United States has produced more sculptors of individual genius in the last half-century than Great Britain. American architecture conveys to the educated and art-loving Englishman no other idea than that of twenty-storey "sky-scrapers" built of steel and glass. Richardson is not even a name to him. He knows nothing of all the beauty and virility of the work that has been done in the last thirty years. In the minor arts, he may have heard of Rookwood pottery and have a vague notion that the Americans turn out some quite original things in silver work; but of American stained glass—of Tiffany and La Farge—he has never heard. It would do England a world of good—it would do international relations a world of good—if a thoroughly representative exhibition of American painting and sculpture could be made in London. I commend the idea to some one competent to handle it; for it would, I think, be profitable to its promoters. It would certainly be a revelation to Englishmen.

The English indifference to—nay, disbelief in the existence of—American art is precisely on a par with the American incredulity in the matter of British humour; and the removal of each of the misconceptions would tend to the increase of international good-will. Americans believe the British Empire to be a sanguinary and ferocious thing. They believe themselves to be possessed of a sense of humour, a sense of chivalry, and an energy quite lacking in the Englishman; and each one of the illusions counts for a good deal in the American national lack of liking for Great Britain. Similarly, Englishmen believe Americans to be a money-loving people without respectable achievement in art or literature. I am not sure that it would make the Englishman like the American any the more if the point of view were corrected, but at least he would like him more intelligently, and it would prevent him from saying things—in themselves entirely good-humoured and quite unintentionally offensive—which hurt American feelings. We cannot correct an error without recognising frankly that it exists, and the first step towards making the American and the Englishman understand what the other really is must be to help each to see how mistaken he is in supposing the other to be what he is not.

That the American should hold the opinions that he does of England is no matter of reproach. Not only is it natural, but inevitable. Absorbed as he has been with his own affairs and his own history, and viewing Great Britain only in her occasional relations thereto, seeing nothing of her in her private life or of her position and policies in the world at large, how could the American have other than a distorted view of her—how could she assume right proportions or be posed in right perspective? Nor is the Englishman any more to be blamed. America has been beyond and below his horizon, and among the travellers' tales that have come to him of her people and her institutions has been much misinformation; and if he has not yet—as in the realms of literature and art—come to any realisation of America's true achievements, how should he have done so, when Americans themselves have only just shaken off the morbid sensitiveness and diffidence of their youth, and have so recently arrived at some partial comprehension of those achievements themselves?

Probably the most successful joke which *Life* ever achieved (Americans will please believe that it is not with any disrespect that I explain to English readers that *Life* is the *Punch* of New York), successful, that is, measured by the continent-wide hilarity which it provoked, had relation to the New York dandy who turned up the bottoms of his trousers because it was "raining in London." That was published—at a guess—some twenty years ago.

Some ten years later a Chicagoan (one James Norton—he died, alas! all too soon afterwards) leaped into something like national notoriety by a certain speech which he delivered at a semi-public dinner in New York. In introducing Mr. Norton as coming from Chicago the chairman had made playful reference to the supposed characteristic lack of modesty of Chicagoans and their pride in their city. Norton, in acknowledgment, confessed that there was justice in the accusation. Chicagoans, he said, were proud of their city. They had a right to be. They were as proud of Chicago as New Yorkers were of London! And the quip ran from mouth to mouth across the continent.

It would be too much to say that those jokes are meaningless to-day, but to the younger generation of Americans they have lost most of their point, for Anglomania has ceased to be the term of reproach that once it was—it has, at least, dropped from daily use—partly because the official relations of the country with Great Britain have so much improved, but much more because the United States has come to consider herself as Great Britain's equal and, in the new consciousness of her greatness, the idea of toadying to England has lost its sting. It is already difficult to throw one's mind back to the conditions of twenty years ago—to remember the deference which (in New York and the larger cities at least) was paid to English ideas, English manners, English styles in dress—the enthusiasm with which any literary man was received who had some pretension to an English reputation—the disrepute in which all "domestic" manufactured articles were held throughout the country in comparison with the "imported," which generally meant English. In all manufactured products this was so nearly universal that "domestic" was almost synonymous with inferior and "imported" with superior grades of goods. That an immense proportion of American manufactured articles were sold in the United States masquerading as "imported"—and therefore commanding a better price—goes without saying, and in some lines, in which the British reputation was too well established and well deserved to be easily shaken, the practice still survives; but in the great majority of things, the American now prefers his home-made article, not merely from motives of patriotism but because he believes that it is the better article. It is not within our present province to discuss how far this opinion is correct, or how far the policy of protection, by assisting manufacturers to obtain control of their own markets and so distract attention from imported goods, has helped to bring about the change. The point is that the change has taken place. And, so far as the ordinary commodities of commerce are concerned, the Englishman is in a measure aware of what has occurred. He could not be otherwise with the figures of his trade with the United States before him. Nor can he conceal from himself the fact that the change of opinion in America may have some justification when he sees how many things of American manufacture he himself uses daily and prefers—patriotism notwithstanding—to the British-made article.

But Englishmen have little conception as yet that the same revolution has taken place in regard to the less material—less easily exploited—commodities of art and literature. American novels and the drawings of Mr. Gibson have made their way in England in the wake of American boots and American sweetmeats; but Americans would be unwilling to believe that their creative ability ends with the production of Western romances and drawings of the American girl.

Until recent years, the volume as well as the quality of the literary and artistic output of Great Britain was vastly superior to that of the United States. The two were not comparable; but they are comparable to-day, though England is as yet unaware of it. In time, Englishmen will awake to a realisation of the fact; but what the relative standing of the two countries will be by that time it is impossible to say. Englishmen would, perhaps, not find it to their disadvantage, and it would certainly (if not done in too condescending a spirit) not be displeasing to the people of the United States, if they began, even now, to take a livelier interest in the work that the other is doing.

FOOTNOTES:

[153:1] At this point my American friend, to the value of whose criticisms I have already paid tribute, interjects marginally: "none the less *Fliegende Blätter* presents more real humour in a week than is to be found in *Punch* in a month." To which I can but make the obvious reply that I have already said that Americans think so. He points out, however, further that, while the Munich paper is always to be found in the higher-class American clubs, it is comparatively infrequent in the clubs of Great Britain, which is undoubtedly true; and that is a subject (the relative breadth of outlook on the world-literature of the day in the two countries) which will necessarily receive attention later on.

[155:1] Lest any American readers should assume that some personal feeling is responsible for my point of view (which would entirely destroy any value in my argument) it seems necessary to explain that I have become calloused to being told that I am the only Englishman the speaker ever met with an American sense of humour. Sometimes I have taken it as a compliment.

[159:1] It is merely pathetic to find such a paper as the London *Academy* at this late day summing up the American æsthetic impulse as follows: "Their culture is now a borrowed thing animated by no life of its own. Their art is become a reflection of French art, their literature a reflection of English literature, their learning a reflection of German learning. A velleity of taste in their women of the richer class seems to be all that maintains in their country the semblance of a high, serious, and disinterested passion for the things of the mind."

It would be interesting to learn from the *Academy* what school of English writers it is that the American humourists "reflect," who among English novelists are the models for the present school of Western fiction, where in English historiography is to be found the prototype of the great histories of their country, collaborated or otherwise, which the Americans are now producing, which journals published in England are responsible for American newspapers, what English magazine is so happy as to be the father of the *Century*, *Harper's*, or *Scribner's*. The truth is that the writer in the Academy, like most Englishmen, knows nothing of American literature as a whole, or he would know that, whether good or bad, the one quality which it surely possesses is that it is individual and peculiar to the people. The *Academy*, it is only fair to say, has recently changed hands and I am not sure that under its present direction it would make the same mistake.

CHAPTER VII

ENGLISH AND AMERICAN EDUCATION

The Rhodes Scholarships—"Pullulating Colleges"—Are American Universities Superior to Oxford or Cambridge?—Other Educational Forces—The Postal Laws—Ten-cent Magazines and Cheap Books—Pigs in Chicago—The Press of England and America Compared—Mixed Society—Educated Women—Generals as Booksellers—And as Farmhands—The Value of War to a People.

It may be presumed that when Cecil Rhodes conceived the idea of establishing the Rhodes scholarships at Oxford, it did not occur to him that Americans might not care to come to Oxford—might think their own universities superior to the English. Nor is it likely that there will in the immediate future be any dearth of students anxious to take those scholarships, for the mere selection has a certain amount of *kudos* attaching to it and, at worst, the residence abroad should be of advantage to any young American not destined to plunge at once into a business life. If it were a mere question of the education to be received, it is much to be feared that the great majority of Americans, unless quite unable to attend one of their own universities, would politely decline to come to England. At the time when the terms of the will were made public, a good many unpleasant things were said in the American press; and it was only the admiration of Americans for Mr. Rhodes (who appealed to their imagination as no other Englishman, except perhaps Mr. Gladstone, has appealed in the last fifty years), coupled with the fact that he was dead, that prevented the foundation of the scholarships from being greeted with resentment rather than gratitude.

There was a time, of course, when the name of Oxford sounded very large in American ears; and it will probably be a surprise to Englishmen to be told that to-day the great majority of Americans would place not only Harvard and Yale, but probably also several other American universities, ahead of either Oxford or Cambridge. Nor is this the opinion only of the ignorant. Trained educational authorities who come from the United States to Europe to study the methods of higher education in the various countries, seldom hesitate to say that the education to be obtained at many of the minor Western colleges in America is fully as good as that offered by either of the great English universities, while that of Harvard and Yale is far superior to it.[167:1] And it must be remembered that education itself, as an art, is incomparably more studied, and more systematically studied in America than in England.

Matthew Arnold spoke of the "pullulating colleges and universities" of America—"the multitude of institutions the promoters of which delude themselves by taking seriously, but which no serious man can so take"; and he would be surprised to see to what purpose some of those institutions have "pullulated" in the eighteen years that have passed since he wrote—to note into what lusty and umbrageous plants have grown such institutions as the Universities of Chicago and Minnesota, though one of those is further west by some distance than he ever penetrated. That these or any other colleges have more students than either Oxford or Cambridge need not mean much; and they cannot of course acquire in twenty years the old, history-saturated atmosphere. Against that are to be set the facts that the students undoubtedly work, on the average, much harder than do English undergraduates and that the teaching staffs are possessed of an enthusiasm, an earnestness, a determination not merely to fill chairs but to get results, which would be almost "bad form" in some Common (or Combination) Rooms in England. Wealth, moreover, and magnificence of endowment can go a considerable way towards even the creation of an atmosphere—not the same atmosphere as that of Oxford or Cambridge, it is true; for no money can make another Addison's Walk out of Prairie Avenue, or convert the Mississippi by St. Anthony's Falls into new "Backs."

"We may build ourselves more gorgeous habitations,
Fill our rooms with painting and with sculpture,
We cannot buy with gold the old associations———."

But an atmosphere may be created wholly scholastic, and well calculated to excite emulation and inspire the ambition of youths.

Nor is it by any means certain that the American people would desire to create the atmosphere of an old-world university if they could. The atmosphere of Oxford produces, as none other could, certain qualities; but are they the qualities which, if England were starting to make her universities anew, she would set in the forefront of her endeavour?[169:1] Are they really the qualities most desirable even in an Englishman to-day? Are they approximately the qualities most likely to equip a man to play the noblest part in the life of modern America? The majority of American educators would answer unhesitatingly in the negative. There are things attaching to Oxford and Cambridge which they would dearly love to be able to transplant to their own country, but which, they recognise, nothing but the passage of the centuries can give. Those things are unattainable; and, frankly, if they could only be attained by transplanting with them many other attributes of English university life, they would rather forego them altogether.

What Englishmen most value in their universities is not any book-learning which is to be acquired thereat, so much as the manners and rules for the conduct of life which are supposed to be imparted in a university course,—manners and rules which are of an essentially aristocratic tendency. Without wishing to push a point too far, it is worth noting that that aristocratic tendency is purely Norman, quite out of harmony with the spirit of the Anglo-Saxon. It would never occur to an Anglo-Saxon, pure and simple, to make his university anything else than an institution for scholastic training, in which every individual should be taught as much, and as equally, as possible. The last thing that would occur to him would be to make it a weapon of aristocracy or an institution for perpetuating class distinctions. The aim and effect of the English universities in the past has been chiefly to keep the upper classes uppermost.

That there are too many "universities" in America no one—least of all an educated American—denies; but with the vast distances and immense population of the country there is room for, perhaps, more than Matthew Arnold eighteen years ago could have foreseen, and not a few of those establishments which in his day he would doubtless have unhesitatingly classed among those which could not be taken seriously, have more than justified their existence.

To the superiority of the American public school system over the English, considered merely as an instrumentality for the general education of the masses of a people, and not for the production of any especially privileged or cultivated class, is generally ascribed the confessedly higher average of intelligence and capacity among (to use a phrase which is ostensibly meaningless in America) the lower orders. But the educational system of the country has been by no means the only factor in producing this result; and it may be worth while merely as a matter of record, and not without interest to American readers, to note what some of those other factors have been during the last twenty years—factors so temporary and so elusive that even now they are in danger of being forgotten.

First among these factors I would set the American postal laws, an essential feature of which is the extraordinarily low rates at which periodical literature may be transmitted. A magazine which may be sent to any place in the United States for from an eighth of a penny to a farthing, according to its weight, will cost for postage in England from two-pence-halfpenny to fourpence. It is not the mere difference in cost of the postage to the subscriber that counts, but the low American rate has permitted the adoption by the publishers of a system impossible to English magazine-makers, a system which has had the effect of making magazines, at least as good as the English sixpenny monthlies, the staple reading matter of whole classes of the population, the classes corresponding to which in England never read anything but a local weekly, or halfpenny daily, paper. It might be that the reading matter of a magazine would not be much superior to that of a small weekly paper. But at least it encourages somewhat more sustained reading and, what is the great fact, it accustoms the reader to handling something *in the form of a book*. That is the virtue. A people weaned from the broad-sheets by magazines readily takes next to book-reading.

Moreover, under the American plan, books themselves, if issued periodically, used to have the same postal advantages as the magazines.[17].[1] A so-called "library" of the classical English, writers could be published at the rate of a book a month, call itself a periodical, and be sent through the post in precisely the same way. The works of Scott, Dickens, Thackeray, or anybody else could be published in weekly, fortnightly, or monthly parts. If in monthly parts at sixpence, the cost to the subscriber would be practically the same as that of a monthly magazine, only that the reader would accumulate at the rate of twelve volumes a year—and read at the rate of one a month—the works of Scott, or Dickens, or Thackeray. Of course much worthless literature, fiction of the trashiest, has been circulated in the same way—much more perhaps than of the better class. But even so, the reading matter was superior to that previously accessible, and the vital fact still remains that the people acquired the habit of book-reading.

In America, the part thus played by some of the periodical libraries was of much importance, but it was probably not comparable to the influence of the ten-cent magazine. In the United States itself, the immense beneficence of that influence has hardly been appreciated. The magazines came into vogue, and the people accepted the fact as they accept the popularity of a new form of "breakfast food." The quickening of the national intelligence which resulted was no more immediate, no more readily traceable or conspicuous to the public eye, than would be the improvement in the national stamina which might result from the introduction of some new article of diet. A change which takes five or ten years to work itself out is lost sight of, becomes invisible, amid the jostling activities of a national life like the American. Moreover, several causes were contributing to the same end and, had any one stopped to endeavour to do it, it would not have been at any time easy to unravel the threads and show what proportion of the fabric was woven by each; but if it had been possible to affix an intellect-meter to the aggregate brain of the American people during the last twenty years, of such ingenious mechanism that it would have shown not only what the increase in total mental power had been but also what proportions of that increase were ascribable to the various contributing causes—education, colonial expansion, commercial growth, ten-cent magazines, and so forth—and if, further, the "readings" of that meter could be interpreted into terms of increase in national energy, national productiveness, national success, I do not think that Parliament would lose one unnecessary day in passing the legislation necessary to reform the English postal laws.

One other point is worth dwelling upon—equally trivial in seeming, equally important in its essence—which is the selling of books by the great department stores, the big general shops, in America. Taking all classes of the British population together and both sexes—artisans and their wives, peasants in country districts, slum residents in London and other large cities,—what proportion of the population of the British Isles do of set purpose go into a bookseller's shop once a year or once in their lives? Is it ten per cent.—or five per cent.—or two per cent.? The exact proportion is immaterial; but the number must be very small. In America some years ago, the owners of department stores and publishers found that there was considerable profit to be made in the handling of books—cheap reprints of good books in particular. The combined booksellers' and stationers' shops in the cities of the United States are in themselves more frequent and more attractive than in England: and I am going back to the days before the drug-store library which is as yet too recent an institution to have had an easily measurable influence. But incomparably more influential than these, in bringing the multitude in immediate contact with literature, have been the department stores, of almost every one of which the "book and stationery" department is a conspicuously attractive, and generally most profitable, feature. Here every man or woman who goes to do any shopping is brought immediately within range of the temptation to buy books—is involuntarily seduced into a bookshop where the wares are temptingly displayed and artfully pressed on the attention of customers. New books of all kinds are sold at the best possible discount; but what was of chief importance was the institution of the cheap libraries of the "Classics"—tables heaped with them in paper at fourpence, piles of them shoulder high in cloth at ninepence, shelves laden with them in glittering backs and by no means despicable in typography at one and sevenpence. Thus simultaneously with the inculcation of the book-reading habit by the magazines came the facility for book-buying, and, always remembering the difference in the scale of prices in the two countries, it was easy for the woman doing her household shopping to fall a victim to the importunities of the salesman and lavish an extra eighteen or thirty-eight cents on a copy of *The Scarlet Letter* or *Ivanhoe*, Irving's *Alhambra*, or *Bleak House*, to take home as a surprise. In this way, whole classes in America, the English counterparts of which rarely read anything more formidable than a penny paper, acquired the habit of book-buying and the ambition to form a small library. The benefit to the people cannot be computed.

Incidentally, as we know, not a little injustice was done to English authors by the pirating of their books, without recompense, while the copyright still lived. It was after I went to America, though I had heard Ruskin lecture at

Oxford, that I first read *Fors Clavigera* and *Sesame and Lilies* in Lovell's Library, at five-pence a volume, and, about the same time, Tolstoi's *War and Peace* in the *Franklin Square Library*, at the same price. Of older works, I can still remember Lamb and part of De Quincey, *Don Quixote* and *Rasselas* (those four for some reason stand out in my mind from their fellows in the row), all bought for the modest ten-cent piece per volume—the price of two daily newspapers (for all newspapers in America then cost five cents) or one blacking of one's shoes. Much has, of course, been done of late years in England in popularising the "Classics" in the form of cheap libraries; but the facilities for buying the books—or rather the temptations to do so—are incomparably less, while the relative prices remain higher.

Even at fourpence halfpenny (supposing them to be purchasable at the price) Lamb's Essays still cost more in London than a drink of whiskey. In America, more than twenty years ago, the whiskey cost half as much again as the book.

All of which is in the nature of a digression, but it has not led us far from the main road, for the object that I am aiming at is to convey to the English reader some idea of what the forces are which are at work on the education of the American people. The Englishman generally knows that in the United States there is nothing analogous to the great public schools of England—Winchester, Westminster, Eton, and the rest—and that they have a host of more or less absurd universities in no way to be compared to Oxford or Cambridge. The American, as has been said, challenges the latter statement bluntly; while, as for the public schools, he maintains that it is not the American ideal (if he wished to fortify his position, he might say it was not an Anglo-Saxon ideal) to produce a limited privileged and cultivated class, but that the aim is to educate the whole nation to the highest level; that, barring such qualities as their mere selectness may enable the great English schools to give to their pupils, the national high schools of America do, as a matter of fact, prepare pupils just as efficiently for the university as do the English institutions, while the great system of common schools secures for the mass of the people a much better education than is given in England to the same classes. Added to which, various other causes co-operate with the avowedly educational instrumentalities to produce a higher level of intellectual alertness and a more general love of reading in the people.

And what is the result? Is the American people as well educated or as well informed or as well cultivated as the English? To endeavour to make a comparison between the two is to traverse a very morass, full of holes, swamps, sloughs, creeks, inlets, quicksands, and pitfalls of divers and terrifying natures. If it is to be threaded at all, it must be only with the greatest caution and, at times, indirectness.

The charming English writer, the author of *Sinners and Saints*, affected, on alighting from the train in the railway station at Chicago, to be immensely surprised by the fact that there was not a pig in sight. "I had thought," he said, "Chicago was all pigs." There are a good many English still of the same opinion.

The one institution in any country of which the foreigner sees most, and by which perhaps every people is, if unwittingly, most commonly judged by other peoples, is its press; and it is difficult for a superficial observer to believe that the nation which produces the newspapers of America is either an educated or a cultivated nation. Max O'Rell's comment on the American press is delightful: "Beyond the date, few statements are reliable." Matthew Arnold called the American newspapers "an awful symptom"—"the worst features in the life of the United States." Americans also—the best Americans—have a great dislike of the London papers.

The fact is that merely as newspapers (as gatherers of news) the American papers are probably the best in the world. What repels the Englishman is primarily the form in which the news is dressed—the loudness, the sensationalism but if he can overcome his repugnance to these things sufficiently to be able to judge the paper as a whole, he will find, apart from the amazing quantity of "news" which it contains, a large amount of literary matter of a high order. I am not for one moment claiming that the American paper (not the worst and loudest, which are contemptible, nor the best, which are almost as non-sensational as the best London papers, but the average American daily paper) is, or ought to be, as acceptable reading to a cultivated man—still less to a refined woman—as almost any one of the penny, or some halfpenny, London papers. But the point that I would make and which I would insist on very earnestly is that the two do not stand for the same thing in relation to the peoples which they respectively represent.

We have seen the same thing before in comparing the consular and diplomatic services of the two countries. Just as in the United States the consuls are plucked at random from the body of the people, whereas in England they are a carefully selected and thoroughly trained class by themselves, so the press of the United States represents the people in its entirety, whereas the English press represents only the educated class. The London papers (I am omitting consideration of certain halfpenny papers) are not talking for the people as a whole, nor to the people as a whole. Consciously or unconsciously they are addressing themselves always to the comparatively small circle of the educated class. When they speak of the peasant or the working man, even of the tradesman, they discuss him as a third person: it is not to him that they are talking. They use a language which is not his language; they assume in their reader information, sentiments, modes of thought, which belong not to him, but only to the educated class—

that class which, whether each individual thereof has been to a public school and a university or not, is saturated with the public school and university traditions.

It was said before that the English people has a disposition to be guided by the voice of authority—to follow its leaders—as the American people has not. The English newspaper speaks to the educated class, trusting, not always with justification, that opinion once formulated in that class will be communicated downwards and accepted by the people. The American newspaper endeavours to speak to the people direct.

That English papers are immensely more democratic than once they were goes without saying. A man need not be much past middle age to be able to remember when the *Daily Telegraph* created, by appealing to, a whole new stratum of newspaper readers. The same thing has been done again more recently by the halfpenny papers, some of which come approximately near to being adapted to the intelligences, and representing the tastes, of the whole population, or at least the urban population, down to the lowest grade. But it is not by those papers that England would like to be judged. Yet when Englishmen draw inferences about the American people from the papers which they see, they are doing what is intrinsically as unjust. It would be no less unjust to take the first hundred men that one met with, on Broadway or State Street, and compare them—their intellectuality and culture—with one hundred members of the London university clubs.

Let us also remember here what was said of the Anglo-Saxon spirit—that spirit which is so essentially non-aristocratic, holding all men equal in their independence. We have seen how this spirit is more untrammelled and works faster in the United States than in England; but where, in any case, it has moved ahead among Americans the tendency in England generally is to follow in the same lines, not in imitation of America but by the impulse of the common genius of the peoples.

The American dailies, even the leading dailies, are made practically for those hundred men on Broadway; the London penny papers are addressed in the main to the university class. Judging from the present trend of events in England it may not be altogether chimerical to imagine a time when in London only two or three papers will hold to the class tradition and will still speak exclusively in the language of the upper classes (as a small number of papers in New York do to-day), while the great body of the English press will have followed the course of the American publishers; and when the English papers are frankly adapted to the tastes and intelligence of as large a proportion of the English people as are now catered for by the majority of the American papers, he would be a rash Englishman whose patriotism would persuade him to prophesy that the London papers would be any more scholarly, more refined, or more chastened in tone than are the papers of New York or Chicago.

And while the Englishman is generally ready to draw unfavourable inferences from the undeniably unpleasant features of the majority of American daily papers, he seldom stops to draw analogous inferences from a comparison of the American and English monthly magazines. Great Britain produces no magazines to compare with *Harper's, The Century*, or *Scribner's*. Those three magazines combined have, I believe, a number of readers in the United States equalling the aggregate circulation of the London penny dailies; which is a point that is worth consideration. When, moreover, the cheaper magazines became a possibility, how came it that such publications as *McClure's* and *The Cosmopolitan* arose? The illustrated magazines of the United States are indeed a fact of profound significance, for which the Englishman when he measures the taste and intellectuality of the American people by its press makes no allowance. Magazines of the same excellence cannot find the same support in England. At least two earnest attempts have been made in late years to establish English monthlies which would compare with any of the three first mentioned above, and both attempts have failed.

What has been said about the much more representative character of the American daily press—the fact that the same papers are read by a vastly larger proportion of the population—brings us face to face with a root-fact which vitiates almost any attempt at a rough and ready comparison between the peoples. In America, there exist the counterparts of every class of man who is to be found in England—men as refined, men no less crass and brutal—some as vulgar and some as full of the pride of birth. Most Englishmen will be surprised to hear that the American, democrat though he is, is as a rule more proud of an ancestor who fought in the Revolutionary War than is an Englishman of one who fought in the Wars of the Roses. I am sure that he sets more store by a direct and authentic descent from one of the company of the *Mayflower* than the Englishman does by an equally direct and authentic line back to the days of William the Conqueror. Incidentally it may be said that the American will talk more about it. But while in America all classes exist, they are not fenced apart, as in England, in fact any more than they are in theory. The American people (*pace* the leaders of the New York Four Hundred) "comes mixed"; dip in where you will and you bring up all sorts of fish. In England if you go into educated society, you are likely to meet almost exclusively educated people—or at least people with the stamp of educated manners. Sir Gorgius Midas is not of course inexorably barred from the society of duchesses. Her Grace of Pentonville must have met him frequently. But in America the duchesses have to rub shoulders with him every day. And—which is worth noting—their husbands also rub shoulders with his wife.

Which brings us to the second root-fact, which is almost as disturbing and confounding to casual observation as the first, namely, the much larger part in the intellectual life of the country played by women in America. Intellectuality or culture in its narrower sense—meaning a familiarity with art and letters—is not commonly regarded by Englishmen as an essential possession in a wife. The lack of it is certainly not considered by the American woman a cardinal offence in a husband. I know many American men who, on being consulted on any matter of literary or artistic taste, say at once: "I don't know. I leave all that to my wife."

An Englishman in an English house, looking at the family portraits, may ask his hostess who painted a certain picture.

"I don't know," she will say, "I must ask my husband. Will, who is the portrait of your grandfather by—the one over there in his robes?"

"Raeburn," says Will.

"Of course," says the wife. "I never can remember the artists' names; they are so confusing—especially the English ones."

The Englishman thinks no worse of her; but the American woman, listening, wishes that she had a portrait of her husband's grandfather by Raeburn and opines that she would know the artist's name.

The same Englishman goes to America and, being entertained, asks a similar question of his host.

"I don't know," says the man, "I must ask my wife. Mary, who painted that picture over there—the big tree and the blue sky?"

"Rousseau," says Mary.

"Of course," says the husband. "I never can remember the names of these fellows. They mix me all up—especially the French ones."

And the Englishman returning home tells his friends of the queer fellow with whom he dined over there—"an awfully good chap, you know"—who owned all sorts of jolly paintings—Rousseaux and things—and did not even know the names of the artists: "Had to ask his wife, by Jove!"

It is not for one moment claimed that there are not in England many women fully as cultured as the most cultured and fairest Americans; that there are not many Englishwomen much better informed, much more widely read, than their husbands. The phenomenon, however, is not nearly as common as in America, where, it has already been suggested, it is probably the result of the fact that the women have at the outset received precisely the same education as the men and, since leaving school or college, have had more leisure, being less engrossed in business and material things.

But this feminine predominance in matters of æsthetics in the United States does not as a rule increase the Englishman's opinion of the intellectuality or culture of the people as a whole. He still judges only by the men. Indeed, he is not entirely disposed to like so much intellectuality in women—such interest in politics, educational matters, art, and literature. Not having been accustomed to it he rather disapproves of it. Blue regimentals are only fit for the blue horse or the artillery.

The Englishman in an American house meets a man more rough and less polished than a man holding a similar position in society would be in England; and he thinks poorly of American society in consequence. He also meets that man's wife, who shows a familiarity with art, letters, and public affairs vastly more comprehensive than he would expect to find in a woman of similar position in England. But he does not therefore strike a balance and re-cast his estimate of American society, any more than in his estimate of the American press he makes allowance for the American magazines. He only thinks that the woman's knowledge is rather out of place and conjectures it to be probably superficial. Wherein he is no less one-sided in his prejudice than the American who will not believe in English humour because he cannot understand it.

Philistinism is undoubtedly more on the surface in educated society in the United States than in Great Britain; but in England outside that society it is nearly all Philistinism. Step down from a social class in England, and you come to a new and lower level of refinement and information. In America the people still "come mixed."

Twenty-five years ago in England, you did not expect a stock-broker, and to-day you do not expect a haberdasher (even though he may have been knighted), to know whether Botticelli is a wine or a cheese. In America, because the Englishman meets that stock-broker or that haberdasher in a society in which he would not be likely to meet him in England, he does expect him to know; and I suspect that if a census were taken there would be found more stock-brokers and haberdashers in America than in England who do know something of Botticelli. I am quite certain that more of their wives do. Matthew Arnold spoke not too pleasantly of the curious sensation that he experienced in addressing a bookseller in America as "General." The "bookseller" in question was a man widely respected in the United States, the head of a great house of publishers and booksellers, a conspicuously public-spirited citizen, and a *bona fide* General who saw stern service in the Civil War. To Englishmen, knowing nothing of the background, the mere fact as stated by Matthew Arnold is curious.

But if civil war were to break out in Great Britain—England and Wales against Scotland and Ireland—and the conflict assumed such titanic proportions that single armies of a million men took the field, then would Tennyson's "smooth-faced snub-nosed rogue" indeed have to "leap from his counter and till and strike, were it but with his cheating yard-wand, home." The entire population of England that was not actually needed at home would be compelled to take the field, and in the slaughter (it is curious how little English men know of the terrific proportions of the conflict between the North and South) the demand for officers would be so great that there would not be enough men of previous training to fill the places. Men would rise from the ranks by merit and among those who rose to be generals there might well be a publisher or bookseller or two. On the termination of the war, the soldiers would turn from their soldiering to their old trades and it might be General Murray or General Macmillan or General Bumpus; and the thing would not then be strange to English ears.

An American story tells how, soon after the close of the Civil War, a stranger asked a farmer if he needed any labourers; and the farmer replied in the negative. He had just taken on three new ones, he said, all of them disbanded soldiers. One, he added, had been a private, one a captain, and one a full-blown colonel.

"And how do you find them?" asked the other.

"The private's a first-class workman," said the farmer, "and the captain he isn't bad."

"And the colonel?"

"Well, I don't want to say nothing agin a man as fit as a colonel in the war," said the farmer, "but I know I ain't hiring no brigadier-generals if they come this way."

They are growing old now, and fewer, the men who held commissions in the war that ended over forty years ago; but during those forty years there has been no community, no trade or profession or calling, in which they have not been to be found, indistinguishable from their civilian colleagues, except by the tiny button in the lapels of their coats. Until Mr. Roosevelt, (and he won his spurs in another war) there has been no man elected President of the United States, except Mr. Cleveland, the one Democrat, who had not a distinguished record as an officer in the Union armies—Grant, Hayes, Garfield, Harrison, and McKinley were all soldiers. You may still see that little button in many pulpits. Farmers wear it, and cabinet ministers, millionaires, and mechanics.

The Anglo-Saxon is a fighting breed. The population of the British Isles sprang from the loins of successive waves of fighting men. It was not the weaklings of the Danes or Normans, Jutes, Saxons, or Angles who came to conquer Britain, but the bold, the hardy, the venturesome of each tribe or people. It was not the mere mixture of bloods that made the English character what it was, the race a race of empire builders; it was because of each blood there came to Britain only of the most adventurous. And through the centuries it has been the constant stress and training of the perpetual turmoil in which the people have lived that have kept the stock from degeneration. There has never been a time in English history, save when the people have been struggling in wars among themselves, when there has been an English family that has not at any given moment had sons or fathers, uncles or cousins out somewhere doing the work of the Empire.

And some are drowned in deep water,
And some in sight of shore,
And word goes back to the weary wife
And ever she sends more.

For since that wife had gate or gear
And hearth and garth and bield
She willed her sons to the white Harvest,
And that is a bitter yield.

. . . .

The good wife's sons come home again
With little into their hands,
But the lore o' men that ha' dealt wi' men
In the new and naked lands,

But the faith o' men that ha' brothered men
By more than the easy breath,
And the eyes o' men that ha' read wi' men
In the open book of death.[188:1]

I have already explained how far Americans are from understanding the British Empire. It is a pity; they would understand Englishmen better and like them better. And what the building of the Empire and the keeping of it have done for Englishmen, the Civil War did in large measure for the Americans. Even the struggle with their own wilderness might not have sufficed to keep the people hard and sound of heart and limb through a century of peace and growing prosperity. The Civil War is already beginning to slip into the farther reaches of the people's memory; but twenty-five years ago the echoes of the guns had hardly died away—the minds of the people were still inspired. It was an awful, and a splendid, experience for the nation. It is not necessary, with Emerson, "always to respect war hereafter"; but there have been times when it has seemed to me that I would rather be able to wear that little tri-colour button of the American Loyal Legion than any other decoration in the world.[189:1]

It is the great compensation of war that it does not breed in a people only a fighting spirit. All history shows that it is in the mental exhilaration and the moral uplift after a period of war successfully waged that a people puts forth the best that is in it, in the production of works of art and in its literature. It is an old legend—older than Omar—that the most beautiful flowers spring from the blood of heroes. And it is true. When the genius of a nation has been ploughed up with cannon-shot and bayonets and watered with blood— then it is that it breaks into the most nearly perfect blossom. It has been so through all history, back beyond the times of gun and bayonet, when spears and swords were the plough-shares, as far as we can see and doubtless farther. In America, the necessities of the case compelled the people to turn first to material works; it was to the civilising of their continent, the repairing of their shattered commercial and industrial structure (shattered when it was yet only half built), that their new inspiration had perforce to turn first. But there was impetus enough for that and to spare, and, after satisfying their mere physical needs, they swept on with a sort of inspired hunger for things to satisfy their minds and souls. Europeans are accustomed to think that the American desire for culture is something superficial—something put on for appearance's sake; and nothing could well be farther from the truth. It is an intense, deep-seated, national craving. War on the scale of the Civil War ploughs deep. It may be impossible for a nation to make itself cultivated— to grow century-old shrubberies and five-century-old turf—in ten years or forty; and when the Americans in their ravening famine reach out to grasp at once all that is good and beautiful in the world, it may be that at first they cannot assimilate all that they draw to them—they can grasp, but not absorb. To that extent there may be much that is superficial in American culture. But every year and every day they are sucking the nourishment deeper—the influences are penetrating, percolating, permeating the soil of their natures (yes, I know that I am running two metaphors abreast, but let them run)— and it is a mistake to conclude because in some places the culture lies only on the surface that there are not others where it has already sunk through and through. Above all is it a mistake to suppose that the emotion itself is shallow or that the yearning is not as deep as their—or any human—natures.

It is possible that some critics may be found cavilling enough to accuse me of inconsistency in thus celebrating the praise of War in a work which is avowedly intended for the promotion of Peace. Carlyle wisely, if somewhat brutally, pointed out that if an Oliver Cromwell be assassinated "it is certain you may get a cart-load of turnips from his carcase." But one does not therefore advocate regicide for the sake of the kitchen-gardens.

FOOTNOTES:

[167:1] What is said above—or at least what can be read between the lines—may throw some light on the fact, on which the English press happens as I write to be commenting in some perplexity, that whereas certain Australians among the Rhodes scholars have distinguished themselves conspicuously in the schools, the only honours that have fallen to Americans have been those of the athletic field. Those journals which have inferred therefrom a lack of aptitude for scholarship on the part of American youth in general may be amiss in their diagnosis.

[169:1] To avoid misapprehension, let me say that, as an Oxford man, I have all the Oxford prejudices as fully developed as any Englishman could wish. Rather a year of Oxford than five of Harvard or ten of Minnesota. How much of this is sentiment, and worthless, and how much reason, it would be hard to say and is immaterial. The personal prepossession need not blind one either to the greatness of the work which the other institutions do, nor to the defensibility of that point of view which sets other qualities, in an institution the professed object of which is to educate and to fit youths for life, above even those possessed by Oxford or Cambridge.

[171:1] In 1906, under a stricter definition of the term "periodical," the privilege of sending as second-class matter books issued at regular intervals was withdrawn.

[188:1] Rudyard Kipling, "The Sea Wife" (*The Seven Seas*).

[189:1] The Loyal Legion is the society of those who held commissions as officers on the side of the North. The Grand Army of the Republic is the society which includes all ranks.

CHAPTER VIII

A COMPARISON IN CULTURE

The Advantage of Youth—Japanese Eclecticism and American—The Craving for the Best—*Cyrano de Bergerac*—Verestschagin—Music and the Drama—Culture by Paroxysms—Mr. Gladstone and the Japanese—Anglo-Saxon Crichtons—Americans as Linguists—England's Past and America's Future—Americanisms in Speech—Why they are Disappearing in America—And Appearing in England—The Press and the Copyright Laws—A Look into the Future.

Ruskin, speaking of the United States, said that he could never bring himself to live in a country so unfortunate as to possess no castles. But, with its obvious disadvantages, youth in a nation has also compensations. Max O'Rell says that to be American is to be both fresh and mature, and I have certainly known many Americans who were fresh. The shoulders are too young for the head to be very old. But when a man—let us say an Englishman of sixty—full of worldly wisdom, having travelled much and seen many men and cities, looks on a young man, just out of the university, perhaps, very keen on his profession, very certain of making his way in the world, with a hundred interests in what seem to the other "new-fangled" things—telephones and typewriters and bicycles and radio-activity and motor cars, things unknown to the old man's youth,—talking of philosophies and theories and principles which were not taught at college when the other was an undergraduate, the elder is likely to think that the young man's judgment is sadly crude and raw, that his education has been altogether too diffused and made up of smatterings of too many things, and to say to himself that the old sound, simple ways were better. Yet it may be—is it not almost certain?—that the youth has had the training which will give him a wider outlook than his father ever had, and will make him a broader man.

In our grandfathers' days, a man of reasonable culture could come approximately near to knowing all that then was known and worth the knowing. The wisdom and science of the world could be included in the compass of a modest bookshelf. But the province of human knowledge has become so wide that, however much "general information" a man may have, he can truly know nothing unless he studies it as a specialist. It is, perhaps, largely as a reaction against the Jacksonian theory of universal competence that the avowed ideal of American education to-day is to cultivate the student's power of concentration—to give him a survey, elementary but sound, of as wide a field as possible, but above all to teach him so to use his mind that to whatever corner of that field he may turn for his walk in life, he will be able to focus all his intellect upon it—to concentrate and bring to bear all his energies on whatever tussock or mole-hill it may be out of which he has to dig his fortune. When the youth steps out into life, it may be that his actual store of knowledge is superficial—a smattering of too many things—but superficiality is precisely the one quality which, in theory at least, his training has been calculated not to produce. Englishmen know that the American throws tremendous energy and earnestness into his business. They know that he throws the same earnestness into his sports. Is it not reasonable to suppose that he will be no less earnest in the study of Botticelli? And it is a great advantage (which the American nation shares with the American youth) to have the products, the literature, the art, the institutions of the whole world to choose from, with practically no traditions to hamper the choice.

When the Japanese determined to adopt Western ways, seeing that so only could they hold their own against the peoples of the West, they did not model their civilisation on that of any one European country. They sent the most intelligent of their young men abroad into every country, each with a mission to study certain things in that country; and so, gathering for comparison the ways of thought and the institutions of all peoples, they were able to pick and choose from each what seemed best to them and to reject all else. They did not propose to make themselves a nation of imitation Englishmen or Germans or Americans. "But," we can imagine them saying, "if we take whatever is best in each country we ought surely to be able to make ourselves into a nation better than any." They modelled their navy on the British, but not their army, nor their banking system, nor did they copy much from British commercial or industrial methods—nor did they take the British system of education.

The United States has been less free to choose. The Japanese had a new house, quite empty, and they could do their furnishing all at once. The American nation, though young, has, after all, a century of domestic life behind it, in the course of which it has accumulated a certain amount of furniture in the form of institutions, prejudices, and traditions, some of which are fixtures and could not be torn out of the structure if the nation wished it; others, though movable, possess associations for the sake of which it would not part with them if it could. Fortunately, however, the house has been much built on to of late years and what goods, or bads, are already amassed can all be stowed away in a single east wing. All the main building (the eastern wing used to be the main building, but it is not now), and particularly the western end and the annex to the north, are new and empty, to be decorated and furnished as the owner pleases. And while the owner, like a sensible man, intends to do all that he can to encourage home manufactures, he does not hesitate to go as far afield as he likes to fill a nook with something better than anything that can be turned out at home.

Nothing strikes an Englishman more, after he comes to know the people, than this eclectic habit, paradoxically combined as it is with an intense—an over-noisy—patriotism. "The best," the American is fond of saying, "is good enough for me"; and it never occurs to him that he has not entire right to the best wherever he may find it. In England it is only a small part of the population which considers itself entitled to the best of anything. The rest of the people may covet, but the best belongs to "their betters." The American knows no "betters." He comes to England and walks, as of right, into the best hotels, the best restaurants, the best seats at the theatres—and the best society. He buys, so far as his purse permits, and often his purse permits a great deal, the best works of art. The consequence is that the world brings him of its best. It may defraud him once in a while into buying an imitation or a second-class article patched up; but, on the whole, the American people has something like the best of the world to choose from. And what is true of the palpable and material things is equally true of the intangible and intellectual.

Englishmen have long been familiar with one aspect of this fact, in the honours which America has in the past been ready to shower on any visiting Englishman of distinction: in the extraordinary number of dollars that she has been willing to pay to hear him lecture. Of this particular commodity—the lecturing Englishman—the people has been fairly sated; but because Americans are no longer eager to lionise any English author or artist with some measure of a London reputation, it does not by any means imply that they are not still seeking for, and grappling, the best in art and letters wherever they can find it. They only doubt whether the Englishman who comes to lecture is, after all, the best.

A Frenchman has pronounced American society to be the wittiest in the world. A German has said that more people read Dante in Boston than in Berlin. I take it that many more read Shakespeare in the United States than in Great Britain—and they certainly try harder to understand him. Nor need it be denied that they have to try harder. Without any knowledge of actual sales, I have no doubt that the number of copies of the works of any continental European author, of anything like a first-class reputation, sold in America is vastly greater than the number sold in England. Tolstoi, Turgeniev, Sienkiewicz, Ibsen, Maeterlinck, Fogazzaro, Jokai, Haeckel, Nietzsche—I give the names at random as they come—of any one of these there is immeasurably more of a "cult" in the United States than in England—a far larger proportion of the population makes some effort to master what is worth mastering in each. Rodin's works—his name at least and photographs of his masterpieces—are familiar to tens of thousands of Americans belonging to classes which in England never heard of him. Helleu's drawings were almost a commonplace of American illustrated literature six years before one educated Englishman in a hundred knew his name. Zörn's etchings are almost as well known in the United States as Whistler's. Englishmen remain curiously engrossed in English things.

It may be a very disputable judgment to say that the most nearly Shakespearian literary production of modern times—at least of those which have gained any measure of fame—is M. Rostand's *Cyrano de Bergerac*. Immediately on its publication it was greeted in America with hardly less enthusiasm than in Paris; and within a few weeks it became the chief topic of conversation at a thousand dinner tables. In a few months I had seen the play acted by three different companies—all admirable, scholarly productions, of which the most famous and most "authorised" was by no means the best—and soon thereafter I came to England, for a short visit, but with the determination to find time to make the trip to Paris to see M. Coquelin as "Cyrano." I found Englishmen—educated Englishmen, including not a few authors and critics to whom I spoke—practically unaware of the existence of such a play. Of those who had heard of it and read *critiques*, I met not one who had read the work itself. Some time after, Sir Charles Wyndham produced it in London and it was, I believe, not a success. To-day *Cyrano de Bergerac* (I am speaking of it not as an acting play but as literature) is practically unknown even to educated Englishmen, except such as make French literature their special study.

Cyrano may or may not be on a level with any but the greatest of Shakespeare's plays (it is evident from his other work that M. Rostand is not a Shakespeare) but that it was an immeasurably finer thing than ninety-nine per cent of the books of the year which English people were reading that winter on the advice of English critics is beyond question. The nation which was reading and discussing M. Rostand's work was conspicuously better engaged than the nation which was reading and discussing the English novels of the season.

Again when poor Vasili Verestschagin met his death so tragically off Port Arthur, his name meant little or nothing to the great majority of educated Englishmen, though there had been exhibitions of his work in London—the same exhibitions as were made throughout the larger cities of the United States. In America regret for him was wide-spread and personal, for he stood for something definite in American eyes—rather unfortunately, perhaps, in one way, because Verestschagin, too, had painted those miserable sepoys being eternally blown from British guns.

The general English misapprehension of the present condition of art and literature in America sometimes shows itself in unexpected places. I have a great love for *Punch*. Since the time when the beautifying of its front cover with gamboge and vermilion and emerald green constituted the chief solace of wet days in the nursery, I doubt if, in the course of forty years, I have missed reading one dozen copies of the London *Charivari*. After a period of exile in regions where current literature is unobtainable one of the chief delights of a return to civilisation is "catching up" with the back numbers of *Punch*; nor, in spite of gibes to the contrary, has the paper ever been more brilliant than under its present editorship. Yet *Punch* in this present week of September 11, 1907, represents an American woman, apparently an American woman of wealth and position (at all events she is at the time touring in Italy), as saying on hearing an air from *Il Trovatore*: "Say, these Italians ain't vurry original. Guess I've heard that tune on our street organs in New York ever since I was a gurl."

The weaknesses of the peoples of other nations are fair game; but it is the essence of just caricature that it should have some verisimilitude. *Punch* could not publish that drawing with the accompanying legend unless it was the belief of the editor or the staff that such a solecism was more or less likely to proceed from the mouth of such an American as is depicted; which is precisely the error of the Frenchman who believes that Englishmen sell their wives at Smithfield. Thirty years ago, the lampoon would have had some justification; but at the present time both the actual number and the percentage of women who are familiar with the Italian operas is, I believe, vastly greater in America than in England. This statement will undoubtedly be received with incredulity by the majority of Englishmen who know nothing about the United States; but no one who does know the people of the country will dispute it. In England, the opera is still, for all the changes that have occurred in the last quarter of a century, largely a pleasure of a limited class. It may be (and personally I believe) that in that class there is a larger number of true musicians who know the operas well and love them appreciatively than is to be found in the United States; but the number of people who have a reasonable acquaintance with the majority of operas, and are familiar with the best known airs from each and with the general characteristics of the various composers, is immensely larger in America. It is only the same fact that we have confronted so often before—the fact of the greater homogeneousness or uniformity of tastes and pursuits in the American people.

It must be clearly understood, here as elsewhere, that I am not comparing merely the people of New York with the people of London, but the people of the whole United States of all classes, urban and provincial, industrial and peasant, East and West, with the whole population of all classes in the British Isles; for a large percentage of the mistakes which Englishmen make about America arises from the fact that they insist on comparing the educated classes of London with such people as they may chance to have met in New York or one or two Eastern cities, under the impression that they are thereby drawing a comparison between the two peoples. Senator Hoar's opinion of

Matthew Arnold has been already quoted; and the truth is that very few Englishmen who have written about America have lived in the country long enough to grasp how much of the United States lies on the other side of the North River. Not only does not New York alone, but New York, Boston, Philadelphia, and Washington combined do not bear anything like the same relation to America as a whole as London bears to the British Isles. Englishmen take no account of, for they have not seen and no one has reported to them, the intense craving for and striving after culture and self-improvement which exists (and has existed for a generation) not only in such larger cities as Chicago, Cincinnati, St. Louis, Milwaukee, and New Orleans, but in many hundreds of smaller communities scattered from the Atlantic to the Pacific. One must have such a vision of the United States as a whole as will enable him to imagine all this endeavour, now dissipated over so vast a stretch of country, as all massed together into a territory no larger than the British Isles before he can arrive at an intelligent basis of comparison between the peoples. What is centralised in England in America is diffused over half a continent and much less easily measurable.

It happens that as I am correcting the proofs of the chapter the London newspapers of the day (January 25, 1908) contain announcements of the death in New York of Edward MacDowell. He was often spoken of as "the American Grieg"; but it was a phrase which irritated many good musical critics in America, for the reason that they considered their countryman the greater man of the two. They would have had Grieg spoken of as the Norwegian MacDowell. In that judgment they may have been right or they may have been wrong; but it is characteristic of the attitudes of the British and American peoples that, whereas the people of the United States know Grieg better than he is known in England (that is to say, that a larger proportion of the people, outside the classes which professedly account themselves musical, have more or less acquaintance with his music), just as they know the work of half a dozen English composers, MacDowell, though he had played his pianoforte concertos in London, remained almost unknown in England outside of strictly musical circles. It is certain that had MacDowell been an Englishman he would have been immensely better known in America than, being an American, he ever was in England.

In the kindred field of the drama the general English idea of the American stage is based chiefly on acquaintance with that noisy type of "musical comedy" of which so many specimens have in recent years been brought to England from the other side of the Atlantic. It is as if Americans judged English literature by Miss Marie Corelli and Guy Thorne. Those things are brought to England because they are opined by the managers to be the sort of thing that England wants or which is likely to succeed in England, not because they are what America considers her best product. To attempt any comparison of the living playwrights or actors in the two countries would be a thorny and perilous undertaking; and if any comparison is to be made at all it must be done lightly and as far as possible examples must be drawn from those who are no longer actively on the boards. Madame de Navarro (Miss Mary Anderson) has deliberately put on record her opinion of Miss Clara Morris as "the greatest emotional actress I ever saw." It is not likely that when Madame de Navarro pronounced that estimate she was forgetting either Miss Terry or Mrs. Campbell—or Mesdames Rejane and Bernhardt or Signora Duse. Madame de Navarro is no mean judge: and those who have read Miss Morris's wonderful book, *Life on the Stage*, will think the judgment in this case not incredible.

Similarly I believe that in Mr. Richard Mansfield the United States has just lost an actor who had not his peer in earnestness, scholarship, restraint, and power on the English stage. I am not acquainted with an English actor to-day who, in the combination of all these qualities, is in his class. His "Peer Gynt" was a thing which, I believe, no living English actor could have approached, and I gravely doubt whether England would have furnished a public who would have appreciated it in sufficient numbers to make its presentation a success if it had been achieved in London.

It was said that in any effort to arrive at an estimate of American culture, or to state that culture in terms of English culture, we should have to find landmarks in trifles. All these things are such trifles. Let us concede that *Cyrano* is not the greatest literature, nor is Verestschagin's work the highest art; still neither the one nor the other is properly a negligible quantity in the sum-total of the creative work of the generation. There may be many American women who do not know their Verdi, and it may be that Madame de Navarro's estimate of Miss Morris, mine of Mr. Mansfield, and that of certain American critics of Edward MacDowell are equally at fault; but it still remains absurd to take ignorance of the Italian operas as characteristic of American women or to talk contemptuously, as many Englishmen do, of the American theatre, because they have no knowledge of it beyond what they have seen of the one class of production from *The Belle of New York* to *The Prince of Pilsen*, or of American music, because their acquaintance with it begins and ends with Sousa and the writers of "coon songs."

It will be urged that successive "crazes" for individual artists or authors, for particular productions or even isolated schools, are no evidence of any general culture. Conceding this, it remains impossible to avoid the question: supposing a nation or an individual to spend each successive six months in a new enthusiasm—six months on Plato and Aristotelianism,—six months, taking the *Light of Asia*, Mr. Sinnett, and *Kim* as a starting point, on Buddhism and esoteric philosophy,—six months, inspired by Fitzgerald, on Omar, Persian literature and history and the various ramifications thereof,—six months on M. Rodin, his relation to the art of sculpture in general and particularly to the sculpture of the Greeks,—a similar six months devoted to Mr. Watt with like excursions into his environment, proximate and remote,—six months to Millet, Barbizon, and the history of French painting,—six months of Russian art with Verestschagin and six with Russian literature and politics working outwards from Count Tolstoi,—six months of philosophic speculation radiating from Haeckel,—six months absorbed in Japanese art,—six months burrowing in Egyptian excavations and Egyptian history—the question is, I say, supposing a nation or an individual to have passed through twenty such spasms (of which I have suggested ten, every one of which ten is a subject which I have in my own experience known to become the rage in America more or less wide-spread and for a greater or lesser period) and supposing that nation or that individual to be possessed of extraordinary earnestness and power of concentration, with a great desire to learn, how far will that nation or that individual have travelled on the road toward something approaching culture? Let it be granted that the individual or the nation starts with something less of the æsthetic temperament, less well grounded in, or disposed towards, artistic or literary study than the average Englishman who has made decent use of his opportunities at school, at the university, and in the surroundings of his every-day life; the intellectual condition of that individual or nation will not at the end of the ten years of successive *furores* be the same intellectual condition as that of the Englishman who, after leaving college, has spent ten years in the ordinary educated society of England, but it is probable that, besides the accumulation of a great quantity of information, some not entirely inadequate or incorrect general standards of taste and criticism will have been arrived at. It is worth remembering that at least one eminently competent English critic has declared that while there may be less erudition in America, there is conspicuously more culture.

When the Englishman hears the American, and especially the American woman, slip so glibly from Rodin to Rameses, from Kant to kakemonos, he dubs her superficial. Perhaps she is, considering only the actual knowledge possessed compared with the potentiality of knowledge on any one of the topics. There is a story which has been fitted to many persons and many occasions, but which thirty years ago was told of Mr. Gladstone, though for all I know it may go back to generations before he was born. Mr. Gladstone, so the story ran, was present at a dinner where among the guests was a distinguished Japanese; and, as not seldom happened, Mr. Gladstone monopolised the conversation, talking with fluency and seeming omniscience on a vast range of subjects, among which Japan came in for its share of attention. The distinguished stranger was asked later for his opinion of the English statesman. "A wonderful man," he said, "a truly wonderful man! He seems to know all about everything in the world except Japan. He knows nothing at all about Japan."

The specialist in a single subject can always find the holes in the information on that subject of the "universal specialist." But it is worth noticing that, like almost every other salient trait of the American character, this American desire to become a universal specialist—this reaching after the all-culture and all-knowledge—is an essentially Anglo-Saxon or English characteristic. The German may be content to spend his whole life laboriously probing into one small hole. The Frenchman (let me say again that I thoroughly recognise that all national generalisations are unsound) will cheerfully wave aside with a *la-la-la* whole realms of knowledge which do not interest him. But all Englishmen and all Americans would be Crichtons and Sydneys if they could. And—perhaps on the principle of setting a thief to catch a thief—although the all-round man is the ideal of both peoples, each is equally suspicious of an intellectual rotundity (in another person) too nearly complete.

Americans rather like to repeat that story of Mr. Gladstone, when the talk is of English culture.

The American as a rule is a better linguist than the Englishman,—he is quicker, that is, to pick up a modern language and likely to speak it with a better accent. "Never trust an Englishman who speaks French without an English accent," said Prince Bismarck; and the remark, however unjust it may be to an occasional individual, showed a shrewd insight into the English character. There is always to be recognised the fact that there are tens—perhaps hundreds—of thousands of Englishmen who speak Hindustani, Pushtu, or the language of any one of a hundred remote peoples with whom the Empire has traffic, while the American has had no contact with other peoples which called for a knowledge of any tongue but his own, except that in a small way some Spanish has been useful. But so far as European languages go, the Englishman, in more or less constant and intimate relation with each of the peoples of Europe, has been so well satisfied of his own superiority to each that it has seemed vastly more fitting that they should learn his language than that he should trouble to learn theirs. Under any circumstances, is it not obviously easier for each one of the European peoples to learn to talk English than for the Englishman to learn eight European tongues with eighty miscellaneous dialects?

When an Englishman does learn a foreign language, it is most commonly for literary or scholastic purposes, rather than (with the exception of French in certain classes) for conversational use. The American on the other hand, having had no need of languages in the past, coming now in contact with the world, sees that there are three or four languages of Europe which it is most desirable that he should know, if only for commercial purposes; and a language learned for commercial purposes must be mastered colloquially and idiomatically. The American is not distracted by the need of Sanskrit or of any one of the numerous more or less primitive tongues which a certain proportion of the English people must acquire if the business of the Empire is to go on. Nor is his vision confused by seeing all the European tongues jumbled, as it were, together before him at too close range. He can distinguish which are the essential or desirable languages for his purposes; and the rising generation of Americans is learning those languages more generally, and in a more practical way, than is the rising generation of Englishmen.

And yet we have not crossed that morass;—nor perhaps, however superior in folly we may be to the angels, is it desirable that we should in plain daylight. We have at most found some slight vantage-ground: thrown up a mole-hill of a Pisgah from which we can attain a distant view of what lies beyond the swamp, even if perchance we have taken some mirages and *ignes fatui* for solid landscape and actual illuminations.

The ambitions and ideals of the two peoples are fundamentally alike; nor is there so great a difference as appears on the surface in their method of striving to attain those ideals and realise those ambitions, albeit the American uses certain tools (modern he calls them, the Englishman preferring to say new-fangled) to which the Englishman's hands have not taken kindly. It is natural that the English nation, having a so much larger past, should be more influenced by it than the American. It is natural that the American, conscious that his national character has but just shaped itself out of the void, with all the future before it, should look more to the present and the future than the Englishman.

The Englishman prefers to turn almost exclusively to the study of antiquity— the art and philosophies and letters of past ages—for the foundation of his work, and thence to push on between almost strictly British lines. The American seeks rather to absorb only so much of the wisdom and taste of antiquity as may serve for an intelligent comprehension of the world-art, the world-philosophies, the world-literature of to-day, and then, borrowing what he will from each department of those, to strive on that foundation to build something better than any. There are many scholars and students in America who would prefer to see the people less eager to push on. There are many thinkers and educators in England who hold that English scholarship and training dwell altogether too much in the past and that it were better if England would look more abroad and would give larger attention to the conditions of modern life—the conditions which her youth will have to meet in the coming generation.

If an American were asked which of the two peoples was the more cultivated, the more widely informed, he would probably say: "You fellows have been longer at the game than we have. You've had more experience in the business; but we believe we've got every bit as good raw material as you and a blamed sight better machinery. Also we are more in earnest and work that machinery harder than you. Maybe we are not turning out as good goods yet—and maybe we are. But it's a dead sure thing that if we aren't yet, we're going to."

A common index to the degree of cultivation in any people is found in their everyday language—their spoken speech; but here again in considering America from the British standpoint we have to be careful or we may be entrapped into the same fallacy as threatens us when we propose to judge the United States by its newspapers. In the first place the right of any people to invent new forms of verbal currency to meet the requirements of its colloquial exchange must be conceded. There was a time when an Americanism in speech was condemned in England because it was American. When so many of the Americanisms of ten years ago are incorporated in the daily speech even of educated Englishmen to-day, it would be affectation to put forward such a plea nowadays. Going deeper than this, we undoubtedly find that the educated Englishman to-day speaks with more precision than the educated American. The educated Englishman speaks the language of what I have already called the public school and university class. But while the Englishman speaks the language of that class, the American speaks the language of the whole people. That is not, of course, entirely true, for there are grades of speech in the United States, but it is relatively true—true for the purpose of a comparison with the conditions in Great Britain. The Englishman may be surprised at the number of solecisms committed in the course of an hour's talk by a well-to-do New Yorker whom he has met in the company of gentlemen in England. He would perhaps be more surprised to find a mechanic from the far West commit no more. The tongue of educated Englishmen is not the tongue of the masses—nor is it a difference in accent only, but in form, in taste, in grammar, and in thought. If in England the well-to-do and gentle classes had commercial transactions only among themselves, it is probable that a currency composed only of gold and silver would suffice for their needs; copper is introduced into the coinage to meet the requirements of the poor. American speech has its elements of copper for the same reason—that all may be able to deal in it, to give and take change in its terms. It is the same fact as we have met before, of the greater homogeneousness of the American people—the levelling power (for want of a better phrase) of a democracy.

The Englishman may object, and with justice, that because an educated man must incorporate into his speech words and phrases and forms which are necessary for communication with the vulgar, there is no reason why he should not be able to reserve those forms and phrases for use with the vulgar only. A gentleman does not pay half-a-crown, lost at the card table to a friend, in coppers. Why cannot the educated American keep his speech silver and gold for educated ears? All of which is just. There are people in the United States who speak with a preciseness equal to that of the most exacting of English precisians, but they are not fenced off as in England within the limits of a specified class; while the common speech of the American people, which is used by a majority of those who would in England come within the limits of that fenced area, is much more careless in form and phrase than the speech of educated Englishmen. It may be urged that it is much less careless, and better and vastly more uniform, than any one of the innumerable forms of speech employed by the various lower classes in England; which is true. The level of speech is better in America; but the speech of the educated and well-to-do is generally much better in England. All this, however (which is mere commonplace) may be conceded, but, though educated Americans may use a more debased speech than educated Englishmen, the point is that it is not safe to argue therefrom to an inferiority in culture in America; because the American uses his speech for other and wider purposes than the Englishman. The different American classes, just as they dress alike, read the same newspapers and magazines, and, within limits, eat the same food, so they speak the same language. It is unjust to compare that language with the language used in England only by the educated classes.

But, what is an infinitely larger fact, the inferiority of the American speech to the English is daily and rapidly disappearing. Twenty years ago, practically all American speech fell provincially on educated English ears. That is far from being the case to-day; and what is most interesting is that the alteration has not come about as the result of a change in the diction of Americans only. The change has been in Englishmen also. To whatever extent American speech may have improved, it is certain also that English speech has become much less precise—much less uniform among the educated and "gentlemanly" classes—and English ears are consequently less exacting.

With the gradual elimination of class distinctions in England, or rather with the blurring of the lines which separate one class from another, a multitude of persons pass for "gentlemen" in England to-day who could not have dreamed—and whose fathers certainly did not dream—of being counted among the gentry thirty-five years ago. The fact may be for good or ill; but one consequence has been that the newcomers, thrusting up into the circles above them, have taken with them the speech of their former associates, so that one hears now, in nominally polite circles, tones of voice, forms of speech, and the expression of points of view which would have been impossible in the youth of people who are now no more than middle-aged.

There was a time when the dress proclaimed the man of quality at once. That distinction began to pass away with the disappearance of silk and ruffles and wigs from masculine costume. For a century longer, the shibboleths of voice and manner kept their force. But now those too are going; and the result is that the English speech of the educated class has become less precise and less uniform. The same speech is now common to a larger proportion of the people. In the days when nearly all the members of educated society—we are speaking of the men only, for they only counted in those days—had been to one or other of the same "seven great public schools" (which not one public school man in a hundred can name correctly to-day) and to one or other of the same two universities, they kept for use among themselves all through their after life the forms of speech, the catchwords, the classical references which passed current in their school and undergraduate days. It was a free-masonry of speech on which the outsider could not intrude. To-day, when not a quarter of the members of the same circles have been to one of those same seven schools nor a half to the same universities, when at least a quarter have been to no recognised classical school at all, it is impossible that the same free-masonry should prevail. There were a hundred trite classical quotations (no great evidence of scholarship, but made jestingly familiar by the old school curricula) which our fathers could use with safety in any chance company of the society to which they were accustomed; but even the most familiar of them would be a parlous experiment in small talk to-day. They have vanished from common conversation even more completely than they have disappeared from the debates of the House of Commons. And this is only a type of the change which has come over the educated speech of England, which we may regret or we may welcome. It may be sad that the English gentleman should speak in less literary form than he did thirty years ago, but the loss may be outweighed many times by the fact that so much larger a proportion of the people speak the same speech as he—not so refined as his used to be, but materially better than the majority of those who use it to-day could then have shaped their lips to frame. Few Englishmen at least would acquiesce in the opinion that it showed a decay of culture in England—that the people were more ignorant or less educated. It may not be safe to draw an analogous conclusion in the case of the American people.

A story well-known to most Englishmen has to do with the man who, arriving at Waterloo station to take a train, went into the refreshment room for a cup of coffee. In his haste he spilled the coffee over his shirt front and thereupon fell to incontinent cursing of "this d——d London and South-Western Railway."

An American variant of, or pendant to, the same story tells of the Eastern man who approached Salt Lake City on foot and sat by the wayside to rest.

By ill luck he sat upon an ants' nest. Shortly he rose anathematising the "lustful Mormon city" and turned his face eastward once more, a Mormon-hater to the end of his days.

Not much less illogical is an Englishman I know who, having spent some three weeks in the United States, loathes the people and all the institutions thereof, almost solely (though the noise of the elevated trains in New York has something to do with it) because he found that they applied the name of "robin" to what he calls "a cursed great thrush-beast." Nearly every English visitor to the United States has been irritated at first by discovering this, or some similar fact; but it is not necessary on that account to hate the American people, to express contempt for their art and literature, and to belittle their commercial greatness and all the splendours of their history.[214:1] Rather ought Englishmen to like this application by the early colonists to the objects of their new environment of the cherished names of the well-known things of home. It shows that they carried with them into the wilderness in their hearts a love of English lane and hedgerow, and strove to soften the savagery of their new surroundings by finding in the common wild things the familiar birds and flowers which had grown dear to them in far-off peaceful English villages.

We will not now potter again over the well-trodden paths of the differences in phraseology in the two peoples which have been so fruitful a source of "impressions" in successive generations of English visitors to the United States, for the thing grows absurd when "car," and "store," and "sidewalk," and "elevator" are commonplaces on the lips of every London cockney; nor is there any need here to thread again the mazes of the well-worn discussion as to how far the peculiarities of modern American speech are only good old English forms which have survived in the New World after disappearance from their original haunts.[215:1] The subject is worth referring to, however, for the very reason that its discussion *has* become almost absurd,—because by a process which has been going on, as we have already said, on both sides of the ocean simultaneously, the differences themselves are disappearing, the tongues of the two peoples are coming together and coalescing once more. The two currents into which the stream divided which flowed from that original well of English are drawing together—are, indeed, already so close that it will be but a very short time when the word "Americanism" as applied to a peculiarity in language will have ceased to be used in England. The "Yankee twang" and the "strong English accent" will survive in the two countries respectively for some time yet; but the written and spoken language of the two nations will be—already almost is—the same, and English visitors to the United States will have lost one fruitful source of impressions.

The process has been going on in both countries, but in widely different forms. And this seems to me a peculiarly significant fact. In America the language of the people is constantly and steadily tending to improve; and this tendency is, Englishmen should note, the result of a deliberate and conscious effort at improvement on the part of the people. This can hardly be insisted upon too strongly.

The majority of "Americanisms" in speech were in their origin mere provincialisms—modes of expression and pronunciation which had sprung up unchecked in the isolated communities of a scattered people. They grew with the growth of the communities, until they threatened to graft themselves permanently on the speech of the nation. The United States is no longer a country of isolated and scattered communities. After the Civil War, and partly as a result thereof, but still more as a result of the knitting together of the whole country by the building of the American railway system, with the consequent sudden increase in intimacy of communication between all parts, there developed in the people a new sense of national unity. England saw a revolution in her means of communication when railways superseded stage-coaches and when the penny post was established; but no revolution comparable to that which has taken place in the United States in the present generation. Prior to 1880—really until 1883—Portland, Oregon, was hardly less removed from Portland, Maine, than Capetown is from Liverpool to-day, and the discomforts of travel from one to the other were incomparably greater. Now they are morally closer together than London and Aberdeen, in as much as nowhere between the Atlantic and Pacific is there any such consciousness of racial difference as separates the Scots from the English.

The work of federation begun by the original thirteen colonies is not yet completed, for the individuality of the several States is destined to go on being continuously more merged—until it will finally be almost obliterated—in the Federal whole; but it may be said that in the last twenty-five years, and not until then, has the American people become truly unified—an entity conscious of its oneness and of its commercial greatness in that oneness, thinking common thoughts, co-operating in common ambitions, and speaking a common speech. Into that speech were at first absorbed, as has been said, the peculiarities, localisms, and provincialisms which had inevitably grown up in different sections in the days of non-communication. But precisely those same causes—the settlement of the country, the construction of the railways, the development of the natural resources—which contributed to the unification and laid the foundations of the greatness, produced, with wealth and leisure, new ambitions in the people. The desire for art and literature and, what we have called the all-culture, was no new growth, but an instinct inherited from the original English stock. Quickened it must have been by the moral uplifting of the people by the Civil War, but, as we have already seen, for some time after the close of that war the whole energies of the people were necessarily devoted to material things.

Only with the completion of the repairing of the ravages of that war, and with the almost coincident settlement of the last great waste tracts of the country, were the people free to reach out after things immaterial and æsthetic; and only with the accession of wealth, which again these same causes produced, came the possibility of gratifying the craving for those things. And in the longing for self-improvement and self-culture, thus newly inspired and for the first time truly national, one of the things to which the people turned with characteristic earnestness was the improvement of the common speech. The nation has set itself purposefully and with determination to purify and prevent the further corruption of its language.

The movement towards "simplification" of the spelling may or may not be in the direction of purification, but it will be observed that the movement itself could not have come into being without the national desire for improvement. The American speech is now the speech of a solidified and great nation; and it cannot be permitted to retain the inelegancies and colloquialisms which were not intolerable, perhaps, in the dialect of a locality in the days when that locality had but restricted intercourse with other parts of the country. This effort to purify the common tongue is conscious, avowed, and sympathised with in all parts of the country alike.

When any point of literary or grammatical form is under discussion in a leading American newspaper to-day, the dominant note is that of a purism more strict than will appear in a similar discussion in England. In many American newspaper offices the rules of "style" forbid the use of certain words and phrases which are accepted without question in the best London journals. There have of course always been circles—as, notoriously, in and around Boston, and, less notoriously but no less truly, in Philadelphia and New York—wherein the speech, whether written or spoken, has been as scrupulous in form and grammar as in the most scholarly circles in Great Britain. These circles corresponded to what we have called the public-school and university class of England, and, no more than it, did they speak the common speech of their country. Only now is the people as a whole consciously striving after an uplifting of such common speech.

In England, on the other hand, the process that has been going on has been quite involuntary and is as yet almost entirely unconscious.

We have spoken so far of only one factor in that process—namely, the democratisation of the English people which is in progress and the blurring of the lines between the classes. Co-operating with this are other forces. Just as the most well-bred persons can afford on occasions to be most careless of their manners—just as only an old-established aristocracy can be truly reckless of the character of new associates whom it may please to take up—so it may be that the well-educated man, confident of his impeccability and altogether off his guard, more readily absorbs into his daily speech cant phrases and even solecisms than the half-educated who is ever watchful lest he slip. The American has a way of writing, figuratively, with a dictionary at his elbow and a grammar within reach. There are few educated Englishmen who do not consider their own authority—the authority drawn from their school and university training—superior to that of any dictionary or grammar, especially of any American one.[220:1] So it has come about that, while the tendency of the American people is constantly to become more exact and more accurate in its written and spoken speech, the English tendency is no less constantly towards a growing laxity; and while the American has been sternly and conscientiously at work pruning the inelegancies out of his language, the Briton has been lightheartedly taking these same inelegancies to himself. It is obviously impossible that such a twofold tendency can go on for long without the gulf between the quality of the respective languages becoming appreciably narrower.

The American writers who now occupy places on the staffs of London journals are thoroughly deserving of their places. They have earned these and retain them on the ground of their capacity as news gatherers, and through the brilliancy of their descriptive writing. They possess what is described as "newspaper ability" as opposed to "literary ability." It is, nevertheless, the fact that in the majority of the newspaper offices, the "copy" of these writers is permitted to pass through the press with an immunity from interference on the part either of editor or proof-reader, which, a decade back, would not have been possible in any London office. Thus the British public, unwarned and unconscious, is daily absorbing at its breakfast table, and in the morning and evening trains, American newspaper English, which is the output of English newspaper offices. It is not now contended that this English is any worse than the public would be likely to receive from the same class of English writers, but the fact itself is to be noted. I am not prepared to agree with Mr. Andrew Lang in holding the English writer necessarily blameworthy who "in serious work introduces, needlessly, into our tongue an American phrase." Such introductions, however needless, may materially enrich the language, and I should, even with the permission of Mr. Lang, extend the same latitude to the introduction of Scotticisms.

A more important matter for consideration is the present condition of the copyright laws of the two countries. English publishers understand well enough why it is occasionally cheaper, or, taking all the conditions together, more advantageous to have put into type in the United States rather than in Great Britain the work of a standard English novelist, and to bring the English edition into print from a duplicate set of American plates. On the other hand, it is exceptional for a novel, or for any book by an American writer, to be put into type in England for publication in both countries. For the purpose of bringing the text of such books into line with the requirements of English readers, it is the practice of the leading American publishers to have one division of their composing-rooms allotted to typesetting by the English standard, with the use by the proof-readers of an English dictionary. It occasionally happens, however, that the attention of these proof-readers to the task of securing an English text limits itself to a few typical examples, such as spelling "colour" with a "u" and seeing that "centre" does not appear as "center," while all that constitutes the essence of American style, as compared with the English style, is passed unmolested and without change.

Such a result is, doubtless, inevitable in the case of a work by an American writer who has his own idea of literary expression and his own standard of what constitutes literary style, but the resulting text not infrequently gives ground for criticism on the part of English reviewers, and for some feeling of annoyance on the part of cultivated English readers.

In the case of books by English authors which are put into type in American printing-offices, there is, of course, no question of modification of style or of form of expression, but with these, as stated, the proof-readers are not always successful in eliminating entirely the American forms of spelling.

The English publisher, even though he give a personal reading to the book in the form in which it finally leaves his hands, (and, in the majority of cases, having read it once in manuscript, he declines to go over the pages a second time, but contents himself with a cursory investigation of the detail of "colour," of "centre,") is not infrequently dissatisfied, but it is too late for any changes in the text, and he can only let the volume go out. In the case of books printed in England from plates made in America, there is nothing at all to warn the reader; while in the case of books bound in England from sheets actually printed in the United States, there is nothing which the reader is likely to notice; and in nine cases out of ten the Englishman is unconscious that he is reading anything but an English book. The critic may understand, and the man who has lived long in the United States and who can recognise the characteristics of American diction, assuredly will understand, but these form, of course, a very small class in the community; and when the rest of the public is constantly reading American writing without a thought that it is other than English writing, it is hardly strange that American forms of speech creep daily more and more largely into the English tongue. What is really strange is that the educational authorities have been prepared to accept and to utilise in English schools many American educational books carrying American forms of speech and American spelling.

The morality or the wisdom of the English copyright laws is not at the moment under discussion, but it is my own opinion (which I believe to be the opinion of every Englishman who has given any attention to the matter) that not on any ground of literary criticism, or because of any canons of taste, but merely as a matter of pounds, shillings, and pence to England, and for the sake of securing additional employment for British labour, the laws of copyright are in no less radical and urgent need of amendment than the English postal laws. What we are here concerned with, however, is the effect of the present condition of these laws as one of the contributory factors which are co-operating to lessen the difference, once so wide and now so narrow, between the American and the English tongue.

Nor can there be any doubt of the result of this twofold process if it be allowed to continue indefinitely, working in England towards a democratisation and Americanisation of the speech, and in America towards a higher standard of taste, based on earlier English literary models. The two currents, once divergent, now so closely confluent, will meet; but will they continue to flow on in one stream? Or will the same tendencies persist, so that the currents will cross and again diverge, occupying inverse positions?

In a hundred years from now, when, as a result of the apparently inevitable growth of the United States in wealth, in power, and in influence, its speech and all other of its institutions will come to be held in the highest esteem, is it possible that Londoners may vehemently put forward their claim to speak purer American than the Americans themselves—just as many Americans assert to-day that their speech is nearer to the speech of Elizabethan England than is the speech of modern Englishmen? Is it possible that it will be only in the common language of Englishmen that philologists will be able to find surviving the racy, good old American words and phrases of the last decades of the nineteenth century—a period which will be to American literature what the Elizabethan Age is to English. It may, of course, be absurd, but already there are certain individual Americanisms which have long been *taboo* in every reputable office in the United States, but are used cheerfully and without comment in London dailies.

Once more it seems necessary to take precaution lest I be interpreted as having said more than I really have said. It would be a mere impertinence to affect to pronounce a general judgment on the level of culture or of achievement of the two peoples in all fields of art and effort; and the most that an individual can do is to take such isolated examples drawn from one or from the other, as may serve in particular matters as some sort of a standard of measurement. What I am striving to convey to the average English reader is, of course, not an impression of any inferiority in the

English, but only the fact that the Englishman's present estimate of the American is almost grotesquely inadequate.

FOOTNOTES:

[214:1] Mr. Archer, I find, has this delightful story: "A friend of mine returned from a short tour in the United States, declaring that he heartily disliked the country and would never go back again. Enquiry as to the grounds of his dissatisfaction elicited no more definite or damning charge than that 'they' (a collective pronoun presumed to cover the whole American people) hung up his trousers instead of folding them—or *vice versa*, for I am heathen enough not to remember which is the orthodox process."

[215:1] But I cannot resist recording my astonishment at finding in Ben Jonson the phrase "to have a good time" used in precisely the sense in which the American girl employs it to-day, or at learning from Macaulay that Bishop Cooper in the time of Queen Elizabeth spoke of a "platform" in its exact modern American political meaning.

[220:1] Though it is worth noting that incomparably the best dictionary of the English language yet completed is an American one.

CHAPTER IX

POLITICS AND POLITICIANS

The "English-American" Vote—The Best People in Politics—What Politics Means in America—Where Corruption Creeps in—The Danger in England—A Presidential Nomination for Sale—Buying Legislation—Could it Occur in England?—A Delectable Alderman—Taxation while you Wait—Perils that England Escapes—The Morality of Congress—Political Corruption and the Irish—Democrat and Republican.

The American people ought cordially to cherish Englishmen who come to the United States to live, if only for the reason that they have never organised for political purposes. In every election, all over the United States, one hears of the Irish vote, the German vote, the Scandinavian vote, the Italian vote, the French vote, the Polish vote, the Hebrew vote, and many other votes, each representing a *clientèle* which has to be conciliated or cajoled. But none has ever yet heard of the English vote or of an "English-American" element in the population. It is not that the Englishman, whether a naturalised American or not, does not take as keen an interest in the politics of the country as the people of any other nation; on the contrary, he is incomparably better equipped than any other to take that interest intelligently. But he plays his part as if it were in the politics of his own country, guided by precisely the same considerations as the American voters around him.[227:1]

The individual Irishman or German will often take pride in splitting off from the people of his own blood in matters political and voting "as an American." It never occurs to the Englishman to do otherwise. The Irishman and the German will often boast, or you will hear it claimed for them, that they become assimilated quickly and that "in time," or "in the second generation," they are good Americans. The Englishman needs no assimilation; but feels himself to be, almost from the day when he lands (provided that he comes to live and not as a tourist), of one substance and colour with the people about him. Not seldom he is rather annoyed that those around him, remembering that he is English, seem to expect of him the sentiments of a "foreigner," which he in no way feels.

More than once, it is true, during my residence in America I have been approached by individuals or by committees, with invitations to associate myself with some proposed political organisation of Englishmen "to make our weight felt;" but in justice to those who have made the suggestion it should be said that it has always been the outcome of exasperation at a moment either when Fenianism was peculiarly rampant in the neighbourhood, or when members of other nationalities were doing their best to create ill-will between Great Britain and the United States. The idea of organising, as the members of other nationalities have organised, for the mere purpose of sharing in the party plunder, has, I believe, never been seriously contemplated by any Englishmen in America; though there are many communities in which their vote might well give them the balance of power. It would, as a rule, be easier to pick out—say, in Chicago—a Southerner who had lived in the North for ten years than an Englishman who had lived there for the same length of time. It would certainly be safer to guess the Southerner's party affiliation.

The ideas of Englishmen in England about American politics are vague. They have a general notion that there is a great deal of politics in America, that it is mostly corrupt, and that "the best people" do not take any interest in it. As for the last proposition, it is only locally or partially true, and quite untrue in the sense in which the Englishman understands it.

The word "politics" means two entirely separate things in England and in the United States. Understanding the word in its English sense, it is conspicuously untrue that the "best people" in America do not take at least as much an interest in politics as the "best people" take in England. Selecting as a representative of the "best people" of America, any citizen eminent in his particular community—capitalist, landed proprietor or "real-estate owner," banker, manufacturer, lawyer, railway president, or what not,—that man as a usual thing takes a very active interest in politics, and not in the politics of the nation only, but of his State and his municipality. He is known to be a pillar of one party or the other; he gives liberally of his own funds and of the funds of his firm or company to the party treasury[229.1]; he is consulted by, and advises with, the local committees; representatives of the national committees or from other parts of the State call upon him for information; he concerns himself intimately with the appointments to political office made from his section of the country; he attends public meetings and entertains visiting speakers at his house; as far as may be judicious (and sometimes much further), he endeavours by his example or precept to influence the votes and ways of thought of those in his service. The chances of his being sent to Congress or to the Senate, of his becoming a cabinet minister, being appointed to a foreign mission, or accepting a position on some commission of a public character, are vastly greater than with the man of corresponding position in England. So far from not taking an interest in politics, as Englishmen understand the phrase, he is commonly a most energetic and valuable supporter of his party.

But—and here is the nub of the matter—politics in America include whole strata of political work which are scarcely understood in England. When the English visitor is told in the United States that "our best people will not take any interest in politics," it is usually in the office of a financier, or at a fashionable dinner table, in New York or some other of the great cities. What is intended to be conveyed to him is that the "best people" will not take part in the active work in municipal politics or in that portion of the national politics which falls within the municipal area. The millionaire, the gentleman of refinement and leisure, will not "take off his coat" and attend primary meetings, or make tours of the saloons and meet Tammany or "the City Hall gang" on its own ground. As a matter of fact it is rather surprising to see how often he does it; but it is spasmodically and in occasional fits of enthusiasm for Reform, "with a large R." And, whatever temporary value these intermittent efforts may have (and they have great value, if only as a warning to the "gangs" that it is possible to go too far), they are in the long run of little avail against the constant daily and nightly work of the members of a "machine" to whom that work means daily bread.

I have said that it is surprising to see how often these "best people" do go down into the slums and begin work at the beginning; and the tendency to do so is growing more and more frequent. The reproach that they do not do it enough has not the force to-day that once it had. Meanwhile in England there is little complaint that the same people do not do that particular work, for the excellent reason that that work does not exist to be done. It would only be tedious here to go into an elaborate explanation of why it does not exist. The reason is to be found in the differences in the political structure of the two countries—in the much more representative character of the government (or rather of the methods of election to office) in America—in the multiplication of Federal, State, county, and municipal office-holders—in the larger number of offices, including many which are purely judicial, which are elective, and which are filled by party candidates elected by a partisan vote—in the identification of national and municipal politics all over the country.

Of all these causes, it is probably the last which is fundamentally most operative. The local democracy, local republicanism everywhere, is a part of the national Democratic or Republican organisation. The party as a whole is composed of these municipal units. Each municipal campaign is conducted with an eye to the general fortunes of the party in the State or the nation; and the same power that appoints a janitor in a city hall may dictate the selection of a presidential candidate.

Until very recently, this phenomenon was practically unknown in England. The "best person"—he who "took an interest in politics" as a Liberal or as a Conservative—was no more concerned, as Liberal or Conservative, in the election of his town officers than he was accustomed to take part in the weekly sing-song at the village public house. National politics did not touch municipal politics. Within the last two decades or so, however, there has been a marked change, and not in London and a few large cities alone.

Englishmen who have been accustomed to believe that the high standard of purity in English public life, as compared with what was supposed to be the standard in America, was chiefly owing to the divorcement of the two, are not altogether gratified at the change or easy in their mind as to the future. London is still a long way from having such an organisation as Tammany Hall in either the Moderate or Progressive party; but it is not easy to see what insuperable obstacles would exist to the formation of such an organisation, with certain limitations, if a great and unscrupulous political genius should arise among the members of either party in the London County Council and should bend his energies to the task. It is not, of course, necessary that, because Englishmen are approximating to the American system in this particular, they should be unable to avoid adopting its worst American abuses. But it will do no harm if Englishmen in general recognise that what is, it is to be hoped, still far from inevitable, was a short time ago impossible. If Great Britain must admit an influence which has, even though only incidentally, bred pestilence and corruption elsewhere, it might be well to take in time whatever sanitary and preventive measures may be available against similar consequences.[232:1]

Meanwhile in the United States there is continually being raised, in ever increasing volume, the cry for the separation of local and national politics. It is true that small headway has yet been made towards any tangible reform; but the desire is there. Again, therefore, it is curious that in politics, as in so many other things, there are two currents setting in precisely opposing directions in the two countries—in America a reaction against corruptions which have crept in during the season of growth and ferment and an attempt to return to something of the simplicity of earlier models, and, simultaneously in England, hardly a danger, but a possibility of sliding into a danger, of admitting precisely those abuses of which the United States is endeavouring to purge itself. The tendencies at work are exactly analogous to those which, as we have seen, are operating to modify the respective modes of speech of the two peoples. What the ultimate effect of either force will be, it is impossible even to conjecture. But it is unpleasant for an Englishman to consider even the remotest possibility of a time coming, though long after he himself is dead, when the people of America will draw awful warnings from the corrupt state of politics in England, and bless themselves that in the United States the municipal rings which dominate and scourge the great cities in England are unknown.

At present that time is far distant, and there can be no reasonable doubt that there is much more corruption in public affairs in the United States than in

England. The possibilities of corruption are greater, because there are so many more men whose influence or vote may be worth buying; but it is to be feared that the evil does not exceed merely in proportion to the excess of opportunity. Granted that bribery and the use of undue influence are most obvious and most rampant in those spheres which have not their counterpart in Great Britain—in municipal wards and precincts, in county conventions and State legislatures—it still remains that the taint has spread upwards into other regions which in English politics are pure. There is every reason to think that the Englishman is justified in his belief that the motives which guide his public men and the principles which govern his public policy are, on the whole, higher than those which guide and inspire and govern the men or policies of any other nation. Bismarck's (if it was Bismarck's) confidence in the *parole de gentleman* is still justified. In America, a similar faith in matters of politics would at times be sorely tried.

Perhaps as good an illustration as could be cited of the greater possibilities of corruption in the United States, is contained in a statement of the fact that a very few thousand dollars would at one time have sufficed to prevent Mr. Bryan from becoming the Democratic candidate for the Presidency in 1896. This is not mere hearsay, for I am able to speak from knowledge which was not acquired after the event. Nor for one moment is it suggested that Mr. Bryan himself was thus easily corruptible, nor even that those who immediately nominated him could have been purchased for the sum mentioned.

The fact is that for a certain specified sum the leaders of a particular county convention were willing to elect an anti-Bryan delegation. The delegation then elected would unquestionably control the State convention subsequently to be held; and the delegation to be elected again at that convention would have a very powerful influence in shaping the action of the National Convention at St. Louis. The situation was understood and the facts not disputed. Those to whom the application for the money was made took all things into consideration and determined that it was not worth it; that it would be better to let things slide. They slid. If those gentlemen had foreseen the full volume of the avalanche that was coming, I think that the money would have been found.

It was, however, better as it was. The motives which prompted the refusal of the money were, as I was told, not motives of morality. It was not any objection to the act of bribery, but a mere question of expediency. It was not considered that the "goods" were worth the money. But, as always, it was better for the country that the immoral act was not done. The Free Silver poison was working in the blood of the body politic, and it was better to let the malady come to a head and fight it strenuously than to drive it back and let it go on with its work of internal corruption. Looking back now it is easy to see that the fight of 1896 must have come at some time, and it was best that it came when it did. The gentlemen who declined to produce the few thousand dollars asked of them (the sum was fifteen thousand dollars, if I remember rightly, or three thousand pounds) would, a few weeks later, have given twice the sum to have the opportunity back again. Now, I imagine, they are well content that they acted as they did.

As illustrating the methods which are not infrequent in connection with the work of the State legislatures, I may mention that I once acted (without premeditation) as witness to the depositing of two thousand dollars in gold coin in a box at a safety deposit vault, by the representative of a great corporation, the key of which box was afterwards handed to a member of the local State legislature. The vote and influence of that member were necessary for the defeat of certain bills—bills, be it said, iniquitous in themselves—which would have cost that particular corporation many times two thousand dollars; and two thousand dollars was the sum at which that legislator valued the aforesaid vote and influence.

It is not always necessary to take so much precaution to secure secrecy as was needed in this case. The recklessness with which State legislators sometimes accept cheques and other easily traceable media of exchange is a little bewildering, until one understands how secure they really are from any risk of information being lodged against them. A certain venerable legislator in one of the North-western States some years ago gained considerable notoriety, of a confidential kind, by being the only member of his party in the legislature at the time who declined to accept his share in a distribution which was going on of the mortgage bonds of a certain railway company. It was not high principle nor any absurd punctiliousness on his part that made him decline. "In my youth," said he to the representative of the railway company, "I was an earnest anti-slavery man and I still recoil from bonds." It was said that he received his proportion of the pool in a more negotiable form.

It would be easy, even from my own individual knowledge, to multiply stories of this class; but the effect would only be to mislead the English reader, while the American is already familiar with such stories in sufficiency. The object is not to insist upon the fact that there is corruption in American public life, but rather to show what kind of corruption it is, and that it is largely of a kind the opportunity for indulgence in which does not exist in England. The method of nominating candidates for Parliament in England removes the temptation to "influence" primaries and bribe delegations. In the absence of State legislatures, railway and other corporations are not exposed to the same system of blackmail.

Let us suppose that each county in England had its legislature of two chambers, as every State has in America, the members of these legislatures being elected necessarily only from constituencies in which they lived, so that a slum district of a town was obliged to elect a slum-resident, a village a resident of that village; let us further suppose that by the mixture of races in the population certain districts could by mere preponderance of the votes be expected to elect only a German, a Scandinavian, or an Irishman—in each case a man who had been perhaps, but a few years before, an immigrant drawn from a low class in the population of his own country; give that legislature almost unbridled power over all business institutions within the borders of the county, including the determination of rates of charge on that portion of the lines of great railway companies which lay within the county borders—is there not danger that that power would be frequently abused? When one party, after a long term of trial in opposition, found itself suddenly in control of both houses, would it always refrain from using its power for the gratification of party purposes, for revenge, and for the assistance of its own supporters? Local feeling sometimes becomes, even in England, much inflamed against a given railway company, or some large employer of labour, or great landlord, whether justly or not. It may be that in the case of a railway, the rates of fare are considered high, the train service bad, or the accommodations at the stations poor. At such a time a local legislature would be likely to pass almost any bill that was introduced to hurt that railway company, merely as a means of bringing pressure to bear upon it to correct the supposed shortcomings. It obviously then becomes only too easy for an unscrupulous member to bring forward a bill which will have plausible colour of public-spirited motive, and which if it became a law would cost the railway company untold inconvenience and many tens of thousands of pounds; and the railway company can have that bill withdrawn or "sidetracked" for a mere couple of hundred.

Personally I am thankful to say that I have such confidence in the sterling quality of the fibre of the English people (so long as it is free, as it is in England, from Irish or other alien influence) as to believe that, even under these circumstances, and with all these possibilities of wrong-doing, the local legislatures would remain reasonably honest. But what might come with long use and practice, long exposure to temptation, it is not easy to say. Some things occur in the colonies which are not comforting. If, then, the corruption in American politics be great, the evil is due rather to the system than to any inherent inferiority in the native honesty of the people. Their integrity, if it falls, has the excuse of abundant temptation.

The most instructive experience, I think, which I myself had of the disregard of morality in the realm of municipal politics was received when I associated myself, sentimentally rather than actively, with a movement at a certain election directed towards the defeat of one who was probably the most corrupt alderman in what was at the time perhaps the corruptest city in the United States. Of the man's entire depravity, from a political point of view, there was not the least question among either his friends or his enemies. Nominally a Democrat, his vote and policy were never guided by any other consideration than those of his own pocket. On an alderman's salary (which he spent several times over in his personal expenditure each year), without other business or visible means of making money, he had grown wealthy— wealthy enough to make his contributions to campaign funds run into the thousands of dollars,—wealthy enough to be able always to forget to take change for a five-dollar or a ten-dollar bill when buying anything in his own ward,—wealthy enough to distribute regularly (was it five hundred or a thousand?) turkeys every Thanksgiving Day among his constituents. No one pretended to suggest that his money was drawn from any other source than from the public funds, from blackmail, and from the sale of his vote and influence in the City Council. In that Council he had held his seat unassailably for many years through all the shifting and changing of parties in power. But a spirit of reform was abroad and certain public-spirited persons decided that it was time that the scandal of his continuance in office should be stopped. The same conclusion had been arrived at by various campaign managers and bodies of independent and upright citizens on divers preceding occasions, without any result worth mentioning. But at last it seemed that the time had come. There were various encouraging signs and portents in the political heavens and all auguries were favourable. There were, it is true, experienced politicians who shook their heads. They blessed us and wished us well. They even contributed liberally to our campaign fund; but the most experienced among them were not hopeful.

It was a vigorous campaign—on our side; with meetings, brass bands, constant house-to-house canvassing, and processions *ad libitum*. On the other side, there was no campaign at all to speak of; only the man whom we were seeking to unseat spent some portion of every day and the whole of every night going about the ward from saloon to saloon, always forgetting the change for those five-dollar and ten-dollar bills, always willing to cheer lustily when one of our processions went by, and, as we heard, daily increasing his orders for turkeys for the approaching Thanksgiving season.

So far as the saloon keepers, the gamblers, the owners and patrons of disorderly houses went, we had no hope of winning their allegiance; but, after all, they were a small numerical minority of the voters of the ward. The majority consisted of low-class Italians, unskilled labourers, and it was their votes that must decide the issue. There was not one of them who was not thoroughly talked to, as well as every member of his family of a reasoning age. There was not one who did not fully recognise that the alderman was a thief and an entirely immoral scamp; but their labour was farmed by, perhaps, half a dozen Italian contractors. These men were the Alderman's henchmen. As long as he continued in the Council, he was able to keep their men employed—on municipal works and on the work of the various railway and other large corporations which he was able to blackmail. We, on our part, had obtained promises of employment, from friends of decent government regardless of politics in all parts of the city, for approximately as many men as could possibly be thrown out of work in case of an upheaval. But of what use were these, more or less unverifiable, promises, when on the eve of the election the half a dozen contractors (who of course had grown rich with their alderman's continuance in office) gave each individual labourer in the ward to understand clearly that if the present alderman was defeated each one of them would have to go and live somewhere—live or starve,—for not one stroke of work would they ever get so long as they lived in that ward?

It was, as I have said, a vigorous campaign on our side; and the Delectable One was re-elected by something more than his usual majority. On the night of the election it was reported—though this may have been mere rumour—that the bills which he laid on the counter of each saloon in the ward (and always forgot to take any change) were of the value of fifty dollars each. That was some years ago, but I understand that he is still in that same City Council, representing that same ward.

It was in the same city that one year I received notice of my personal property tax, the amount assessed against me being about ten times higher than it ought to have been. Experience had taught me that it was useless to make any protest against small impositions, but a multiplication of my obligations by tenfold was not to be submitted to without a struggle. I wrote therefore to the proper authority, making protest, and was told that the matter would be investigated. After a lapse of some days, I was invited to call at the City Hall. There I was informed by one of the subordinate officials that it was undoubtedly a case of malice—that the assessment had been made by either a personal or a political enemy. I was then taken to see the Chief. The Chief was a corpulent Irishman of the worst type. My guide leaned over him and in an undertone, but not so low that I did not hear, gave him a brief *résumé* of the story, stating that it was undoubtedly a case of intentional injustice, and concluding with an account of myself and my interests which showed that the speaker had taken no little trouble to post himself upon the subject. He emphasised the fact of my association with the press. At this point for the first time the Chief evinced some interest in the tale. His intelligence responded to the word "newspapers" as promptly as if an electrical current had suddenly been switched into his system. "H'm! newspapers!" he grunted.

Then, heaving his bulk half round in his chair so as partially to face me——

"This is a mistake," he said. "We will say no more about it. Your assessment's cancelled."

"I beg your pardon," I said, "I have no objection to paying one-tenth of the amount. If an '0' is cut off the end——"

"That's all right," he said. "The whole thing is cut off."

I made another protest, but he waved me away and my guide led me from the room. Because it was opined that, through the press, I might be able to make myself objectionable if the imposition was persisted in, I paid no tax at all that year. Which was every whit as immoral as the original offence.

Stories of this class it would be easy to multiply indefinitely; but again I say that it is not my desire to insist on the corruptness which exists in American political life, but rather to explain to English readers what the nature of that corruptness is and in what spheres of the political life of the country it is able to find lodgment. What I have endeavoured to illustrate is, first, how the peculiar political system of the United States may, under some exceptional conditions, make it possible for even the nomination of a President to be treated as a matter of purchase, though the candidate himself and those who immediately surround him may be of incorruptible integrity; second, the unrivalled opportunities for bribery and other forms of political wrong-doing furnished by the existence of the State legislatures, with their eight thousand members, drawn necessarily from all ranks and elements of the population, and possessing exceptional power over the commercial affairs of the people of their respective States; and, third, the methods by which, in certain large cities, power is attained, used, and abused by the municipal "bosses" of all degrees, a condition of affairs which is in large measure only made possible by the identification of local and national politics and political parties. In each case the conditions which make the corruption possible do not exist in England, even though in the last named (the identification of local with national politics and parties) the tendency in Great Britain is distinctly in the direction of the American model. It is, perhaps, an inevitable result of the working of the Anglo-Saxon "particularistic" spirit, which ultimately rebels against any form of national government or of national politics in which the individual and the individual of each locality, is debarred from making his voice heard.

As for the corruptness which is supposed to exist in Congress itself, this I believe to be largely a matter of partisan gossip and newspaper talk. It may be that every Congress contains among its members a few whose integrity is not beyond the temptation of a direct monetary bribe; and it would perhaps be curious if it were not so. But it is the opinion of the best informed that the direct bribery of a member of either the Senate or the House is extremely rare. It happens, probably, all too frequently that members consent to acquire at a low figure shares in undertakings which are likely to be favourably affected by legislation for which they vote, in the expectation or hope of profit therefrom; but it is exceedingly difficult to say in any given case whether a member's vote has been influenced by his financial interest (whether, on public grounds, he would not have voted as he did under any circumstances), and at what point the mere employment of sound business judgment ends and the prostitution of legislative influence begins. The same may be said of the accusations so commonly made against members of making use of information which they acquire in the committee room for purposes of speculation.

Washington, during the sessions of Congress is full of "lobbyists"—*i. e.*, men who have no other reason for their presence at the capital than to further the progress of legislation in which they are interested or who are sent there for the purpose by others who have such an interest; but it is my conviction (and I know it is that of others better informed than myself) that the instances wherein the labours of a lobbyist go beyond the use of legitimate argument in favour of entirely meritorious measures are immensely fewer than the reader of the sensational press might suppose. The American National Legislature is, indeed, a vastly purer body than demagogues, or the American press, would have an outsider believe.

There is no doubt that large manufacturing and commercial concerns do exert themselves to secure the election to the House, and perhaps to the Senate, of persons who are practically their direct representatives, their chief business in Congress being the shaping of favourable legislation or the warding off of that which would be disadvantageous to the interests which are behind them. Undoubtedly also such large concerns, or associated groups of them, can bring considerable pressure to bear upon individual members in divers ways, and there have been notorious cases wherein it has been shown that this pressure has been unscrupulously used. Except in the case of the railways, which have only a secondary interest in tariff legislation, this particular abuse must be charged to the account of the protective policy, and its development in some measure would perhaps be inevitable in any country where a similar policy prevailed.

In the British Parliament there are, of course, few important lines of trade or industry which are not abundantly represented, and both Houses contain railway directors and others who speak frankly as the representatives of railway interests, and lose thereby nothing of the respect of the country or their fellow-members. It is not possible here to explain in detail why the assumption, which prevails in America, that a railway company is necessarily a public enemy, and that any argument in favour of such a corporation is an argument against the public welfare, does not obtain in England. It will be necessary later on not only to refer to the fact that fear of capitalism is immensely stronger in America than it is in England, but also to explain why there is good reason why it should be so. For the present, it is enough to note that it is possible for members of Parliament to do, without incurring a shadow of suspicion of their integrity, things which would damn a member of Congress irreparably in the eyes alike of his colleagues and of the country. There is hardly a railway bill passed through Parliament the supporters of which would not in its passage through Congress have to run the gauntlet of all manner of insinuation and abuse; and when the sensational press of the United States raises a hue and cry of "Steal!" in regard to a particular measure, the Englishman (until he understands the difference in the conditions in the two countries) may be bewildered by finding on investigation that the bill is one entirely praiseworthy which would pass through Parliament as a matter of course, the only justification for the outcry being that the legislation is likely, perhaps most indirectly, to prove advantageous to some particular industry or locality. The fact that the measure is just and deserving of support on merely patriotic grounds is immaterial, when party capital can be made from such an outcry. I have on more than one occasion known entirely undeserved suffering to be inflicted in this way on men of the highest character who were acting from none but disinterested motives; and he who would have traffic with large affairs in the United States must early learn to grow callous to newspaper abuse.

In wider and more general ways than have yet been noticed, however, the members of Congress are subjected to undue influences in a measure far beyond anything known to the members of Parliament.

In the colonial days, governors not seldom complained of the law by which members of the provincial assemblies could only be elected to sit for the towns or districts in which they actually resided. The same law once prevailed in England, but it was repealed in the time of George III., and had been disregarded in practice since the days of Elizabeth.[247:1] Under the Constitution of the United States it is, however, still necessary that a member of Congress should be a resident (or "inhabitant") of the State from which he is elected. In some States it is the law that he must reside in the particular district of the State which elects him, and custom has made this the rule in all. A candidate rejected by his own constituency, therefore, cannot stand for another; and it follows that a member who desires to continue in public life must hold the good will of his particular locality.

So entirely is this accepted as a matter of course that any other system (the British system for instance) seems to the great majority of Americans quite unnatural and absurd; and it has the obvious immediate advantage that each member does more truly "represent" his particular constituents than is likely to be the case when he sits for a borough or a Division in which he may never have set foot until he began to canvas it. On the other hand, it is an obvious disadvantage that when a member for any petty local reason forfeits the good will of his own constituency, his services, no matter how valuable they may be, are permanently lost to the State.

The term for which a member of the Lower House is elected in America is only two years, so that a member who has any ambition for a continuous legislative career must, almost from the day of his election, begin to consider the chance of being re-elected. As this depends altogether on his ability to hold the gratitude of his one constituency, it is inevitable that he should become more or less engrossed in the effort to serve the local needs; and a constituency, or the party leaders in a constituency, generally, indeed, measure a man's availability for re-election by what is called his "usefulness."

If you ask a politician of local authority whether the sitting member is a good one, he will reply, "No; he hasn't any influence at Washington at all. He can't do a thing for us!" Or, "Yes, he's pretty good; he seems to get things through all right." The "things" which the member "gets through" may be the appointment of residents of the district to minor government positions, the securing of appropriations of public moneys for such works as the dredging or widening of a river channel to the advantage of the district or the improvement of the local harbour, and the passage of bills providing for the erection in the district of new post-offices or other government buildings. Many other measures may, of course, be of direct local interest; but a member's chief opportunities for earning the gratitude of his constituency fall under the three categories enumerated.

It is obvious that two years is too short a term for any but an exceptionally gifted man to make his mark, either in the eyes of his colleagues or of his constituency, by conspicuous national services. Even if achieved, it is doubtful if in the eyes of the majority of the constituencies (or the leaders in those constituencies) any such impalpable distinction would be held to compensate for a demonstrated inability to get the proper share of local advantages. The result is that while the member of Parliament may be said to consider himself primarily as a member of his party and his chief business to be that of co-operating with that party in securing the conduct of National affairs according to the party beliefs, the member of Congress considers himself primarily as the representative of his district and his chief business to be the securing for that district of as many plums from the Federal pie as possible.

Out of these conditions has developed the prevalence of log-rolling in Congress: "You vote for my post-office and I'll help you with your harbour appropriation." Such exchange of courtesies is continual and, I think, universal. The annual River and Harbour Bill (which last year appropriated $25,414,000 of public money for all manner of works in all corners of the country) is an amazing legislative product.

Another result is that the individual member must hold himself constantly alert to find what his "people" at home want: always on the lookout for signs of approval or disapproval from his constituency. And the constituency on its side does not hesitate to let him know just what it thinks of him and precisely what jobs it requires him to do at any given moment. Nor is it the constituency as a whole, through its recognised party leaders, which alone thinks that it has a right to instruct, direct, or influence its representative, but individuals of sufficient political standing to consider themselves entitled to have their private interest looked after, manufacturing and business concerns the payrolls of which support a large number of voters, labour unions, and all sorts of societies and organisations of various kinds—they one and all assert their right to advise the Congressman in his policies or to call for his assistance in furthering their particular ends, under threat, tacit or expressed, of the loss of their support when he seeks re-election. The English member of Parliament thinks that he is subjected to a sufficiency of pressure of this particular sort; but he has not to bear one-tenth of what is daily meted out to his American *confrère*, nor is he under any similar necessity of paying attention to it.

Under such conditions it is evident that a Congressman can have but a restricted liberty to act or vote according to his individual convictions. It is only human that, in matters which are not of great national import, a man should at times be willing to believe that his personal opinions may be wrong when adherence to those opinions would wreck his political career. So the Congressman too commonly acquires a habit of subservience which is assuredly not wholesome either for the individual or for the country; and sometimes the effort to trim sails to catch every favouring breeze has curious oblique results. As an instance of this may be cited the action taken by Congress in regard to the army canteen. A year or more back, the permission to army posts to retain within their own limits and subject to the supervision of the post authorities, a canteen for the use of soldiers, was abolished. The soldiers have since been compelled to do their drinking outside, and, as a result, this drinking has been done without control or supervision, and has produced much more serious demoralisation. The action of Congress was taken in the face of an earnest and nearly unanimous protest from experienced army officers—the men, that is, who were directly concerned with the problem in question. The Congressmen acted as they did under the pressure of the Woman's Christian Temperance Union, and with the dread lest a vote for the canteen should be interpreted as a vote for liquor, and should stand in the way of their own political success.

From what has been said it will be seen that the member of Congress is compelled to give a deplorably large proportion of his time and thought to paltry local matters, leaving a deplorably small portion of either to be devoted to national questions; while in the exercise of his functions as a legislator he is likely to be influenced by a variety of motives which ought to be quite impertinent and are often unworthy. These things however seem to be almost inevitable results of the national political structure. The individual corruptibility of the members of either House (their readiness, that is to be influenced by any considerations, other than that of their re-election, of their own interests, financial or otherwise), I believe to be grossly exaggerated in the popular mind. Certainly a stranger is likely to get the idea that the Congress is a much less honourable and less earnest body than it is.

The subject of the corruptness of the public service in the larger cities brings up again a matter which has been already touched upon, namely the extent to which this corruptness is in its origin Irish and not an indigenous American growth. Under the favourable influences of American political conditions the Irish have developed exceptional capacity for leadership (a capacity which they are also showing in some of the British colonies) and they do not generally use their ability or their powers for the good of the community. The rapidity with which the Irish immigrant blossoms into political authority is a commonplace of American journalism:

"Ere the steamer that brought him had got out of hearing,
He was Alderman Mike introducing a bill."

It is commonly held by Americans that all political corruptness in the United States (certainly all municipal wickedness) is chargeable to Irish influence; but it is a position not easy to maintain in the face of the example of the city of Philadelphia, the government of which has from the beginning been chiefly in the hands of Americans, many of whom have been members of the oldest and best Philadelphia families. Yet the administration of Philadelphia has been as corrupt and as openly disregardful of the welfare of the community as ever was that of New York. While Irishmen are generally Democrats, both Philadelphia and the State of Pennsylvania, are overwhelmingly Republican and devoted to the protective policy under which so many of the industries of the State have prospered exceedingly. Those who have fought for the cause of municipal reform in Philadelphia find that, while the masses of the people of the city would prefer good government, it is almost impossible to get them to reject an official candidate of the Republican party. The Republican "bosses" have thus been able to impose on the city officials of the worst kind, who have served them faithfully to the disaster of the community.[253:1] None the less, notwithstanding particular exceptions, it is a fact that as a general rule the corrupt maladministration of affairs in American cities is the direct result of Irish influence.

The opportunities of the Irish leaders for securing control of the city administration, or of certain important and lucrative divisions of this administration, have been furthered, particularly in such cities as New York and San Francisco, by the influence they are able to gain over bodies of immigrants who are also in the fold of the Roman Catholic Church, and who, on the ground of difference of language and other causes, have less quickness of perception of their own political opportunities. The Irish leaders have been able to direct in very large measure the votes of the Italians (more particularly the Italians from the South), the Bohemians, and the other groups of immigrants from Catholic communities. As the Irish immigration has decreased both absolutely and relatively, the numbers of voters supporting the leadership of the bosses of Tammany Hall and of the similar organisations in Chicago and San Francisco have been made good, and in fact substantially increased, by the addition of Catholic voters of other nationalities.

I wish the English reader to grasp fully the significance of these facts before he allows the stories which he hears of the municipal immorality which exists in the United States to colour too deeply his estimate of the character of the American people. That immorality is chiefly Irish in its origin and is made continuously possible by the ascendency of the Irish over masses of other non-Anglo-Saxon peoples. The Celts were never a race of individual workers either as agriculturists or in handicraft. That "law of intense personal labour" which is the foundation of the strength of the Anglo-Saxon communities never commanded their full obedience, as the history of Ireland and the condition of the country to-day abundantly testify. It is not, then, the fault of the individual Irishman that when he migrates to America, instead of going out to the frontier to "grow up" with the territory or taking himself to agricultural work in the great districts of the West which are always calling for workers, he prefers to remain in the cities to engage when possible in the public service, or, failing that, to enter the domestic service of a private employer.

It should not be necessary to say (except that Irish-American susceptibilities are sometimes extraordinarily sensitive) that I share to the full that admiration which all people feel for the best traits in the Irish character; but, in spite of individual exceptions, I urge that it is not in the nature of the race to become good and helpful citizens according to Anglo-Saxon ideals, and that, as far as those qualities are concerned which have made the greatness of the United States, the contribution from the Irish element has been inconsiderable. The deftness of the Irishman in political organisation and his lack of desire for individual independence, as a result of which he turns either to the organising of a governing machine or to some form of personal service (in either case merging his own individuality) is as much foreign to the American spirit as is the docility of the less intelligent class of Germans under their political leaders—a docility which, until very recently has caused the German voters in America to be used in masses almost without protest.

It is the Anglo-Saxon, or English, spirit which has played the dominant part in moulding the government of the United States, which has made the nation what it is, which to-day controls its social usages. The Irish invasion of the political field may fairly be said to be in its essence an alien invasion; and, while it may be to the discredit of the American people that they have allowed themselves in the past to be so engrossed in other matters that they have permitted that invasion to attain the success which it has attained, I do not fear that in the long run the masterful Anglo-Saxon spirit will suffer itself to be permanently over-ridden (any more than it has allowed itself to be kept in permanent subjection in England), even in the large cities where the Anglo-Saxon voter is in a small minority. Ultimately it will throw off the incubus. In the meanwhile it is unjust that Englishmen or other Europeans should accept as evidence of native American frailty instances of municipal abuses and of corrupt methods in a city like New York, where it has not been by native Americans that those abuses and those methods were originated or that their perpetuation is made possible. On the contrary the American minority fights strenuously against them, and I am not sure that, being such a minority as it is, it has not made as good a fight as is practicable under most difficult conditions. The American people as a whole should not be judged by the conditions to which a portion of it submits unwillingly in certain narrow areas.

It may be well to explain here (for it is a subject on which the Englishman who has lived in America is often consulted) that the Republican party may roughly be said to be the equivalent of the Conservative party in England, while the Democrats are the Liberals. It happens that a precisely reverse notion has (or had until very recent years) some vogue in England, the misconception being an inheritance from the times of the American Civil War.

British sympathy was not nearly so exclusively with the South at the time of the war as is generally supposed in the United States; none the less, the ruling and aristocratic classes in England did largely wish to see the success of the

Southern armies. The Southerner, it was understood, was a gentleman, a man of mettle and spirit, and in many cases the direct descendant of an old English Cavalier family; while the Northerners were for the most part but humdrum and commercially minded people who inherited the necessarily somewhat bigoted, if excellent, characteristics of their Dutch, Puritan, or Quaker ancestors. The view had at least sufficient historical basis to serve as an excuse if not as a justification. So it came about that those classes which came to form the backbone of the Conservative party were largely sympathisers with the South; and, after the war, that sympathy naturally descended to the Democratic party rather than to the Northern Republicans. Except, however, in one particular the fundamental sentiments which make a man a Republican or a Democrat to-day have nothing to do with the issues of war times.

I do not know that any one has successfully defined the fundamental difference either between a Conservative and a Liberal, or between a Republican and a Democrat, nor have I any desire to attempt it; and where both parties in each country are in a constant state of flux and give-and-take, such a definition would perhaps be impossible. It may be that Ruskin came as near to it as is practicable when he spoke of himself as "a Tory of the old school,—the school of Homer and Sir Walter Scott."

Many people in either country accept their political opinions ready made from their fathers, their early teachers, or their chance friends, and remain all their lives believing themselves to belong to—and voting for—a party with which they have essentially nothing in sympathy. If one were to say that a Conservative was a supporter of the Throne and the Established Church, a Jingo in foreign politics, an Imperialist in colonial matters, an advocate of a strong navy and a disbeliever in free trade, tens of thousands of Conservatives might object to having assigned to them one or all of these sentiments, and tens of thousands of Liberals might insist on laying claim to any of them. Precisely so is it in America. None the less the Republican party in the mass is the party which believes in a strong Federal government, as opposed to the independence of the several States; it is a party which believes in the principle of a protective tariff; it conducted the Cuban War and is a party of Imperial expansion; it is the party which has in general the confidence of the business interests of the country and fought for and secured the maintenance of the gold standard of currency. It is obvious that, however blurred the party lines may be in individual cases, the man who in England is by instinct and conviction a Conservative, must in America by the same impulse be a Republican.

In both countries there is, moreover, a large element which furnishes the chief support to the miscellaneous third parties which succeed each other in public attention and whenever the lines are sharply drawn between the two great parties, the bulk of these can be trusted to go to the Liberal side in England and to the Democratic side in America. Nor is it by accident that the Irish in America are mostly Democrats.

I am acutely aware of the inadequacy of such an analysis as the foregoing and that many readers will have cause to be dissatisfied with what I say; but I have known many Englishmen of Conservative leanings who have come to the United States understanding that they would find themselves in sympathy with the Democrats and have been bewildered at being compelled to call themselves Republicans. Whatever the individual policy of one or the other party may be at a given moment, ultimately and fundamentally the English Conservative, especially the English Tory, is a Republican, and the Liberal, especially the Radical, is a Democrat. Both Homer and Sir Walter Scott today would (if they found themselves in America) be Republicans.

FOOTNOTES:

[227:1] For myself, I confess that my interest began somewhat prematurely. I had been in the country but a few months and had taken no steps towards naturalisation when I voted at an election in a small town in a Northwestern Territory where I had been living only for a week or two. My vote was quite illegal; but my friends (and every one in a small frontier town is one's friend) were all going to vote and told me to come along and vote too. The election, which was of the most friendly character, like the election of a club committee, proved to be closely contested, one man getting in (as City Attorney or Town Clerk or something) only by a single vote—my vote. Since then, the Territory has become a populous State, the frontier town has some hundred thousand inhabitants, and the gentleman whom I elected has been for some years a respected member of the United States Senate. I have never seen any cause to regret that illegal vote.

[229:1] The laws governing expenditures for electoral purposes, and the conduct of elections generally, are stricter in England than in the United States, and I think it is not to be questioned that there is much less bribery of voters. Largely owing to the exertions of Mr. Roosevelt, however, laws are now being enacted which will make it more difficult for campaign managers to raise the large funds which have heretofore been obtainable for election purposes.

[232:1] In as much as a demand that the control of the police force should be vested in the County Council has appeared in the programme of one political party in London, it may be well to call the attention of Englishmen to the fact that it is precisely the association of politics with the police which gives to American municipal rings their chief power for evil.

[247:1] See Bryce, *The American Commonwealth*, vol. i., p. 188.

[253:1] Inasmuch as I have twice within a small space referred to evils which incidentally grow out of the protective system, lest it be thought that I am influenced by any partisan feeling, I had better state that my personal sympathies are strongly Republican and Protectionist.

CHAPTER X

AMERICAN POLITICS IN ENGLAND

The System of Parties—Interdependence of National and Local Organisations—The Federal Government and Sovereign States—The Boss of Warwickshire—The Unit System—Prime Minister Crooks—Lanark and the Nation—New York and Tammany Hall—America's Superior Opportunities for Wickedness—But England is Catching up—Campaign Reminiscences—The "Hell-box"—Politics in a Gravel-pit—Mr. Hearst and Mr. Bryan.

The subject of this chapter will, perhaps, be more easy of comprehension to the English reader if he will for a moment surrender his imagination into my charge while we transfer to England certain political conditions of the United States.

There are in the first place, then, the great political parties, in the nation and in Parliament (Congress); with the fact always to be borne in mind that the members of Congress are not nominated by any central committee or association, but are selected and nominated by the people of each district. A candidate is not "sent down" to contest a given constituency. He is a resident of that constituency, selected in small local meetings by the voters themselves.

Next, every County (State) has its own machinery of government, including a Governor, Lieutenant-Governor, and other County officials as well as a bi-cameral Legislature, with a membership ranging from seventy in some Counties to over three hundred in others. In these County Legislatures and governments, parties are split on precisely the same lines as in the nation and in Parliament. Members of the House of Commons have usually qualified for election by a previous term in the County Legislature, while members of the House of Lords are actually elected direct, not by the people in the mass, but by the members of the County Legislatures only, each county sending to Westminster two members so elected. Nor is it to be supposed that these County governments are governments in name only.

It is not easy to imagine that in England the Counties, each with its separate and sovereign government, preceded the National Government and voluntarily called it into existence only as a federation of themselves. But that, we must for the present understand, was indeed the course of history; and when that federation was formed, the various Counties entrusted to the Central Government only a strictly limited list of powers. The Central Government was authorised to treat with foreign nations in the name of the United Counties; to maintain a standing army of limited size, and to create a navy; to establish postal routes, regardless of County boundaries; to regulate commerce between the different Counties, to care for the national coast line and all navigable waters within the national dominions, and to levy taxes for national purposes. All powers not thus specifically conceded to the central authority were, in theory at least, reserved by the individual Counties to themselves; and to-day a County government, except that it cannot interfere with the postal service within its borders, nor erect custom-houses on its County lines to levy taxes on goods coming in from neighbouring Counties, is practically a sovereign government within its own territory.

It is only within the last ten years that the right of the Central Government—the Crown—to use the King's troops to protect from violence the King's property, in the shape of the Royal mails, in defiance of the wishes of the Governor of a County, was established by a decision of the Supreme Court. The Governor protested that the suppression of mobs and tumults within his County borders was his business, his County police and militia being the proper instruments for the purpose, and for the Crown to intervene without his request and sanction was an invasion of the sovereign dignity of the County.

Although so much has been said on this subject by various English writers, from Mr. Bryce downwards, few Englishmen, I think, have comprehended the theoretical significance of this independence of the individual States, and fewer still grasp its practical importance. Perhaps the most instructive illustration of what it means is to be found in the dilemma in which the American government has, on two occasions in recent years, found itself from its inability to compel a particular State to observe the national treaty obligations to a foreign power.

The former of the two cases arose in Louisiana when a number of citizens of New Orleans (including not only leading bankers and merchants but also, it is said, at least one ex-Governor of the State and one Judge), finding that a jury could not, because of terrorisation, be found to convict certain murderers, Italians and members of the Mafia, took the murderers out of gaol and hanged them in a public square in broad daylight. The Italian government demanded the punishment of the lynchers, and the American government had to confess itself entirely unable to comply with the request. Whether it would have given the satisfaction if it could is another question; but the dealing with the criminals was a matter solely for the Louisiana State authorities, and the Federal Government had no power to interfere with them or to dictate what they should do. The only way in which it could have obtained jurisdiction over the offenders would have been by sending Federal troops into the State to take them by force, a proceeding which the State of Louisiana would certainly have resisted by force, and civil war would have followed. Ultimately, the United States, without acknowledging any liability in the matter, paid to the Italian government a certain sum of money as a voluntary *solatium* to the widows and families of those who had been killed, and the incident was closed.

The second case, which has recently strained so seriously the relations between the United States and Japan, arose with the State of California, which refused to extend to Japanese subjects the privileges to which they are unquestionably entitled under the "most favoured nation" clause of the treaty between the two governments. It is a matter which cannot be dealt with fully here without too long a digression from the path of our present argument, and will be referred to later. It is enough for the present to point out that once again the National Government—or what we have called the Crown— has been seen to be entirely incapable, without recourse to civil war, of compelling an individual State—or County—to respect the national word when pledged to a treaty with a foreign power.[264:1]

The States then, or Counties, are independent units, in each of which there exists a complete party organisation of each of the great parties, which organisations control the destinies of the parties within the County borders and have no concern whatever with the party fortunes outside. The great parties in the nation and in Parliament must look to the organisations within the several Counties for their support and existence. The loss of a County, say Hampshire, by the local Conservative organisation will mean to the Conservative party in the nation not merely that the members to be elected to the lower house of Parliament by the Hampshire constituencies will be Liberal, but that the County Legislature will elect two Liberal Peers to the upper house as well; and it is likely that in one or other of the two houses parties may be so evenly balanced that the loss of the members from the one County may overthrow the government's working majority. Moreover, the loss of the County in the local County election will probably mean the loss of that County's vote at the next presidential election, which may result in the entire dethronement of the party from power.

Wherefore it is obviously necessary that the party as a whole—in the nation and in Congress—should do all that it can to help and strengthen the party leaders in the County. This it does in contests believed to be critical, and particularly just in advance of a national election, by contributing to the local campaign funds when a purely County (State) election is in progress (with which, of course, the national party ought theoretically to have nothing to do) and in divers other ways; but especially by judicious use of the national patronage in making appointments to office when the party is in power.

The President—or let us say the Prime Minister—would rarely presume to appoint a postmaster at Winchester or Petersfield, or a collector of the port of Portsmouth or Southampton, without the advice and consent of the

Hampshire Peers or Senators. And the advice of the Hampshire Peers, we may be sure, would be shaped in accordance with their personal political interests or by considerations of the welfare of the party in the County. They would not be likely to recommend for preferment either a member of the opposite party or a member of their own party who was a personal opponent. Moreover, besides the appointments in the County itself, there are many posts in the government offices in Whitehall, as well as a number of consulates and other more remote positions, to be filled. In spite of much that has been done to make the United States civil service independent of party politics, it remains that the bulk of these posts are necessarily still filled on recommendations made by the Congressmen or party leaders from the respective Counties, and again it is the good of the party inside those Counties which inspires those recommendations.

Thus we see how the national party when in power is able to fatten and strengthen the hands of the party organisations within the several Counties; and strengthen them it must, for if they lose control of the voters within their territory then is the national party itself ruined and dethroned.

And below the County party organisations, the County governments, are the organisations and governments in the cities, which again are split on precisely the same lines of cleavage. The City Council of Petersfield or Midhurst is divided into Conservatives and Liberals precisely as the Hampshire Legislature or the Parliament at Westminster. Jealousies often arise between the County organisations and those in the cities. The influence of Birmingham might well become overpowering in the Warwickshire Legislature, whereby it would be difficult for any but a resident of Birmingham to become Governor of the County or to be elected to the House of Lords. If the Birmingham municipal organisation chanced to be controlled by a strong hand, it is not difficult to see how he might impose his will upon the County Legislature and the County party organisation, how he might claim more than his share of the sweets and spoils of office for his immediate friends and colleagues in the city, to the disgust of the other parts of the County. For the most part, however, such quarrels, between the city and County organisations of the same party, when they arise, are but lovers' quarrels, rarely pushed to the point of endangering the unity of the party in the State at election time.

But now if we remember what was said at first, that no candidates for Parliament or other elected functionaries are "sent down" by a central organisation, but all are "sent up" from the bottom, the impulse starting from small meetings in public-house parlours and the like (in the case of cities, meetings being held by "precincts" to elect delegates to a meeting of the "ward," which meeting again elects delegates to the meeting of the city), when we see how the city can coerce the County and the County sway the nation, then we have also no difficulty in seeing how it is, as has been said already, that the same power that appoints a janitor in a town-hall may dictate the nomination of a President. Even more than the County organisation is to the national party, is the city organisation to the County. The party, both as a national and as a County organisation, must fatten and strengthen the hands of the city machine. Thus comes it that such an alderman as the Delectable One is unassailable. His power reaches far beyond the city. The party organisation in the city cannot dispense with him, because he can be relied upon always to carry his ward, and that ward may be necessary, not to the city machine only, but to the County and the nation.

It is hardly necessary to explain that in a general election in England the party which is returned to power need not necessarily have a majority of the votes throughout the country. A party may win ten seats by majorities of less than a hundred in each and lose one, being therein in a minority of a thousand; with the result that, with fewer votes than were cast for its opponents, it will have a clear majority of nine in the eleven seats. This is of course well understood.

But in an American general or presidential election, this anomaly is immensely aggravated by the fact that the electoral unit is not a city or a borough but a whole County or State. The various States have a voice in proportion to their population, but that vote is cast as a unit. A majority of ten votes in New York carries the entire thirty-seven votes of that State, while a majority of one thousand in Montana only counts three. There are forty-six States in the Republic, but the thirteen most populous possess more than half the votes, and a presidential candidate who received the votes of those thirteen, though each was won by only the narrowest majority, would be elected over an antagonist who carried the other thirty-three States, though in each of the thirty-three his majority might be overwhelming. Bearing this in mind, we see at once what immense importance may, in a doubtful election, attach to the control of a single populous State.

If in an English election, similarly conducted, the country was known to be so equally divided that the vote of Warwickshire, with, perhaps, twenty votes, would certainly decide the issue, the man who could control Warwickshire would practically control the country. We have seen further, however, that the man who controls Warwickshire will probably be the man who controls Birmingham. He may be the Mayor of Birmingham, or, more likely, the chairman (or "boss") of the municipal machine who nominated and elected the Mayor and whose puppet the Mayor practically is. It then becomes evident that the man who can sway the politics of the nation is not merely the man who controls the single County of Warwickshire, but the man who, inside that County, controls the single city.

To go a step below that again, the control of the city may depend entirely on the control of a given ward in the city. That ward may contain a very large labouring vote, by reason of the existence of a number of big factories within its limits. Unless that labouring vote can be polled for the Liberal party, the ward will not go Liberal, and without it the city will be lost. The loss of the city involves the loss of the County, and the loss of the County means the loss of the nation. The man therefore who by his personal influence, or by his leadership in a perfectly organised party machine in one ward of Birmingham, can be relied on to call out the full Liberal strength in that one ward of a single city may be absolutely indispensable to the success of the party in the country as a whole. And it is even conceivable that that man again may be dependent on one of his own henchmen, the "Captain" of a single precinct in the ward or the man who has the ear and confidence of the hands in the largest of the factories.

Let me not be understood as saying that the personal influence of an individual may not be extremely powerful in an English election; and that power may rest, similarly, on his popularity in, and consequent ability to carry with him into the party fold, one particular district. But there is not the same established form of County government on avowedly national lines, nor the same city government, as in America, through which that influence can make itself definitely and continuously felt.

We will state the situation in another way, which will make it clear to Englishmen from another point of view:

Let it be imagined that at the next general election in England, the decision is to be arrived at by a direct vote of the country as a whole for a Conservative or a Liberal Prime Minister. Instead of each County and borough electing its members of Parliament (they will do that only incidentally) the real struggle will take the form of a direct contest between two men. Each of the great parties will choose its own candidate, and the Conservatives have already nominated Mr. Balfour. It remains for the Liberals to name their man who is to run against Mr. Balfour. The selection is to be made in a National Convention, to be held in Manchester, at which each County will be represented by a number of delegates proportioned to its population. Those delegates have already been elected in each County by local meetings within the Counties themselves, and in nearly every case the delegations so elected will come into the Convention Hall at Manchester prepared to vote and act as a unit. Whether that has been arrived at by choice of the individual Counties when they elected their delegations or whether the Convention itself has decided the matter by adopting the "unit rule" does not matter. The fact is that each county will be compelled to vote in a body, *i. e.*, that if London has forty votes and Kent twenty, those forty votes or those twenty will have to be cast solidly for some one man. They cannot be split into thirty votes for one man and ten for another; or into fifteen for one man and one each for five other men.

The Convention meets and it is plain from the first that the two strongest candidates are Lord Rosebery and Sir Henry Campbell-Bannerman. There are scattering votes for Mr. Morley and Mr. Asquith, each of them getting the vote of one or more small Counties. But after the first ballot, which is always more or less preliminary, it is apparent that neither of those gentlemen can hope to be chosen, so the Counties which voted for them, having expressed their preference, proceed on the next ballot to give their suffrages either to Lord Rosebery or to Sir Henry. The second ballot is completed. Every County has voted, with the result that (out of a total vote of 521, of which 261 are necessary for a choice) there are 248 votes for Lord Rosebery and 253 for Sir Henry Campbell-Bannerman. But there is still one County which has not voted for either. Kent at both ballots has cast its twenty votes for Mr. Will Crooks. The reason why Kent does this is because the representatives from Woolwich and the neighbourhood are a numerical majority of the Kent delegation and those men are devoted to Mr. Crooks.

The third ballot produces the same result: Rosebery 248; Bannerman, 253; Crooks, 20. The fourth, fifth, sixth, and seventh ballots show no change except that once in a while Rutland with three votes and Merioneth with four have amused themselves or caused a temporary flutter by swinging their votes from one side to the other or, perhaps, again casting them for Mr. Morley or Mr. Asquith. There is a deadlock. The Convention becomes impatient. The evening wears on and midnight arrives and still there is no change. Neither Lord Rosebery nor Sir Henry can get the extra dozen votes that are needed: still with regularity when the name of Kent is called the leader of the delegation rises and responds "Kent casts twenty votes for William Crooks."

At last in the small hours of the morning something happens. How it has been arrived at nobody seems to know; but when the roll is called for the thirteenth time, Norfolk, heretofore loyal to Sir Henry, suddenly votes for Crooks. Tremendous excitement follows. The word goes round that Campbell-Bannerman is beaten; his friends have given up and it is useless to vote for him any longer. Meanwhile in the course of the evening feeling between the supporters of Sir Henry and the Roseberyites has grown so bitter that whatever the deserting Bannermanites do, they will not help to elect

Lord Rosebery. Here and there a Scotch County remains firm to its leader, but Oxford swings off to Mr. Morley; Suffolk, amid yells that make it difficult to tell who the vote is cast for, follows Norfolk and plumps for Crooks. Sussex brings in Mr. Asquith again and Warwickshire goes for Crooks. Amid breathless silence the result of the thirteenth ballot is read out: Rosebery, 248; Crooks, 96; Morley, 72; Asquith, 50; Bannerman, 43; etc.

The fourteenth ballot begins. "Aberdeen!" calls the Chairman. The head of the Aberdeen delegation stands up in a suspense so tense that it almost hurts. "Aberdeen casts seventeen votes for Mr. Will Crooks!" In an instant the whole hall is filled with maniacs. County after County rushes to range itself on the winning side. Before the roll is more than half completed it is evident that Crooks must be chosen. Thereafter there is no dissentient voice. The ballot is interrupted by a voice which is known to belong to Lord Rosebery's personal representative. He moves that the nomination of Mr. Crooks be made unanimous. In a din wherein no voice can be heard the erstwhile leader of the Bannermanite forces is seen waving his arms and is known to be seconding the motion. In ten minutes the hall is singing *God Save the King* and Mr. Will Crooks is the chosen candidate of the Liberal party to oppose Mr. Balfour at the coming election.

That is not materially different from what happened when Mr. Bryan was first nominated for the Presidency against Mr. McKinley—except that it did not take so long to accomplish. I have said that Mr. Bryan's nomination could have been defeated if a certain local delegation had been "attended to" in advance. What is to be noted is that Mr. Crooks has been nominated simply because he had a hold which could not be shaken on a small but compact body of men at Woolwich. It is true that it is not often that so dramatic a thing would happen as the nomination of Mr. Crooks himself but more frequently an arrangement—a "trade" or "deal"—would be entered into by which in consideration of the Crooks vote being thrown to one or other of the leading candidates, in the event of the latter's defeating Mr. Balfour and being elected to the Premiership, certain political advantages, in the form of appointments to office and "patronage" generally, would accrue, not necessarily to Mr. Crooks himself, but to his "machine," the citizens of Woolwich, and the Liberal party in the County of Kent at large. We see here how the local "boss" may become all-powerful in national affairs (and this is of course only one of fifty ways) and how the interdependence of the party in the nation with the party organisation in the County or the municipality tends to the fattening of the latter and, it must be added, the debauching of all three.

At the last general election in England, in January, 1906, there is no doubt that the Conservative party owed the loss of a large number of seats merely to the fact that it had been in office for so long, without serious conflict, that the local party organisations had not merely grown rusty but were practically defunct. In the United States the same thing, in anything like the same degree, would be impossible, because between the periods of the general elections (which themselves come every four years) come the State and municipal elections for the purposes of which the local party organisations are kept in continuous and more or less active existence. A State or a city may, of course, be so confirmedly Republican or Democratic that, even though elections be frequent, the ruling party organisation will become, in a measure, soft and careless, but it can never sink altogether out of fighting condition. When a general election comes round, each great party in the nation possesses—or organises for the occasion—a national committee as well as a national campaign organisation; but that committee and that national organisation co-operate with the local organisations in each State and city and it is the local organisations that really do the work—the same organisations as conduct the fight, in intermediate years, for the election of members to the State Legislature or of a mayor and aldermen. And each of those local organisations necessarily tends to come under the control of a recognised "boss."

Let us see another of the fifty ways in which, as has been said, one of these local bosses may be all-powerful in national affairs. A general election is approaching in Great Britain, and, as before, the Liberal party is in doubt whether to select as its candidate for the Premiership Lord Rosebery or Sir Henry Campbell-Bannerman. The political complexion of almost every County is known and there is no chance of changing that complexion—a condition, be it said, which exists in America in the case of a large majority of the States. It is evident that at the coming election the vote is going to be extremely close, the most important of the "doubtful" Counties being Lanarkshire, which has 25 votes; which 25 votes will of course be governed by the course of the working population of Glasgow. Whichever party can secure Lanarkshire's vote will probably be successful; so that the destiny of the country really depends on the temper of the labouring men of Glasgow. Glasgow has, let us suppose, a strong and well-organised local Liberal "machine" which carried the city at the last municipal election, so that the mayor and a large majority of the aldermen of Glasgow are Liberals to-day; and the dictator or "boss" of this machine is (we are merely using a name for the sake of illustration) Lord Inverclyde. Lord Inverclyde does not believe that Lord Rosebery is the right man for the Premiership. So he lets his views be known to the Liberal National Committee. "I am, as you know," he says, "a strong Liberal; but frankly I would rather see Mr. Balfour made Prime Minister than Lord Rosebery. Glasgow will not vote for Lord Rosebery. The party can nominate any other man whom it pleases and we will elect him. I will undertake to carry Lanark for Sir Henry or Mr. Morley or anybody else; but I warn you that if Lord Rosebery is nominated, we will 'knife' him"—

that being the euphonious phrase used to describe the operation when a party leader or party machine turns against any particular candidate nominated by the party.

What are the party leaders to do in such a case? To nominate Lord Rosebery after that warning (Lord Inverclyde is known to be a man of his word) will be merely to invite defeat at the election; consequently, though he may be the actual preference of a large majority of the Liberals of the country, Lord Rosebery does not get the nomination. It goes to some one who can carry Lanarkshire,—some one, that is, who is pleasing to the boss of the local machine of Glasgow. It would be not unlikely that the national leaders might resent the dictation of Lord Inverclyde and might (but not until after the election was safely over) start intriguing in Glasgow politics to have him dethroned from the position of local "boss,"—might, in fact, begin "knifing" him in turn. Whether they would succeed in their object before another general election supervened would depend on the security of his hold on the local Liberal organisation; and that would depend on his personal ability as a politician and—very largely—on his unscrupulousness. For it may, I think, be stated as an axiom that no man can long retain his hold as "boss" of the machine in a large city except by questionable methods,—methods which sometimes involve dishonesty. He must—no matter whether he likes it or not—use his patronage and his power to advance unworthy men; and he must in some measure show leniency to certain forms of lawlessness. Otherwise the influence of the saloons, gamblers, keepers of disorderly houses, and all the other non-law-abiding elements will be thrown against him with sufficient weight to work his downfall.

Unscrupulousness and friendship with wickedness in the slums of a city may thus be the direct road to influence in the councils of the national party. When it is remembered that not a few large cities, and therefore some States, are practically controlled, through the balance of power, by voters of an alien nationality, it is further plain how such an alien vote may become a serious factor in the politics of the nation. Thus is the German element very strong in Milwaukee, and the Scandinavian element in the towns and State of Minnesota. Thus the Irish influence has been almost paramount in New York, though now outnumbered by Germans, Italians, and others; and it is there, in New York, that the conditions which we have imagined in connection with Glasgow and Lord Inverclyde are actually being almost exactly repeated in American Democratic politics as often as a general election comes round.

You may frequently hear it said in America that "as goes New York, so goes the country"; which is to say that in a presidential election the party which carries New York will carry the nation. In theory this is not necessarily so, although it is evident that New York's thirty-six votes in the electoral college must be an important contribution to the support of a candidate. In practice it has proven itself a good rule, partly by reason of the importance of those thirty-six votes, but more, perhaps, because the popular impetus which sways one part of the country is likely to be felt in others—that, in fact, New York goes as the country goes.

But let us assume that the New York vote is really essential to the election of a candidate—that the vote in the country as a whole is evidently so evenly divided that whichever candidate can win New York must be elected the next President. Tammany Hall is a purely local organisation of the Democratic party in New York City. New York State, outside the city, is normally Republican, but many times the great Democratic majority in the Metropolitan district has swamped a Republican majority in the rest of the State. That Democratic vote in the Metropolitan district can only be properly "brought out" and controlled by Tammany; so that the cordial support of Tammany Hall, though, as has been said, it is in reality a strictly local organisation, and as such is probably the worst and most corrupt organisation (as it is also the best managed) that has been built up in the country, may be absolutely vital to the success of a Democratic presidential candidate. Tammany is practically an autocracy, the power of the Chief being almost absolute. England and English society have had some acquaintance with one Chief, and do not like him. But, as Chief of Tammany Hall, it is easy to see how even a coarse-grained Irishman may become for a time influential in American national affairs—even to the dictating of a nominee for the Presidency.

I am not prepared to say that under the same conditions the same things could occur in England. What I am saying is that they do occur in the United States under conditions which do not exist in England; and, while it may be that British civic virtue would be proof against the manifold temptations of a similar political system, we have no sufficient data to justify us in being sure of it, nor is it wise or charitable to assume that because a certain number of American politicians yield to temptations which Englishmen have never experienced, therefore the people are of a less rigid virtue. Mr. Bryce has recorded his opinion that the mass of the public servants in America are no more corrupt than those in England. I prefer not to agree with him for, if it was true when he wrote it, the Americans to-day must be much the better, because since then there has unquestionably been an enormous improvement in the United States, while we have no evidence of a corresponding improvement in England. I believe, not only that many more public men are corrupt in America than in England, but that a larger proportion of the public men are corrupt, which, however, need not imply a lower standard of political incorruptibility: only that there are much greater opportunities of going wrong.

It is interesting to note, moreover, that in the public service the opportunities of malfeasance in public officers in Great Britain are increasing rapidly and, moreover, in precisely those lines wherein they have proved most demoralising in America. I have elsewhere recorded the apprehension with which many Englishmen cannot help regarding the closeness of the relations which are growing up between the national and local party organisations, but in addition to this the urban public bodies are coming to play a vastly larger rôle in the life of the people, while the multiplication of electric car lines and similar enterprises is exposing the members of those bodies to somewhat the same class of untoward influence as has so often proven fatal to the civic virtue of similar bodies in America. Whether, as a result, any large number of cases of individual frailty have exposed themselves, probably only those immediately interested know; the exposure at least has not reached the general public.

It may not, however, be amiss to remember that a century and a half ago, when the conditions in the two countries were widely different from what they are to-day, Benjamin Franklin, coming to England, was shocked and astounded at the corruption then prevalent in English public life.

The procedure of an American presidential campaign has been sufficiently often described for the benefit of English readers. Suffice it to say that it is devastating, at times almost titanic. I have had some experience of the amenities of political campaigning in England, but the most bitterly contested fight in England never produces anything like the intensity of passion that is let loose in the quadrennial upheavals in the United States.

It was my lot to be closely associated with the conduct of a national campaign—as bitterly fought a campaign as the country has seen since the days of the war,—namely that of 1896 when Mr. Bryan was the candidate of the Free Silver Democracy. Early in the fight I began to receive abusive letters, for which a large and capacious drawer was provided in the office, into which they were tossed as they came, on the chance of their containing some reading which might be interesting when the trouble was over. As the fight waxed, they came by every post and in every form, ranging from mere incoherent personal abuse to threats of assassination. Hundreds of them were entirely insane: many hundred more the work, on the face of them, of anarchists pure and simple. A large proportion of them were written in red ink, and in many—very many—cases the passions of the writers had got so far beyond their control that you could see where they had broken their pens in the futile effort to make written words curse harder than they would. The receptacle in which they were placed was officially known in the office as the Chamber of Horrors, but it was, I think, universally spoken of among the staff as the "Hell-box." Before the end of the campaign, capacious though it was, it was crowded to overflowing, and hardly a document that was not as venomous as human wrath could make it. Incidentally I wish to say that never was a campaign—at least as far as my colleagues in our particular department were concerned—more purely in the interest of public morality, without any sort of selfish aims, and less deserving of abuse. What the correspondence of a presidential candidate himself must be in like circumstances, it is horrible to think.[281:1]

The intense feverishness of the campaign is of course increased by the vastness of the country, the tremendous distances over which the national organisation has to endeavour to exercise control, and the immense diversity in the conditions of the people and communities to whom appeal has to be made. The voting takes place all over the country on the same day; and it must be remembered that the area of the United States (not counting Alaska or any external dependencies) is so great that it reaches from west to east about as far as from London to Teheran, and north and south from London to below the southern boundary of Morocco. The difficulty of organisation over such an area can, perhaps, be imagined. In the course of the campaign there came in one day in my mail a letter written on a torn half of a railway time-card. It ran:

"DEAR SIR—There is sixty-five of us here working in a gravel pit and we was going to vote solid for Bryan and Free Silver. Some of your books [*i. e.*, campaign leaflets, etc.] was thrown to us out of a passing train. We have organised a Club and will cast sixty-five votes for William McKinley.—Yours, etc."

So far as those sixty-five were concerned our chief interest thereafter lay in seeing that the existence of that gravel-pit was never discovered by the enemy. A faith which had been so speedily and unanimously embraced might perhaps not have been unassailable.

Before leaving this subject it may be well to say a few words on a recent election in New York which excited, perhaps, more interest in England than any American political event of late years. The eminence which Mr. Hearst has won is an entirely deplorable thing, which has been made possible by the fact, already sufficiently dwelt upon, that political power in the United States is so largely exerted from the bottom up. In their comments on the incident after the event, however, English papers missed some of its significance. Most English writers spoke of Mr. Hearst's appeal to the forces of discontent as a new phenomenon and drew therefrom grave inferences as to what would happen next in the United States. The fact is that the phenomenon is not new in any way. Mr. Hearst, in but a slightly different form, appealed to precisely the same passions as Mr. Bryan aroused—the same as every demagogue has appealed to throughout, at least, the northern and western sections of the country any time in this generation. Mr. Hearst began from the East and Mr. Bryan from the West, but in all essentials the appeal was the same. And Mr. Hearst was not elected. And Mr. Bryan was not elected. What will happen next will be that the next man who makes the same appeal will not be elected also.

It is the allegory of the river and its ripples over again. Englishmen need not despair of the United States, for the great body of the people is extraordinarily conservative and well-poised. In America, man never is, but always to be, cursed. Dreadful things are on the eve of happening, and never happen. There is a great saving fund of common-sense in the people—a sense which probably rests as much on the fact that they are as a whole conspicuously well-to-do as on anything else—which as the last resort shrinks from radicalism. In spite of the yellow press, in spite of all the Socialist and Anarchist talk, in spite of corruption and brass bands and torchlight processions, when the people as a whole is called upon to speak the final word, that word has never yet been wrong. Perhaps some day it will be, for all peoples go mad at times; but the nation is normally sound and sane, with a sanity that is peculiarly like that of the English.

FOOTNOTES:

[264:1] I trust that, because, for the purpose of making an illustration which will bring the matter home familiarly to English minds, I speak of the States as English Counties, I shall not be suspected of thinking (as some writers appear to have thought) that there is really any historical or structural analogy between the two.

[281:1] None the less my friendly American critic (already quoted) holds, and remains firm in, the opinion that "however strenuous the fighting, the political issues produce no such social changes or personal differences in the United States as have frequently obtained in England, say at the time of the leadership of Gladstone, or more recently, in connection with the 'tariff reform' of Chamberlain." It is his contention that Americans take their politics on the whole more good-humouredly than has always been found possible by their English cousins, and that when the campaign is over, there is more readiness in the United States than in England to let pass into oblivion any bitterness that may have found expression during the fighting.

CHAPTER XI

SOME QUESTIONS OF THE MOMENT

Sovereign States and the Federal Government—California and the Senate—The Constitutional Powers of Congress and the President—Government by Interpretation—President Roosevelt as an Inspiration to the People—A New Conception of the Presidential Office—"Teddy" and the "'fraid strap"—Mr. Roosevelt and the Corporations—As a Politician—His Imperiousness—The Negro Problem—The Americanism of the South.

It was said that it would be necessary to refer again to the subject of the relations of the General Government to the several States, as illustrated by the New Orleans incident and the treatment of the Japanese on the Pacific Coast; and the first thing to be said is that no well-wisher of the United States living in Europe can help deploring the fact that the General Government has not the power to compel all parties to the Union to observe the treaties to which the faith of the nation as a whole has been pledged. It is a matter on which the apologist for the United States abroad has, when challenged, no defence. Few people in other countries do not consider the present situation unworthy of the United States; and I believe that a large majority of the American people—certainly a majority of the people east of the Rocky Mountains—is of the same opinion.

It is no excuse to urge that when another Power enters into treaty relations with the United States it does so with its eyes open and with a knowledge of the peculiarities of the American Constitution. This is an argument which belongs to the backwoods stage of American statesmanship. In the past, it is true, the United States has been in a measure the spoilt child among the nations and has been permitted to sit somewhat loosely to the observance of those formalities which other Powers have recognised as binding on themselves; but the time has gone by when the United States can claim, or ought to be willing to accept, any especial indulgences. It cannot at once assert its right to rank as one of the Great Powers and affect to enter into treaties on equal terms with other nations, and at the same time admit that it is unable to honour its signature to those treaties.

This, I say, is the general opinion of thinking men in other countries; but, however desirable it may be that the General Government should have the power to compel the individual States to comply with the requirements of the national undertakings, it is difficult, so long as the several States continue jealous of their sovereignty without regard to the national honour, to see how the end is to be arrived at.

The first obvious fact is that all treaties are made by the President "by and with the advice and consent of the Senate" and no treaty is valid until ratified by a vote of the Senate in which "two thirds of the Senators present concur." The Senate occupies a peculiar position in the scheme of government. It does not represent either the nation as a whole nor, like the House of Representatives, the people as a whole. The Senate represents the individual States each acting in its sovereign capacity[287:1]; and the voice of the Senate is the voice of those States as separate entities. When the Senate passes upon any question it has been passed upon by each several State and it is not easy to see how any particular State can claim to be exempt from the responsibility of any vote of the Senate as a whole.

It would appear to follow of necessity that when the Senate has by a formal two-thirds vote ratified a treaty, every State is bound to accept all the obligations of that treaty, not merely as part of the nation but as a separate unit. The provision in the Constitution which makes the vote of the Senate on any treaty necessary can have no other intent than to bind the several States themselves. As a matter of historical accuracy it had no other intent when it was framed.

In the particular case of the Japanese treaty, the time for the State of California to have made its attitude known was surely when the treaty passed the Senate. The California Senators, or the people of the State, had then two honest courses open to them. They could have let it be known unequivocally that they did not propose to hold themselves bound by the action of the Senate but would, if any attempt were made to force them to comply with the terms of the treaty, secede from the Union; or they could have determined there and then to abide loyally by the terms of the treaty and no matter at what cost to the State, or at what sacrifice of their *amour propre*, to see that all the rights provided in the treaty were accorded to Japanese within the State. Either of these courses would have been honest; and Japanese who came to California would have come with their eyes open. The course which was followed, of allowing them to settle in the State in the expectation of receiving that treatment to which the faith of the United States was pledged, and then denying them that treatment, was distinctly dishonest.

If, however, the State of California, or any other individual State, refuses to acknowledge the responsibilities which it has assumed by the vote of the Chamber of which its representatives are members, there appears no way in which the Federal Government can compel such acknowledgment except those of force and what the believers in the extreme doctrine of State Sovereignty consider Constitutional Usurpation.

It has in many cases been necessary as the conditions of the country have changed so to interpret the phrases of the Constitution as to give to the

General Government powers which cannot have been contemplated by the framers of that instrument. In this case there is every evidence, however, that the framers did intend that the General Government should have precisely those powers which it now desires—or that the individual States should be subject to precisely those responsibilities which they now seek to evade—and if any sentence in the Constitution can be so interpreted as to give to the General Government the power to compel States to respect the treaties made by the nation, it seems unnecessary to shrink from putting such interpretation upon it.

Under the Constitution, Congress has the power to "regulate commerce with foreign nations"—and commerce is a term which has many meanings—as well as "to define and punish offences against the law of nations" and to "make all laws which shall be necessary for carrying into execution the foregoing powers." The President is invested with the power, "by and with the advice of the Senate, to make treaties," and he is charged with the duty of taking "care that the laws be faithfully executed." It would seem that among these provisions there is specific authority enough to cover the case, if the will to use that authority be there. And I believe that in a large majority of the people the will is there.

It would appear to be competent for Congress to "define" any failure on the part of the citizens of any State to comply with whatever requirements in the treatment of foreigners may be imposed on them by a treaty into which the nation has entered, as an "offence against the law of nations." This power of "definition" on the part of Congress is quite unhampered. So also is the power "to make all laws which shall be necessary and proper for carrying into execution" the powers of definition and punishment. And it would be the duty of the President and the Federal Courts to take care that the laws were executed.

If there would be any "usurpation" involved in such an interpretation of the phrases of the Constitution it is certainly less—much less, when regard is had to the intention of the framers of the Constitution—than other "usurpations" which have been effected, and sometimes without protest from the individual States; as, for instance, by the expansion of the right to regulate commerce between the several States into an authority to deal with all manner of details of the control of railways of which the framers of the Constitution never contemplated the existence. It cannot even remotely be compared with such an extension of the Federal power as would be involved in the translation of the authority to "establish post-offices and post-roads" as empowering the government to take an even larger measure of control over those railroads than can be compassed under the right to regulate commerce—a translation which seems to have the approval of President Roosevelt.

Incidentally it may be remarked that it would be peculiarly interesting if, at this day, that authority to construct post-roads should thus be invoked to give the General Government new powers of wide scope, when we remember that it was this same provision of the Constitution which stood sponsor for the very earliest steps which, in the construction of the Cumberland Road and other military or post routes, the young republic took in the path of practical federalism.

To those Americans who received the cause of State Sovereignty as a trust from their fathers and grandfathers before them, the cause doubtless appears a noble one; but to the outsider, unbiassed by such inherited sentiment, it seems evident, first, that the cause, however noble, is also hopeless; and, second, that it is unreasonable that in the forlorn effort to preserve one particular shred of a fabric already so tattered, the United States as a nation should be exposed to frequent dangers of friction with other Powers, and, what is more serious, should be made, once in every decade or so, to stand before the world in the position of a trader who repudiates his obligations.

And if I seem to speak on what is after all a domestic subject with undue vehemence (as I cannot hope that I shall not seem to do to the minds of residents on the Pacific Coast), it is only because it is impossible for an earnest well-wisher of the United States living abroad not to feel acutely (while it does not seem to me that Americans at home are sensible) how much the country suffers in the estimate of other peoples by its present anomalous position. When two business concerns in the United States enter into any agreement, each assumes the other to be able to control its own agents and representatives, nor will it accept a plea of inability to control them as excuse for breach of contract.

It may be that a select circle of the statesmen and foreign office officials in other countries are familiar with the intricacies of the American Constitution, but the masses of the people cannot be expected so to be, any more than the masses of the American people are adepts in the constitutions of those other countries. And it is, unfortunately, the masses which form and give expression to public opinion. In these days it is not by the diplomacies of ambassadors or the courtesies of monarchs that friendships and enmities are created between nations. The feelings of one people towards another are shaped in curious and intangible ways by phrases, sentiments, ideas—often trivial in themselves—which pass current in the press or travel from mouth to mouth. It is a pity that the United States should in this particular expose itself to the contempt of lesser peoples, giving them excuse for speaking lightly of it as of a nation which does not keep faith. It does not conduce to increase the illuminating power of the example of America for the enlightenment of the world.

It might be well also if Americans would ask themselves what they would do if a number of American citizens were subjected to outrage (whether they were murdered as in New Orleans, or merely forced to submit to indignities and inconvenience as in California) in some South American republic, which put forward the plea that under its constitution it was unable to control the people or coerce the administration of the particular province in which the offences were committed. Would the United States accept the plea? Or if the outrages were perpetrated in one of the self-governing colonies of Great Britain and the British Government repudiated liability in the matter? The United States, if I understand the people at all, would not hesitate to have recourse to force to endeavour to compel Great Britain to acknowledge her responsibility.

In the matter of the relation of the general government to the several States the most important factor to be considered at the present moment is undoubtedly the personality of President Roosevelt, and any attempt to make intelligible the change which has come over the United States of recent years would be futile without some recognition of the part which he has played therein. Mr. Roosevelt has been credited with being the author of "a revival of the sense of civic virtue" in the American people. Certainly he has been, by his example, a powerful agent in directing into channels of reform the exuberant energy and enthusiasm which have inspired the people since the great increase in material prosperity and the physical unification of the country bred in it its quickened sense of national life. In the period of activity and expansiveness—one is almost tempted to say explosiveness—which followed the Cuban war, such a man was needed to guide at least a part of the national energy into paths of wholesome self-criticism and reformation. He set before the youth of the country ideals of patriotism and of civic rectitude which were none the less inspiring because easily intelligible and even commonplace.[293:1] The ideals have, it is true, since then, perhaps inevitably and surely not by his will, been dragged about in the none too clean mud of party politics; but the impetus which he gave, before his single voice became largely drowned in the factional hubbub around him, endures and will endure. Whatever comes, the American people is a different people and a better people for his preaching and example.

Moreover, what touches the question of State sovereignty nearly, he has given a new character to the Presidential office. I have expressed elsewhere my belief that the process of the federalising of the country, the concentration of power in the central government, must proceed further than it has yet gone; but it is difficult now to measure, what history will see clearly enough, how much Mr. Roosevelt has contributed to the hastening of the process. No President, one is tempted to say since Washington, but certainly since Lincoln, has had anything like the same conception of the Presidential functions as Mr. Roosevelt, coupled with the courage to insist upon the acceptance of that conception by the country. Whether for good or ill the office of President must always stand for more, reckoned as a force in the national concerns, than it did before it was occupied by Mr. Roosevelt. A weak President may fail to hold anything like Mr. Roosevelt's authority; but the office must for a long time at least be more authoritative, and I think more honourable, for the work which he has done in it.

I first came in contact with Mr. Roosevelt some twenty-five years ago, when his personality already pervaded the country from the Bad Lands of Dakota to the Rocky Mountains. I had a great desire to meet this person about whom, not only in his early life but, as it were, in his very presence, myth was already clustering,—a desire which was almost immediately gratified by chance,—but the particular detail about him which at the time made most impression on my mind was that he was the reputed inventor of the "'fraid strap." The "'fraid strap" is—or was—a short thong, perhaps two feet in length, fastened to the front of the clumsy saddle, which, at signs of contumacy in one's pony, one could, with a couple of hitches, wrap round his hand, in such a way as to increase immensely the chance of a continuity of connection with his seat. The pony of the Plains in those days was not as a rule a gentle beast, and I was moved to gratitude to the inventor of the "'fraid strap"—though whether it was really Mr. Roosevelt's idea or not it is (without confession from himself) impossible to guess, for, as I have said, he was already, though present almost a half-mythical person to the men of the north-western prairie country.

What vexed me no little at the time was that it was with some effort that I could get his name right. I could not remember whether it was Teddy Roosevelt or Roosy Teddevelt. The name now is familiar to all the world; but then it struck strangely on untrained English ears and to me it seemed quite as reasonable whichever way one twisted it round. Mr. Jacob Riis (or Mr. Leupp) has protested against the President of the United States being called "Teddy" and we have his word for it that Mr. Roosevelt's own intimates have never thought of addressing him otherwise than as "Theodore." Doubtless this is correct (certainly I know men who assure me that they call him "Theodore" now) but at least the more friendly "Teddy" has, as is proved by that confusion in my mind of a quarter of a century ago, the justification of long prescription. Nor am I sure that it has not been a fortunate thing both for Mr. Roosevelt and the country that his name has been Teddy to the multitude. I doubt if the men of the West, the rough-riders and the plainsmen, would give so much of their hearts to Theodore.

It is not easy to estimate the value, or otherwise, of Mr. Roosevelt's work in that capacity in which he has of late come to be best known to the world, namely as an opponent of the Trusts; but it is a pity that so many English newspapers habitually represent him as an enemy of all concentrated wealth. He has been called "the first Aristocrat to be elected President." Whether that be strictly true or not, he belongs distinctly to the aristocratic class and his sympathies are naturally with that class. His instincts are not destructive. No one, I have reason to believe, has a shrewder estimate of the worthlessness of the majority of those politicians who use his name as a cloak for their attacks on all accumulated wealth than he. It is only necessary to read his speeches to see how constantly he has insisted that it is not wealth, but the abuse of it, which he antagonises: "We draw the line not against wealth, but against misconduct." He has many times protested against the "outcry against men of wealth," for most of which he has declared "there is but the scantiest justification." Again and again he has proclaimed his desire not to hurt the honest corporation, "but we need not be over-tender about sparing the dishonest."[296:1]

One of the chief difficulties in the practical application of his policies has been that the Government cannot have the power to punish dishonest corporations without first being entrusted with a measure of control over all corporate operations, the concession of which control the honest corporations have felt compelled to resist. Nor is it possible to say that their resistance has not been justified. However wisely and forbearingly Mr. Roosevelt himself might use whatever power was placed in his hands, there has been little in the experience of the corporations in America to make them believe that they can trust either office-holders in general or, for any long term, the Government itself. Dispassionate students of the railway problem in the United States are aware that there is nothing which the corporations have done to the injury of the public worse than the wanton and gratuitous injuries which have been done by the politicians, by the State governments, and even on occasions by the Federal Government itself, to the corporations. If particular railway companies have at times abused the power of which they were possessed as monopolising the transportation to and from a certain section of the country, that abuse has not excelled in wantonness and immorality the abuses of their power over the corporations of which several of the Western States have been systematically guilty. There has been little encouragement to the corporations to submit themselves to any larger measure of public control than has been necessary; and the lessons of the past have shown that it would be injudicious for the railways to surrender uncomplainingly to the State governments authority which the British companies can leave to the Board of Trade without misgiving. And there was a time when the national Interstate Commerce Commission was, if more honest, not much less prejudiced in its dealing with the corporations subject to its authority than were the governments or railway commissions of the individual States.

Mr. Roosevelt's desire may have been (as it is) only to protect the people against the misuse of their power by dishonest corporations; and the honest corporations would be no less glad than Mr. Roosevelt himself to see the dishonest brought to book. But in the necessity of resisting (or what has seemed to the corporations the necessity of resisting) the extensions of the federal power which were requisite before reform could be achieved, the honest have been compelled to make common cause with the dishonest, so that the President has, in particular details, been forced into an attitude of hostility towards all corporations (and the corporations have for the most part been forced to put themselves in an attitude of antagonism to him) in spite of their natural sympathies and common interests.

The result has been unfortunate for business interests generally because the mere fact that the President was "against the companies" (no matter on what grounds, or whether he was against them all or only against some) has encouraged throughout the country the anti-corporation feeling which needed no encouragement. Any time these forty years, or since the early days of the Granger agitation, the shortest road to notoriety and political advancement (at least in any of the Western States) has been by abuse of the railroad companies. A thousand politicians and newspapers all over the country are eager to seize on any phrase or pronouncement of the President which can be interpreted as giving countenance to the particular anti-railroad campaign at the moment in progress in their own locality. A vast number of people are interested in distorting, or in interpreting partially, whatever is said at the White House, so that any phrase, regardless of its context,—each individual act, without reference to its conditions,—which could be represented as an encouragement to the anti-capitalist crusade has been seized upon and made the most of. All over the West there have always, in this generation, been a sufficient number of persons only too anxious, for selfish reasons, to inflame hostility against the railroad companies or against men of wealth; but only within the last few years has it been possible for the most unscrupulous demagogue to find colour and justification for whatever he has chosen to preach in the example and precept of the President—and of a President whose example and precept have counted for more with the masses of the people than have those of any occupant of the White House since the war. In this way Mr. Roosevelt has done more harm than could have been accomplished by a much worse man.

If the corporations have suffered, the course of events has been unfortunate too for Mr. Roosevelt. No one is better aware than he of the misrepresentation to which he is subjected and the unscrupulous use which is made of his example; and it is impossible that at times it can fail to be very bitter. It must also be bitter to find arrayed against him many men whose friendship he must value and whose co-operation in his work it must seem to him that he ought to have. It happens that his is not a character which is swayed by such considerations one hair's breadth from the course which he has marked out for himself; but it is deplorable that a very large proportion of precisely that class of men in which Mr. Roosevelt ought (or at least is justified in thinking that he ought) to find his strongest allies have felt themselves compelled to become his most determined opponents, while those interests which ought (or at least are justified in thinking that they ought) to to find in Mr. Roosevelt, as the occupant of the White House, their strongest bulwark against an unreasoning popular hostility only see that that hostility is immensely inflamed and strengthened by his course and example. The conditions are injurious to the business interests of the country and weaken Mr. Roosevelt's influence for good.

Yet it seems impossible—or certainly impossible for one on the outside—to place the responsibility anywhere except on those general conditions of the country which make possible both the misrepresentation of the position of the President and the wide-spread hostility to the corporations, or on those laxities in political and commercial morality in the past which have put it in the power alternately of the politician to plunder the railways and the railways to prey upon the people. In the ill-regulated conditions of the days of ferment there grew up abuses, both in politics and in commerce, which can only be rooted out with much wrenching of old ties and tearing of the roots of things; but it is worth an Englishman's understanding that the fact that this wrenching and this tearing are now in progress is only an evidence of that effort at self-improvement, an effort determined and conscious, which, as we have already seen more than once, the American people is making. Whatever certain sections of the American press, certain politicians, or certain financial interests, may desire the world to think, there is no need for those at a distance to see in the present conflict evidence either of a wicked and radically destructive disposition in the President or of an approaching disintegration of the American commercial fabric.

Meanwhile, as has been said, one result has been to weaken Mr. Roosevelt's personal influence for good. I have been assured by men of undoubted truthfulness, who are at the head of large financial interests, that he has, in the last few years, become as tricky and unscrupulous in his political methods as the oldest political campaigner; a statement which I believe to be entirely mistaken. "Practical politics," said Mr. Roosevelt once, "is not dirty politics. On the contrary in the long run the politics of fraud and treachery is unpractical politics, and the most practical of all politicians is the one who is clean and decent and upright." There is no evidence which I have been able to find that Mr. Roosevelt does not now believe this as thoroughly and act upon it as consistently as when he first entered the New York State Legislature.

A more reasonable accusation against him, which is made by many of his best friends, is that his imperious will and his confidence in his own opinions make him at times unjust and intolerant in his judgment of others. There have been occasions when he has seemed over-ready to accuse others of bad faith without other ground than his own opinion or the recollection of what has occurred at an interview. He may have been right; but it is certain that he has alienated the friendship of not a few good men by the vehemence and positiveness with which he has asserted his views. And anything, independent of all questions of party, which weakens his influence is, for the country's sake, a thing to be deplored.

The negro question has contributed not a little to Mr. Roosevelt's difficulties, as it has to the misunderstanding of the American people in England. I know intelligent Englishmen who have visited the United States and honestly believe that in the not very distant future the country will again be torn with civil war, a war of black against white, which will imperil the permanence of the Republic no less seriously than did the former struggle. I do not think that the apprehension is shared by many intelligent Americans.

It is perhaps inevitable that Americans should frequently be irritated by the tone of the comments in English papers on the lynchings of negroes which occur in the South. Some of these incidents are barbarous and disgraceful beyond any possibility of palliation, but it is certain that if Englishmen understood the conditions in the South better they would also understand that in some cases it is extremely difficult to blame the lynchers. Many of those people who in London (or in Boston) are loudest in condemnation of outrages upon the negro would if they lived in certain sections of the South not only sympathise with but participate in the unlawful proceedings.

It has already been mentioned that among the men in New Orleans who assisted at the summary execution of the Italian Mafiotes there were, it is believed, an ex-Governor of the State and a Judge: men, that is to say, as civilised and of as humane sentiments as the members of any club in Pall Mall. They were not bloodthirsty ruffians, but gentlemen who did what they did from a stern sense of necessity. It has been my lot to live for a while in a community in which the maintenance of law and order depended entirely on a self-constituted Vigilance Committee; and the operations of that committee were not only salutary but necessary. It has also been my lot to live in a community where the upholders of law and order were not strong enough to organise a Vigilance Committee. I have been one of three or four who behind closed doors earnestly canvassed the possibilities of forming such an organisation, and neither I nor any of the others (among whom I remember were included one attorney-at-law and one mining engineer and surveyor) would have hesitated to serve on such a committee could it have been made of sufficient strength to achieve any useful purpose, but the disparity between our numbers and those of the "bad men" who at that time controlled the community was too obvious to give us any hope of being able to enforce our authority. There may, therefore, be conditions of society infinitely worse than those where order is preserved by lynch law; and I make no doubt that neither I myself nor any fellow-member of my London Club would, if living in one of the bad black districts of the South, act otherwise than do the Southern whites who live there now.

What is deplorable is not the spirit which prompts the acts of summary justice (I am speaking only of one class of Southern "outrage") but the conditions which make the perpetration of those acts the only practicable way of rendering life livable for white people; and for the responsibility for these conditions we must go back either to the institution of slavery itself (for which it should be remembered that England was to blame) or to the follies and passions of half a century ago which gave the negro the suffrage and put him on a plane of political equality with his late masters.[303:1] If, since then, the problem has grown more, rather than less, difficult, it has not been so much by the fault of the Southern white, living under conditions in which only one line of conduct has been open to him, as of Northern philanthropists and negro sympathisers who have helped to keep alive in the breasts of the coloured population ideas and ambitions which can never be realised.

The people of the North have of late years come to understand the South better, and whereas what I have said above would, twenty years ago, have found few sympathisers in any Northern city, I believe that to-day it expresses the opinion of the large majority of Northern men. I also believe that the necessary majority could be secured to repeal so much of the Fourteenth and Fifteenth Amendments to the Constitution as would be necessary to undo the mistake which has been committed. It is true that in some Southern States the majority of the blacks are practically disfranchised now; but it would remove a constant cause of friction and of political chicanery if the fact were recognised frankly that it is not possible to contemplate the possibility of the negro ever becoming the politically dominant race in any community where white people live. There is no reason to believe that the two races cannot live together comfortably even though the blacks be in a large majority, but there must be no question of white control of the local government and of the machinery of justice.

Taking away the franchise from the negro would not, of course, put an end to many of the social difficulties of the situation, but, the present false relations between the two being abolished, those difficulties are no more than have to be dealt with in every community. There would be a chance for the negroes as a race to develop into useful members of the community, *as negroes*, filling the stations of negroes and doing negroes' work, along such lines as those on which Mr. Booker Washington is working. The English have had a wide experience of native races in all parts of the world and they have not yet found the problem of living with them and of holding at least their respect, together with some measure of their active good-will, anywhere insoluble. To an Englishman it does not seem that it should be insoluble in the United States. He is rather inclined to think that the rapidity with which the negro of the South would work out his economic salvation, if once the political difficulty were removed, would depend chiefly on the ability of the race to produce a continuity of men like Mr. Booker Washington, with, perhaps, the concurrent ability of the north to produce men (shall I say, like the late W. H. Baldwin?) to co-operate with the leaders and teachers of the blacks and to interpret them and their work to the country.

The Englishman in England is chiefly impressed by the stories of Southern outrages upon the blacks and he gets therefrom an erroneous idea of the character of the Southern white. An Englishman who studies the situation on the spot is likely to acquire great sympathy with the Southern white and to condemn only the political ineptitude which has made the existing conditions possible.

Whether Mr. Roosevelt's course has been the one best adapted to facilitate a solution of the difficulties it would be idle to enquire. The laws being as they are, and he being the kind of man he is and, as President, entrusted with the duty of seeing that the laws are faithfully executed, he could not have taken a different line. Another man (and an equally good man) might have refrained from making one or two of his appointments and from entertaining Mr. Washington at the White House. But if Mr. Roosevelt did not do precisely those things, he would not do fifty other of the things which have most endeared him to the people.

In this connection, it may be that there will be readers who will think that in many things which I say, when generalising about the American people as a whole, I fail to take into proper account the South and characteristics of such of the people of the South as are distinctively Southern. It is not from any lack of acquaintance with the South; still less from any lack of admiration of or affection for it. But what has been said of New York may in a way be said of the South, for whatever therein is typically Southern to-day is not typically American; and all that is typically Southern is moreover rapidly disappearing. In the tremendous activity of the new national life which has been infused into the country as a result of its solidification and knitting together of the last thirty years, there is no longer room for sectional divergences of character. They are overwhelmed, absorbed, obliterated; and the really vital parts of the South are no longer Southern but American. What has the spirit of Atlanta in Georgia, of Birmingham in Alabama, of any town in the Southwest, from St. Louis to Galveston, to do with the typical spirit of the South? However strong Southern *sentiment* may still be, what is there of the Southern *spirit* even in Richmond or in Louisville? I need hardly say that America produces no finer men than the best Virginian or the best Kentuckian, but, with all his Southern love and his hot rhetoric, the man of this generation who is a leader among his fellows in Kentucky or in Virginia is so by virtue of the American spirit that is in him and not by virtue of any of the dying spirit of the old South.

FOOTNOTES:

[287:1] Mr. Bryce felicitously speaks of the Senate as "a sort of Congress of Ambassadors from the respective States" (*The American Commonwealth*, vol. 1, page 110).

[293:1] "He stands for the commonplace virtues; he is great along lines on which each one of us can be great if he wills and dares" (*Theodore Roosevelt, the Man and Citizen*, by Jacob A. Riis). Mr. Roosevelt has spoken of himself as "a very ordinary man." A pleasant story is told by Mr. Riis of the lady who said: "I have always wanted to make Roosevelt out a hero, but somehow, every time he did something that seemed really great, it turned out, upon looking at it closely, that it was only just the right thing to do."

[296:1] See his *Addresses and Presidential Messages*, with an introduction by Henry Cabot Lodge (Putnams, 1904).

[303:1] To those who would understand the negro question and the mistakes of the people of the North during the Reconstruction period (to which the present generation owes the legacy of the problem in its acute form) I commend the reading of Mr. James Ford Rhodes's *History of the United States from the Compromise of 1850 to the Restoration of Home Rule in the South in 1877* (Macmillan).

CHAPTER XII

COMMERCIAL MORALITY

Are Americans more Honest than Englishmen?—An American Peerage—Senators and other Aristocrats—Trade and the British Upper Classes—Two Views of a Business Career—America's Wild Oats—The Packing House Scandals—"American Methods" in Business—A Countryman and Some Eggs—A New Dog—The Morals of British Peers—A Contract of Mutual Confidence—Embalmed Beef, Re-mounts, and War Stores—The Yellow Press and Mr. Hearst—American View of the House of Lords.

It would seem to be inevitable that any general diffusion of corruption in political circles should act deleteriously on the morals of the whole community. It will therefore seem almost absurd to Englishmen to question whether on the whole the code of commercial ethics in America—the standard of morals which prevails in the every-day transaction of business—is higher or lower than that which prevails in Great Britain. The answer must be almost a matter of course. But, setting aside any expression of individual opinion and all preconceived ideas based on personal experience, let us look at the situation and see, if we can, what, judging only from the circumstances of the two countries, would be likely to be the relative conditions evolved in each. To do this it will be necessary first to clear away a common misapprehension in the minds of Englishmen.

It is somehow generally assumed—for the most part unconsciously and without any formulation of the notion in the individual mind—that American society is a sort of truncated pyramid: that it is cut off short—stops in mid-air—before it gets to the top. Because there are no titles in the United States, therefore there are no Upper Classes; because there is no Aristocracy therefore there is nothing that corresponds to the individual Aristocrat.[309:1] If there were a peerage in the United States, the country would have its full complement of Dukes, Marquises, Earls, Viscounts, and the rest. And—this is the point—they would be precisely the same men as lead America to-day;—but how differently Englishmen would regard them!

The middle-class Englishman, when he says that he is no respecter of titles and declares that it does not make any difference to him whether a man be a Lord or not, may think he is speaking the truth. It is even conceivable that there are some so happily constituted as to be able to chat equally unconcernedly with a Duke and with their wife's cousin, the land agent. Such men, I presume, exist in the British middle classes. But the fact remains that in the mass and, as it were, at a distance the effect of titles on the imagination of the British people is extraordinarily powerful.

That the men in America are precisely the same men, though they have no titles, as they would be if they had, is best shown by the example of Americans who have crossed the Canadian border. If Sir William Van Horne had not gone to Canada in 1881 or thereabouts, he would still be plain "Bill" Van Horne and just as wonderful a man as he is to-day. On the other hand if fortune had happened to place Mr. James J. Hill a little farther north—in Winnipeg instead of in St. Paul—it is just as certain that he would to-day be Lord Manitoba (or some such title) as that his early associates George Stephen and Donald Smith are now Lord Mount Stephen and Lord Strathcona and Mount Royal. But somehow—it were useless to deny it—Englishmen would think of him as quite a different man. Mr. C. M. Hays in Montreal is still what he was in St. Louis—Charlie Hays. He will not change his nature when he becomes Lord Muskoka.

And what is true of a few individuals is no less true all over the United States. In the immediate neighbourhood of Mr. Hill, there should be at least one peerage in the Washburn family and a couple of baronetcies among the Pillsburys. Chicago would have of course one Duke in the head of the McCormick family, Mr. Marshall Field would have died Earl Dearborn, and Mr. Hughitt might be Viscount Calumet. In New York Lord Waldorf would be the title of the eldest son of the (at present third) Duke of Astoria. The Vanderbilt marquisate—of Hudson probably—would be a generation more recent. So throughout the country, from Maine to Mississippi, from Lord Penobscot to the Marquis of Biloxi, there would be a peerage in each of the good old houses—the Adamses, the Cabots, and the Quincys, the Livingstons, the Putnams, and Stuyvesants, the Carters and Randolphs and Jeffersons and Lees.

Americans will say: "Thank Heaven and the wisdom of our Anglo-Saxon forefathers that it is not so!" If it were so, however, a good deal of British misunderstanding of the United States would be removed. Nor will it be contended that any of the Americans whom Englishmen have known best—Mr. Bayard, Mr. Lowell, Mr. Choate, or Mr. Whitelaw Reid, or General Horace Porter—would be other than ornaments to any aristocracy in the world. It would be idle to enquire whether Mr. Roosevelt or Mr. Chamberlain, Mr. Cleveland or Sir Henry Campbell-Bannerman, Mr. Root or Lord Rosebery, Mr. Olney or Sir Edward Grey were the better man, for every Englishman will probably at once concede that the United States does somehow manage to produce individuals of as fine a type as England herself. But what no Englishman confesses in his heart is that there is any class of these men—that there is as good an upper stratum to society there as in England. These remarkable individuals can only be explained as being what naturalists call a "sport"—mere freaks and accidents. This idea exists in the English mind solely, I believe, from the lack of titles in America; which is because the colonists were inspired by Anglo-Saxon and not by Norman ideas. Had Englishmen been accustomed for a generation or two to have relations, diplomatic and commercial, not with Mr. Brown and Mr. Smith, but with Lord Savannah and the Earl of Chicopee, the idea would never have taken root. And if Englishmen knew the United States better, they would be astonished to find how frequent these "sports" and accidents seem to be. And it must be remembered that the country does at least produce excellent Duchesses and Countesses in not inadequate numbers.

Because American society is not officially stratified like a medicine glass and there is, ostensibly at least, no social hierarchy, Englishmen would do well to disabuse themselves of the idea that therefore the people consists entirely of the lower middle class, with a layer of unassimilated foreign anarchists below and a few native and accidental geniuses thrusting themselves above. Democracy, at least in the United States, is not nearly so thorough a leveller as at a first glance it appears. You will, it is true, often hear in America the statement that it is "four generations from shirt-sleeves to shirt-sleeves," which is to say that one man, from the farm or the workshop, builds up a fortune; his son, being born in the days of little things and bred in the school of thrift, holds it together; but his sons in turn, surrounded from their childhood with wealth and luxury, have lost the old stern fibre and they slip quickly back down the steep path which their grandfather climbed with so much toil. But no less often will you hear the statement that "blood will tell."

In a democracy the essential principle of which is that every man shall have an equal chance of getting to the top, it is a matter of course that that top stratum will be constantly changing. The idea of anything in the nature of an hereditary privileged class is abhorrent to the mind of every good American. If he had to have an official Aristocracy, he would insist on a brand new one with each generation; or more likely that it should be re-elected every four years. We are not now discussing the advantages or disadvantages of the hereditary principle; the point that I desire to make is that at any given time American society, instead of being truncated and headless, has the equivalent of an aristocracy, whether the first, second, third, or fifth generation of nobility, just as abundant and complete as if it were properly labelled and classified into Dukes, Marquises, Viscounts, and the rest. And this aristocracy is quite independent of any social *cachet*, whether of the New York Four Hundred or of any other authority.

It is a commonly accepted maxim among thoughtful Americans that the United States Senate is as much superior to the House of Lords as the House of Representatives is inferior to the House of Commons. One may, or may not, agree with that dictum; but it is worth noticing that, in the opinion of

Americans themselves, it is, at least, not by comparison with the hereditary aristocracy that they show to any disadvantage.

Nor need one accept the opinion (in which many eminent Englishmen coincide with the universal American belief) that the United States Supreme Court is the ablest as well as the greatest judicial tribunal in the world. But when one looks at the membership of that Court and at the majority of the members of the Senate (especially those members from the older States which hold to some tradition of fixity of tenure), when one sees the men who constitute the Cabinets of successive Presidents and those who fill the more distinguished diplomatic posts, when, further, one becomes acquainted with the class of men from which, all over the country, the presidents and attorneys of the great railway corporations and banks and similar institutions are drawn (all of which offices, it will be noticed, with the exception of the senatorships, are filled by nomination or appointment and not by popular election)—when one looks at, sees, and becomes acquainted with all these, he will begin to correct his impressions as to the non-existence of an American aristocracy which, though innocent of heraldry, can fairly be matched against the British.

The average Englishman looks at America and sees a people wherein there is no recognised aristocracy nor any titles. Also he sees that it is, through all its classes, a commercial people, immersed in business. Therefore he concludes that it is similar to what the English people would be if cut off at the top of the classes engaged in business and with all the upper classes wiped out. It will be much nearer the truth if he considers the people as a whole to be class for class just like the English people, subject to the accident that there are no titles, but with the difference that all classes, including the untitled Dukes and Marquises and Earls, take to business as to their natural element. The parallel may not be perfect; but it is incomparably more nearly exact than the alternative and general impression.

It is of course necessary to recognise how rapidly the constitution of English society is changing, how old traditions are dying out, and in accordance with the Anglo-Saxon instinct the social scheme is tending to assimilate itself to the American model. The facts in outline are almost too familiar to be worth mentioning, except perhaps for the benefit of some American readers, for Americans in England are continually puzzled by anomalies which they see in English society. In my childhood I was taught that no gentleman could buy or sell anything for profit and preserve either his self-respect or the respect of his fellows. The only conceivable exceptions—and I think I was not informed of them at too early an age—were that a gentleman might deal in horses or in wines and still remain, if somewhat shaded, a gentleman; the reason being that a knowledge of either horses or wines was a gentlemanly accomplishment. The indulgence extended to the vendor of wines did not extend to the maker or seller of beer. I remember the resentment of the school when the sons of a certain wealthy brewer were admitted; and those boys had, I imagine, a cheerless time of it in their schooldays. The eldest of those boys, being now the head of the family, is to-day a peer. But at that time, though brewers or brewers' sons might be admitted grudgingly to the company of gentlemen, they were not gentlemen themselves. An aunt or a cousin who married a manufacturer, a merchant, or a broker—no matter how rich or in how large a way of business—was coldly regarded, if not actually cut, by the rest of the family. There are many families—though hardly now a class—in which the same traditions persist, but even the families in which the horror of trade is as great as ever make an exception as a rule in favour of trade conducted in the United States. The American may be pardoned for being bewildered when in an aristocracy which is forbidden, so he is told, to make money in trade, he finds no lack of individuals who are willing to take shares in any trading concern in which money in sufficient quantities may be made. The person who will not speak to an English farmer except as to an inferior, sends his own sons to the Colonies or to the United States to farm. These things, however, are, to Englishmen, mere platitudes. But though all are familiar with the change which is passing over the British people, few Englishmen, perhaps, have realised how rapidly the peerage itself is coming to be a trade-representing body. Of seventeen peers of recent creation, taken at random, nine owe their money and peerages to business, and the present holders of the title were themselves brought up to a business career. It may not be long before the English aristocracy will be as universally occupied in business as is the American; and it will be as natural for an Earl to go to his office as it is for the American millionaire (perhaps the father of the Countess) to do so to-day.

In spite of all the change that has taken place, however, it still remains very difficult for the English gentleman, or member of a gentle family, to engage actively in business—certainly in trade—without being made to feel that he is stepping down into a lower sphere where there is a new and vitiated atmosphere. The code of ethics, he understands, is not that to which he is accustomed at his club and in his country house. He trusts that it will not be necessary to forget that he himself is a gentleman, but at least he will have to remember that his associates are only business men.

The American aristocrat, on the other hand, takes to business as being the most attractive and honourable career. Setting aside all question of money-making, he believes it to be (and his father tells him that it is) the best life for him. Idleness is not good for any man. He will enjoy his annual month or two of shooting or fishing or yachting all the better for having spent the last ten or eleven months in hard work. Moreover, immersion in affairs will keep him active and alert and in touch with his fellow-men, besides being in itself one of the largest and most fascinating of pastimes. There is also the money; but when business is put on this level, money has a tendency to become only one among many objects. In England no man can with any grace pretend that he goes into business for any other reason than to make money. In America a man goes into it in order to gain standing and respect and make a reputation.

Under these conditions, to return to our original point, in which country, putting other things aside, would one naturally expect to find the better code of business morals? Let us, if we can, consider the matter, as has been said before, without preconceived ideas or individual bias; let us imagine that we are speaking of two countries in which we have no personal stake whatever. If in any two such countries—in Gombroonia and Tigrosylvania, let us say— we should see two peoples approximately matched, of one tongue and having similar political ideals, not visibly unequal in strength, in abilities, or in the individual sense of honour, and if in one we should further see the aristocracy regarding the pursuit of commerce as a thing beneath and unworthy of them, in which they could not engage without contamination, while in the other it was followed as the most honourable of careers,—in which of the two should we expect to find the higher code of commercial ethics?

It does not seem to me that there can be any doubt as to the answer. Other things being equal, and as a matter of theory only, business in the United States ought to be ruled by much higher standards of conduct than in England.

Before proceeding to an analysis of any particular conditions, there is one further general consideration which I would urge on the attention of English readers, most of whom have preconceived ideas on this subject already formed.

I am not among those who believe that trade or commerce of ordinary kinds either requires or tends to develop great intellectuality in those engaged in it. Indeed, my opinion (for which I am willing to be abused) is that any considerable measure of intellect is a hindrance to success in retail trade or in commerce on a small scale. It is a thesis which some one might develop at leisure, showing that it is not merely not creditable for a man to make money in trade but that it is an explicit avowal of intellectual poverty. Whence, of course, it follows that the London tradesman who grows rich and retires to the country or suburbs to build himself a statelier mansion is more justly an object of pity, if not of contempt, than is often consciously acknowledged. Any imaginative quality or breadth of vision which contributes to distract the mind of a tradesman from the one transaction immediately in hand and the immediate financial results thereof is a disqualification. I state my views thus in their extreme form lest the English reader should think that I entertain too much respect (or too little contempt) for the purely commercial brain. At the same time the English reader will concede that commercial enterprises and industrial undertakings may be on such a scale as to offer full exercise to the largest intellects.

As an illustration of this: Cecil Rhodes grew, as we know, wealthy from the proceeds of vast undertakings; but men closely associated with him have assured me that Rhodes was a very indifferent "business man." We may, I think, take it for certain that if Rhodes had been condemned to conduct a retail grocery he would have conducted it to speedy irretrievable disaster. We are probably all agreed that the conduct of a small grocery does not require fineness of intellect; most English readers, I think, will follow me in believing that success in such a sphere of life implies at least an imperfect intellectual development. On the other hand enterprises truly Rhodian do call for intellectual grasp of the largest.

The consideration which I wish to urge is that business in the United States during the period of growth and settlement of the country has been largely on Rhodian lines. The great enterprises by which the country has been developed, and on which most of the large fortunes of individual Americans are based have been of truly imperial proportions. The flinging of railways across thousands of miles of wilderness (England has made peers of the men who did it in Canada) with the laying out of cities and the peopling of provinces; the building of great fleets of boats upon the lakes; the vast mining schemes in remote and inaccessible regions of the country; lumbering enterprises which (even though not always honestly) dealt with virgin forests by the hundreds of square miles; "bonanza" wheat farming and the huge systems of grain elevators for the handling of the wheat and the conveyance of it to the market or the mill; cattle ranching on a stupendous scale (perhaps even the collecting of those cattle in their thousands daily for slaughter in the packing houses); the irrigating of wide tracts of desert;—these things and such as these are the "businesses" out of which the Americans of the last and present generations have largely made their fortunes. And they are enterprises, most of them, not unworthy to rank with Chartered Companies and the construction of railways from the North to the South of Africa.

Not only this, but something of the same qualities of spaciousness, as of trafficking between large horizons, attach to almost all lines of business in the United States,—to many which in England are necessarily humdrum and commonplace. Almost every Englishman has been surprised on making the acquaintance of an accidental American (no "magnate" or "captain of industry" but an ordinary business man) to learn that though he is no more than the manufacturer of some matter-of-fact article, his operations are on a confusing scale and that, with branch offices in three or four towns and agents in a dozen more, his daily dealings are transacted over an area reaching three thousand miles from his home office, in which the interposition of prairies, mountain ranges, and chains of lakes are but incidents. Business in the United States has almost necessarily something of the romance of remote and adventurous enterprises.

It has been said (and the point is worth insisting on) that the Englishman cannot pretend that he goes into business with any other object than to make money. His motives are on the face of them mercenary if not sordid. The American is impelled primarily by quite other ambitions. Similarly, when the Englishman thinks of business, the image which he conjures up in his mind is of a dull commonplace like, on lines so long established and well-defined that they can embrace little of novelty or of enterprise; a sedentary life of narrow outlook from the unexhilarating atmosphere of a London office or shop. To the American, except in small or retail trade in the large cities, the conditions of business are widely different. All around him, lies, both actually and figuratively, new ground, wilderness almost, inviting him to turn Argonaut. The mere vastness and newness of the country make it full of allurement to adventure, the rewards of which are larger and more immediate than can be hoped for in older and more straitened communities.

It has been said that the American people was, by its long period of isolation and self-communion, made to become, in its outlook on the policies of the world, a provincial people; but that the very provincialism had something of dignity in it from the mere fact that it was continent-wide. So it is with American business. The exigencies of their circumstances have made the American people a commercial people; but whereas in England a commercial life may not offer scope for any intellectual activity and may even have a necessary tendency to stunt the mentality of any one engaged in it, business in the United States offers exercise to a much larger gamut of abilities and, by its mere range and variety, instead of dwarfing has a tendency to keep those abilities trained and alert. A business in England has not approximately the same large theatre of operation or the same variety of incident as a business of the same turn over in America. It is almost the difference between the man who furnishes his larder by going out to his farmyard and wringing the necks of tame ducks therein, and him who must snatch the same supply with his gun from the wild flocks in the wilderness.

But, indeed, no argument should be needed on the subject; for one solid fact with which almost every Englishman is familiar is that in any American (let us use the word) shopkeeper whom he may meet travelling in Europe there is a certain mental alertness, freshness, and vigour, however objectionably they may at times display themselves—which are at least not characteristic of the English shopkeeping class.

Just, then, as we have seen that, if we knew nothing about the peoples of the two countries, beyond the broad outlines of their respective social structures, we should be compelled, other things being equal, to look for a higher code of commercial morality in America than in England, so, when we see one further fact, namely that of the difference in the conditions under which business is conducted, we must naturally, other things being equal, look for a livelier intellect and a higher grade of mentality in the American than in the English business man.

Unfortunately other things never are equal. First, there is the taint of the political corruption in America which must, as has been said, in some measure contaminate the community. Then, England is an old country, with all the machinery of society running in long-accustomed grooves; above all it is a wealthy country and the first among creditor nations, to whose interest it has been, and is, to see that every bond and every engagement be literally and exactly carried out. The United States in the nineteenth century was young and undisciplined, with all the ardour of youth going out to conquer the world, seeing all things in rose-colour, but, for the present,—poor. It was, like any other youth confident of the golden future, lavish alike in its borrowings and its spendings, over-careless of forms and formalities. Happily the confidence in the future has been justified and ten times justified, and it is rich—richer than it yet knows—with resources larger even than it has learned properly to appraise or control. Whatever obligations it incurred in the headlong past are trifles to it now,—a few hundreds of college debts to a man who has come into millions. And with its position now assured it has grown jealous of its credit, national and individual.

It was inevitable that the heedless days should beget indiscretions, the memories of which smart to-day. It was inevitable that amid so much recklessness and easy faith there should be some wrong-doing. Above all, was it inevitable that in the realisation of its dreams, when wealth and power grew and money came pouring into it, there should be bred in the people an extraordinary and unwholesome love of speculation which in turn opened their opportunities to the gambler and the confidence-man of all kinds and sizes. They flourished in the land,—the man who wrecked railways and issued fictitious millions of "securities," the man who robbed the government of moneys destined for the support of Indians or the establishment of postal routes in the farther West, the man who salted mines, the "land-grabber" and the "timber-shark" who dealt not in acres but in hundreds of square miles, the bogus trust company, and the fraudulent land and investment agent. When even the smallest community begins to "boom," the people of the community lose their heads and the harvest ripens to the sickle of the swindler. And the entire United States—sometimes in one part, sometimes in another, sometimes all together,—with only an occasional and short-lived panic to check the madness, boomed continuously for half a century.

It is still booming, but with wealth, established institutions, and invested capital, have come comparative soberness and a sense of responsibility. The spirit which governs American industrial life to-day is quite other than that which ruled it two or three decades ago. The United States has sown its wild oats. It was a generous sowing, certainly, for the land was wide and the soil rich. But that harvest has been all but garnered and the country is now for the most part given over to more legitimate crops.

[Tares still spring up among the wheat. The commercial community is not yet as well ordered as that of England or another older country; and since the foregoing paragraphs were written, the panic which fell upon the United States in the closing months of 1907 has occurred. The country had enjoyed a decade of extraordinary financial prosperity, in the course of which, in the spirit of speculation which has already been mentioned, all values had been forced to too high a level, credits had been extended beyond the margin of safety, and the volume of business transactions had swollen to such bulk in proportion to the amount of actual monetary wealth in existence that any shock to public confidence, any nervousness resulting in a contraction of the circulating medium, could not fail to produce catastrophe. The shock came; as sooner or later it had to come. In the stern period of struggle and retrenchment which followed, all the weak spots in the financial and industrial fabric of the country have been laid bare and, while depression and distress have spread over the whole United States, until all parts are equally involved, not only have the exposures of anything approaching dishonest or illegitimate methods been few, but the way in which the business communities at large have stood the strain has shown that there is nothing approaching unsoundness in the general business conditions. With the system of credit shattered and with hardly circulating medium enough to conduct the necessary petty transactions of everyday life, the country is already recovering confidence and feeling its way back to normal conditions. The results have not been approximately as bad as those which followed the panic of 1893; and the difference is an index to the immensely greater stability of the country's industries. Meanwhile there was at first (and still exists) a feeling of intense indignation in all parts of the country that so much suffering should have been thrown upon the whole people by the misbehaviour of a small circle of men in New York. The experience, however painful, will in the long run be salutary. It will be salutary in the first place for the obvious reason that business will have to start again conservatively and with inflated values reduced to something below normal levels. But it will be even more salutary for the less obvious reason that it has intensified the already acute disgust of the business men of the country as a whole with what are known as "Wall Street methods." Englishmen generally have an idea that Wall Street methods are the methods of all the United States; and, while they have had impressed upon them every detail of those financial irregularities in the small New York clique which precipitated the catastrophe, they have heard and know nothing of the coolness and cheery resolution with which the crisis has been faced by the commercial classes as a whole.]

England has not yet forgotten the disclosures in the matter of the Chicago packing houses. That the light which was then turned on that industry revealed conditions that were in some details inconceivably shocking, is hardly to be doubted: and I trust that those are mistaken who say that if similar investigation had been made into the methods of certain English establishments, before warning was given, the state of affairs would have been found not much different. What is certain, however, is that the English public received an exaggerated idea of the extent of the abuses. In part, this was a necessary result of the exigencies of journalism. A large majority of the newspapers even of London—certainly those which reach a large majority of the readers—prefer sensationalism. Even those which are anxious in such cases to be fair and temperate are sadly hampered both by the limitations of space in their own columns and by the costliness of telegraphic correspondence. It is inevitable that the most conservative and judicial of correspondents should transmit to his papers whatever are the most striking items—revelations—accusations in an indictment such as was then framed against the packers. The more damning details are the best news. On the other hand he cannot, save to a ridiculously disproportionate extent, transmit the extenuating circumstances, the individual denials, the local atmosphere. Telegraph tolls are heavy and space is straitened while atmosphere and extenuating circumstances are not news at all. An Englishman is generally astonished when he reads the accounts of some conspicuous divorce case or great financial scandal in England as they appear in the American (or for that matter the French or German) papers, with the editorial comments thereupon. In the picture of any event happening at a great distance the readers of even the best-intentioned journals necessarily have presented to their view only the highest lights and the blackest shadows. In this instance a certain section of the American press—what is specifically known as the "yellow" press—had strong motives, of a political kind, for making the case against the packers as bad as possible. It is unfortunate that many of the London newspapers look much too largely to that particular class of American paper for their American news and their views on current American events.

If we assume that any reasonable proportion of the accusations made against the packing houses were true of some one or other establishment, it still remains that a considerable proportion of the American business community is otherwise engaged than in the canning of meats. There is a story well known in America of a countryman who entered a train with a packet of eggs, none too fresh, in his coat-tail pocket. He sat down upon them; but deemed it best to continue sitting rather than give the contents a chance to run down his person. Meanwhile the smell permeated through the car and at last the passenger sitting immediately behind the countryman saw whence the unpleasantness arose. Whereupon he fell to abusing the other.

"Thunder!" exclaimed the countryman. "What have you got to complain of? You've only got the smell. *I'm sitting in it!*"

This is much how Americans feel in regard to foreign criticisms of the packing house scandals. Whatever wrong-doing there may have been in individual establishments in this one industry in Chicago, is no more to be taken as typical of the commercial ethics of the American people than the discovery of a fraudulent trader or group of traders in one particular line in Manchester or Glasgow would imply that the British trading public was corrupt. The mere ruthlessness with which, in this case, the wrong-doers were exposed ought in itself to be a sufficient evidence to outsiders that the American public is no more willingly tolerant of dishonesty than any other people. Judged, indeed, by that criterion, surely no other country can detest wrong-doing so whole-heartedly.

And I wish here to protest against the habit which the worst section of the English newspapers has adopted during the last year or so of holding "American methods" in business up to contempt. It is true that it is not done with any idea of directing hostility against the United States; and those who use the catchword so freely would undoubtedly much prefer to speak of "German methods" or even "French" or "Russian methods," if they could. All that is meant is that the methods are un-English and alien; but whether the intention is to lessen the public good-will towards the United States or not, that must inevitably be the effect. Even if it were not, the American public is abundantly justified in resenting it.

The idea that America is trust-ridden to the extent popularly supposed in England has been carefully fostered by those extreme journals in America already referred to (it is impossible not to speak of them as the Yellow Press) for personal and political reasons—reasons which Englishmen would comprehend if they understood better the present political situation in the United States. The idea has been encouraged by divers English "impressionist" authors and writers on the English press who, with a superficial knowledge of American affairs, have caught the jargon of the same school of American journalist-politicians. It has been further confirmed by a misunderstanding of the attitude and policy of President Roosevelt himself, which has already been sufficiently dealt with.

England is, in the American sense, much more "trust-ridden" than the United States. It is not merely that (as any reference to statistics will show) wealth is less concentrated in America than in England—that nothing like the same proportion of the capital of the country is lodged in a few hands—for that, inasmuch as the majority of large fortunes in Great Britain are not commercial in their origin, might mean little; but in business the opportunity for the small trader and the man without backing to win to independence is a hundred times greater in America, while the control exercised by "rings" and "cliques" over certain large industries in England and over the access to certain large markets is, I think, much more complete than has been attained, except most temporarily, by any trust or ring in the United States, except, as in the case of oil, where artificial monopoly has been assisted by natural conditions.

The tendency in the United States even in the last twenty years has not been in the direction of a concentration of wealth, but towards its diffusion in a degree unparalleled in any country in the world. The point in which the United States is economically almost immeasurably superior to England is not in the number of her big fortunes but in the enormously greater well-to-do-ness of the middle classes—the vastly larger number of persons of moderate affluence, who are in the enjoyment of incomes which in England would class them among the reasonably rich.

Consolidation and amalgamation are the necessary and unavoidable tendencies of modern business. As surely as the primitive partnership succeeded individual effort and as, later, corporations were created to enlarge the sphere of partnerships, so is it certain that the industrial units which will fight for control of trade in the much larger markets of the modern world will represent vastly larger aggregations of capital than (except in extraordinary and generally state-aided institutions) were dreamed of fifty years ago. That must be accepted as a certainty. It does not by any means necessarily follow that this process entails a concentration of wealth in fewer hands; on the contrary the larger a corporation is, the wider proportionally, as a general rule, is the circle of the shareholders in whom the property is vested. But presuming the commercial growth of the United States to continue for half a century yet on the lines on which it has developed in the last two decades, the country will then, not so much by any concentration of wealth, but by the mere filling up of the commercial field (so that by increase in the intensity of competition the opportunity for the small or new trader to force his way to the surface will be more curtailed, and the gulf between owner or employer and non-owner or employed will become greater and more permanent)—if, I say, that growth should continue for another fifty years then will the conditions in America approximate to those in England. This it is against which the masses in America are more or less blindly and unconsciously fighting to-day. The comparison with European conditions is generally not formulated in the individual mind; but an approach to those conditions is what the masses of America see—or think they see—in the tendency towards greater aggregations of corporate power. It is not the process of aggregation, but the protest against it, which is peculiar to the United States: not the trust-power but the hatred of it.

This being so, for Englishmen or other Europeans to speak of all manifestations of the process itself as "American" is not a little absurd. Besides which, to so speak of it in the tone which is generally adopted is extremely impolite to a kindred people whose good-will Englishmen ought to, and do, desire to keep.

The thing is best illustrated by taking a single example. The term "Trust" is, of course, very vaguely used, being generally taken, quite apart from its proper significance, to mean any form of combination, corporate aggregation, or working agreement which tends to extend control of a company or individual, or group of companies or individuals, over a larger proportion of a particular trade or industry. In the United States, with the possible exception of the Standard Oil Company (which is not properly a trust), the form of corporate power against which there has been the most bitterness is that of the railways, and the specific form of railway organisation most fiercely attacked has been the Pool or Joint Purse—which is, in all essentials, a true trust. In 1887 the formation of a Pool, or Joint Purse Agreement, was made illegal in the United States; but Englishmen can have no conception of the popular hatred of the word "Pools" which exists in America or of the obloquy which has been heaped upon railway companies for entering into them. Few Englishmen on the other hand have any clear idea of what a Joint Purse Agreement is; and they jog along contentedly ignorant that this iniquitous engine for their oppression is in daily use by the British railway companies.

My personal belief is that the prohibition of pools in America was a mistake: that it would have been better for the country from the first to have authorised, even encouraged, their formation, as in England, under efficient governmental supervision. But the point is that the majority of the American people thought otherwise and no other manifestation of the trust-tendency has been more virulently attacked than the—to English ideas—harmless institution of a joint purse. And whether the American people ultimately acted wisely or unwisely, they were justified in regarding any form of association or agreement between railways with more apprehension than would be reasonable in England. It is not possible here to explain why this is so, except to say broadly that the longer distances in America and the lack of other forms of transportation render an American community, especially in the West, more dependent upon the railway than is the case in England. The conditions give the railway company a larger control over, or influence in, the well-being of the people.

An excellent illustration of the difference in the point of view of the two peoples has been furnished since the above was written by the announcements, within a few weeks of each other in December 1907, of the formation of two "working agreements" between British railway companies,—that namely between the Great Northern and Great Central railways and that between the North British and Caledonian. In the former case the Boards of Directors of the two companies merely constituted themselves a Joint Committee to operate the two railways conjointly. In the latter, not many details of the agreement were made public, except that it was intended to control competition in all classes of traffic and, as the first fruits thereof, there was an immediate and not unimportant increase in certain classes of passenger rates. Neither agreement has, I think, yet received the sanction of the proper authorities, but the public generally received the announcement of both with approval amounting almost to enthusiasm. Of these agreements the former, certainly, and presumably the latter, would be flagrantly illegal in the United States. If, moreover, an attempt were made in America to arrive at the same ends in some roundabout way which would avoid technical illegality, the outburst of popular indignation would make it impossible. Personally I sympathise with the English view and believe both agreements to be not only just and proper but in the public interest; but it is certain that they would have created such an uproar in the United States that English newspapers would inevitably have reflected the disturbance, and English readers would have been convinced that once more the Directorates of American railways were engaged in a nefarious attempt to use the power of capital for the plundering and oppression of the public. In the still more recent debate (February 1908) in the House of Commons, the views expressed by both Mr. Lloyd George and Mr. Bonar Law in favour of the lessening of competition between railway companies would have exposed them to the hysterical abuse of a large part of the American press. Both those gentlemen would have been openly accused of being the tools of (if not actually subsidised by) the corporations, and (but for Mr. Bonar Law's company) Mr. Lloyd George's attitude would, I think, be sufficient to ruin an Administration. These statements contain no reflection on the American point of view. The conditions are such that that point of view may, in America, be the right one. But the absurdity is that Englishmen hear these things, or read of them as being said in the United States, and thereupon assume that terrible offences are being perpetrated; whereas nothing is being done which in England would not receive the approval of the majority of sensible men and be temperately applauded by the spokesmen of both the great parties in Parliament. It is not, I say again, the Trust-power, but the hatred of it, which is peculiar to America.

The same is true of the field as a whole. Things harmless in England might be very dangerous in America. We have so far considered the trust power only as a commercial and industrial factor—in its tendency, by crystallisation or consolidation in the higher strata, to depress the economic status of the industrial masses and to make the emergence of the individual trader into independence more difficult. In this aspect capital is immensely more dominant in England than in America. But there is a political side to the problem.

In the United States, owing to the absence of a throne and an established aristocracy, there is, as it were, no counterpoise to the power of wealth. This is, in practice, the chief virtue of the throne in the British constitution, that, in its capacity as the Fountain of Honour, it prevents wealth from becoming the dominant power in the country and thereby (which Americans are slow to understand) is the most democratic of forces, protecting the proletariat in some measure against the possibility of unhindered oppression by an omnipotent capitalism. The English masses are already by the mere impenetrability of the commercial structure above them much worse off than the corresponding masses in the United States. What their condition might be if for a generation the social restraint put upon wealth by the power of the throne and the established aristocracy were to be relaxed, it is not pleasant to consider. Nor need it be considered.[335:1]

It is, I think, evident that in America the danger to the industrial independence of the individual which might arise from the aggregation of wealth in a few hands is much greater than in England. The power would be capable of greater abuse; the evils which would flow from such abuse would be greater. It is not wealth, but the abuse of it that he is attacking, says President Roosevelt—not the wealthy class, but the "wealthy criminal class." The distinction has not been digested by those in England who rail against American methods or who write of American politics. It is necessary—or so it seems to a large number of the American people—that extraordinary checks should be put upon the possibility of the abuse of wealth in the United States, such as do not exist or are not needed (or at least we have heard no energetic demand for them) in England. As a political fact there is need of especial vigilance in the United States lest corporate power be abused. As a commercial fact it is merely preposterous to rail at the modern tendency to consolidation and amalgamation as specifically "American."

It is probably safe to say that if the United States had such a social counterweight as is furnished in England by the throne and the recognised aristocracy, the growth of what is called "trust-power" would be viewed to-day with comparative unconcern. At all events England is able to view with something like unconcern the conditions, as they exist in England, worse than, as has been said, the trust power is humanly capable of imposing on the American people in another half-century of unhindered growth. Which, American readers will please understand, is not a suggestion that the United States would be benefited, even commercially, by the institution of a monarchy.

Give a dog a bad name and hang him. Englishmen long ago acquired the idea that American business methods in what may be called large affairs were too often unscrupulous; and of such methods, there were certainly examples. I have explained why the temptations to, and the opportunities for, dishonesty were very great in the earlier days and it would be impossible to find language too severe to characterise many of the things which were done—not once, but again and again—in the manipulation of railways, the stealing of public lands, and the plundering of the public treasury. The dog deserved as bad a name as he received. But that dog died. The Americans themselves stoned him to death—with precisely the same ferocity as they have recently exhibited when they discovered, as they feared, some of his litter in the Chicago packing houses—or a year before in the offices of certain insurance companies. The present generation of Americans may not be any better men than their fathers (let us hope that they are, if only for the reputation of the vast immigration of Englishmen and Scotchmen which has poured into the country) but at least they are much less tempted. They live under a new social code. They have nothing like the same opportunity for successful dishonesty and immeasurably greater chance of punishment, whether visited on them by the law or by the opinion of their fellows, if unsuccessful or found out. It is not fair that the new dog should be damned to drag around the old dog's name.

There is an excellent analogy in which the relations of the two peoples are reversed.

Americans are largely of the opinion that the British aristocracy is a disreputable class. They gave that dog its name too; and there have been individual scandals enough in the past to justify it. It is useless for an Englishman living in America to endeavour to modify this opinion in even a small circle, for it is only a question of time—probably of a very short time—before some peer turns up in the divorce court and the Englishmen's friends will send him newspaper clippings containing the Court Report and will hail him on street corners and at the club with: "How about your British aristocracy now?"

Americans cannot see the British peerage as a whole; they only hear of those who thrust themselves into unsavoury notoriety. So Englishmen get no view of the American business community in its entirety, but only read with relish the occasional scandal. Of the two, the American has the better, or at least more frequent, justification for his error than has the Englishman; but it is a pity that the two cannot somehow agree to an exchange. Perhaps a treaty might be entered into (if it were not for the United States Senate) which, when ratified, should be published in all newspapers and posted in all public places in both countries, setting forth that:

"IN CONSIDERATION of the Party of the Second Part hereafter cherishing a belief in the marital fidelity and general moral purity of all members of the British peerage, their wives, heirs, daughters, and near relations, and further agreeing that when, by any unfortunate mishap, any individual member of the said Peerage or his wife, daughter, or other relation shall have been discovered and publicly shown to have offended against the marriage laws or otherwise violated the canons of common decency, to understand and take it for granted that such mishap, offence, or violation is a quite exceptional occurrence owing to the unexplainable depravity of the individual and that it in no way reflects upon the other members of the said Peerage, whether in the mass or individually, or their wives, daughters, or near relations: THEREFORE the Party of the First Part hereby agrees to decline to give any credence whatsoever to any story, remark, or reflection to the discredit of the general honesty of the American commercial classes or public men, but agrees that he will hereafter assume them to be trustworthy and truthful whether individually or in the mass, except in such cases as shall have been publicly proven to the contrary, and that he will always understand and declare that such isolated cases are purely sporadic and not in any way to be taken as evidences either of an epidemic or of a general low state of public morality, but that on the contrary the said American commercial classes do, whether in the mass or individually, hate and despise an occasional scoundrel among them as heartily as would the Party of the First Part hate and despise such a scoundrel if found among his own people—as, he confesses, does occasionally occur."

Nonsense? Of course it is nonsense. But the desirable thing is that Englishmen should be brought to understand that after all it is but an inconsiderable portion of the American business community that is permanently employed in the manufacture of wooden nutmegs, in selling canned horrors for food, or in watering railway shares, and that Americans should believe that there are quite a large number of men of high birth in

England who are only infrequently engaged in either beating their own wives or running away with those of other men.

The brief confessional clause at the conclusion of the above draft I take to be an important portion of the document. It is not necessary that a similar confession should be incorporated in the behalf of the Party of the Second Part, not because there are no family scandals in America, but because, in the absence of a peerage, it is not easy to tell when a divorce or other scandal occurs among the aristocracy. "Scandal in High Life" is such a tempting heading to a column that the American newspapers are generous in their interpretation of the term and many a man and woman, on getting into trouble, must have been surprised to learn for the first time that their ambitions had been realised, unknown to themselves, and that they did indeed belong to that class which they had for so long yearned to enter.

This fact also is worth considering, namely, that whereas in England it is not impossible that there may be more scandals of a financial sort, both in official circles and outside, than the public ever hears of through the press; it is reasonably certain that in America the press publishes full details of a good many more scandals than ever occur.

This peculiarity of the American press (for it is still peculiar to America, in degree at least, if not in kind) does not arise from any set purpose of blackening the reputation of the country in the eyes of the outside world, but is entirely the result of "enterprise," of individual ambition, and the extremity of partisan enthusiasm. Other nations may be quite certain that they hear all the worst that is to be told of the people of the United States. Out of the Spanish war arose what came to be known as the "embalmed beef" scandal. American soldiers in Cuba were furnished with a quantity of rations which, by the time they reached the front and an effort was made to serve them out, were entirely unfit for human consumption. Undoubtedly much suffering was thereby caused to the men and probably some disease. But, equally undoubtedly, the catastrophe arose from an error in judgment and not from dishonesty of contractors or of any government official. But, as the incident was handled by a section of the American press, it might well, had the two great parties at the time been more evenly balanced in public favour, have resulted in the ruin of the reputation of an administration and the overthrow of the Republican party at the next election.

If the Re-mount scandals and the Army Stores scandals which arose out of England's South African war had occurred in America, I doubt if any party could have stood against the storm that would have been provoked, and, deriving their ideas of the affairs from the cabled reports, Englishmen of all classes would still be shaking their heads over the inconceivable dishonesty in the American public service and the deplorable standard of honour in the

American army. It may be necessary and wholesome for a people that occasionally certain kinds of dirty linen should be washed in public; but the speciality of the American "yellow press"[342:1] is the skill which it shows in soiling clean linen in private in order to bring it out into the streets to wash.

POSTSCRIPT—Reference has been made in the foregoing chapter to the British peerage and I now propose to have the temerity to enter a serious protest against the tone in which even the thoughtful American commonly refers to the House of Lords. I cherish no such hopeless ambition as that of inducing the American newspaper paragrapher to surrender his traditional right to make fun of a British peer on any and every occasion. I am speaking now to the more serious teachers of the American people; for it is a deplorable fact that even the best of those teachers when speaking of the House of Lords use language which is generally flippant, nearly always contemptuous, and not uncommonly uninformed.

My own belief (and I think it is that of the majority of thinking Englishmen) is that if the discussion in the House of Lords on any large question be laid side by side with the debate on the same question in the House of Commons and the two be read concurrently, it will almost invariably be seen that the speeches in the Upper House show a marked superiority in breadth of view, expression and grasp of the larger aspects and the underlying principles of the subject. I believe that such a debate in the House of Lords is characterised by more ability and thoroughness than the debate on a similar question in either the Senate or the House of Representatives. It does not appear from the respective membership of the chambers how it could well be otherwise.

Let us from memory give a list of the more conspicuous members of the present House of Peers whose names are likely to be known to American readers, to wit: the Dukes of Devonshire and Norfolk; the Marquises of Ripon and Lansdowne; Earls Roberts, Rosebery, Elgin, Northbrook, Crewe, Carrington, Cromer, Kimberley, Minto, Halsbury, Spencer; Viscounts, Wolseley, Goschen, Esher, Kitchener of Khartoum, St. Aldwyn (Hicks-Beach), Milner, Cross; the Archbishop of Canterbury and the Bishop of London; Lords Lister, Alverstone, Curzon of Kedleston, Mount Stephen, Strathcona and Mount Royal, Avebury, Loreburn, and Rayleigh. Let me emphasise the fact that this is not intended to be a list of the ablest members of the House, but only a list of able members something of whose reputation and achievements is likely to be known to the intelligent American reader. If the list were being compiled for English readers, it would have to be twice as long; but, as it stands, I submit that it is a list which cannot approximately be paralleled from among the members of the House of Commons or from among the members of the Senate and House of Representatives combined.

I take it to be incontrovertible that a list representing such eminence and so great accomplishment in so many fields (theology, statesmanship, war, literature, government, science, and affairs) could not be produced from the legislative chambers of any single country in the world.

The mistake which Americans make is that they confuse the hereditary principle with the House of Lords. The former is, of course, spurned by every good American and no one denies his right to express his disapproval thereof in such terms as he sees fit. But few Americans appear to make sufficient allowance for the fact that whatever the House of Lords suffers at any given time by the necessary inclusion among its members (as a result of its hereditary constitution) of a proportion of men who are quite unfit to be members of any legislative body (and these are the members of the British peerage with whom America is most familiar) is much more than counterbalanced by the ability to introduce into the membership a continuous current of the most distinguished and capable men in every field of activity, whose services could not otherwise (and cannot in the United States) be similarly commanded by the State.

We have seen how in the United States a man can only win his way to the House of Representatives, and hardly more easily to the Senate, without earning the favour of the local politicians and "bosses" of his constituency, and how, when he is elected, his tenure of office is likely to be short and must be always precarious. It is probable that in the United States not one of the distinguished men whose names are given in the above list would (with the possible exception of two or three who have devoted their lives to politics) be included in either chamber. They would, so far as public service is concerned (unless they were given cabinet positions or held seats upon the bench), be lost to the State.

It is, of course, impossible that Americans should keep in touch with the proceedings of the House of Lords; nor is there any reason why they should. The number of Americans, resident at home, who in the course of their lives have read *in extenso* any single debate in that House must be extremely small; and first-hand knowledge of the House Americans can hardly have. Then, of the English publicists or statesmen who visit the United States it is perhaps inevitable that those whose conversation on political topics Americans (especially American economic thinkers and sociologists) should find most congenial are those of an advanced Liberal or Radical—even semi-Republican—complexion. I have chanced to have the opportunity of seeing how much certain American economists of the rising school (which has done such admirable work as a whole) have been influenced by the views of particular Englishmen of this class. I should like to mention names, but not a few readers will be able to supply them for themselves. It has not appeared to occur to the American disciples of these men that the views which they impart on English political subjects are purely partisan, and generally very extreme, views. Their opinions of the House of Lords no more represent the judgment of England on the subject than the opinions of an extreme Free Trade Democrat represent the views of America on the subject of Protection.

Merely as a matter of manners and good taste, it would, I think, be well if Americans endeavoured to arrive at and express a better understanding of the legislative work of the Lords. Englishmen have not much more regard for the principle of a quadrennially elected President than Americans have for an hereditary aristocracy; but they do not habitually permit that lack of regard to degenerate into the use of contemptuous language about individual Presidents. Even in contemplating the result of what seems to them so preposterous a system as that of electing a judiciary by popular party vote, Englishmen have generally confined themselves to a complimentary expression of surprise that the results are not worse than they are. Surely, while being as truculent as they please in their attitude towards the hereditary principle, it would be well if Americans would similarly endeavour to dissociate their detestation of that principle from their feelings for the actual personnel of the House of Lords. There is a good deal both in the constitution and work of the House to command the respect even of the citizens of a republic.

I address this protest directly to American economic and sociological writers in the hope that, recognising that it comes from one who is not unsympathetic, some of them may be influenced to speak less heedlessly on the subject than is their wont. I may add that these remarks are suggested by certain passages in the recently published book of an American author for whom, elsewhere in this volume, I express, as I feel, sincere respect.

FOOTNOTES:

[309:1] It is delightful to find, some weeks after this was written, that Mr. Wells makes precisely this common blunder and states it in almost the exact words that I have used later on. His excuse lies in the fact that, as he says, he had it "in his mind before ever he crossed the Atlantic"; but that hardly excuses his failure to disabuse himself after he was across. Most curious is it that Mr. Wells appears to think that this erroneous notion is a discovery of his own and he enlarges on it and expounds it at some length; the truth being, as I say above, that it is the common opinion of all uninformed Englishmen. Mr. Wells is in fact voicing an almost universal—even if unformulated—national prejudice, but it is a pity that he took it over to America and brought it back again.

[335:1] The reader will, of course, understand that the political or industrial power of capital is entirely a separate thing from the ability of wealth to buy luxury, deference or social recognition for its possessor. In this particular there is little to choose between the two and curiously enough, each country has been called by visitors from the other the "paradise of the wealthy."

[342:1] Englishmen often ask the meaning of the phrase "the yellow press." The history of it is as follows: In 1895, Mr. W. R. Hearst, having had experience as a journalist in California, purchased the New York *Journal*, which was at the time a more or less unsuccessful publication, and, spending money lavishly, converted it into the most enterprising, as well as the most sensational, paper that New York or any other American city had ever seen. In catering to the prejudices of the mass of the people, he invaded the province of the New York *World*. In the "war" between the two which followed, one began and the other immediately adopted the plan of using yellow ink in the printing of certain cartoons (or pictures of the *Ally Sloper* type) with which they adorned certain pages of their Sunday editions especially. The term "yellow press" was applied at first only to those two papers, but soon extended to include other publications which copied their general style. The yellow ink was, I believe, actually first employed by the *World*; but the *Journal* was the aggressor in the fight and in most particulars it was that paper which set the pace, and it, or Mr. Hearst, rightly bears the responsibility for the creation of yellow journalism.

CHAPTER XIII

THE GROWTH OF HONESTY

The Superiority of the Anglo-Saxon—America's Resemblance to Japan—A German View—Can Americans Lie?—Honesty as the Best Policy—Religious Sentiment—Moral and Immoral Railway Managers—A Struggle for Self-Preservation—Gentlemen in Business—Peculation among Railway Servants—How the Old Order Changes, Yielding Place to New—The Strain on British Machinery—Americans as Story-Tellers—The Incredibility of the Actual.

My desire is to contribute, if possible, something towards the establishment of a better understanding between the two peoples by correcting certain misapprehensions which exist in the mind of each in regard to the other. At the present moment we are concerned with the particular misapprehension which exists in the English mind in regard to the commercial ethics—the average level of common honesty—in the masses of American business men. I have endeavoured to show, first, that the majority of Englishmen have, even though unconsciously, a fundamental misconception of the character of the American people, arising primarily from the absence of a recognised aristocracy in the United States:—that, in fact, the two peoples are, in the construction of their social fabrics, much more alike than the Englishman generally assumes. I have endeavoured to show, next, that if we were entirely without any knowledge of, or any prejudices in regard to, the code of commercial ethics at present existing in either country, but had to deduce for ourselves *a priori* from what we knew of the part which commerce and business played in the social life of the two countries the probable degree of morality which would be found in the respective codes, we should be forced to look for a higher standard in the United States than in England. We have seen how it comes that Englishmen have, justifiably and even unavoidably, acquired the erroneous notions which they have acquired, first, from the fact that, in the rough days of the past, American business morality was, at least in certain parts of the country, looser than that which prevailed in the older-established and better constituted society of the England of the same day (and in the older communities of the United States itself); and, second, from the fact that the chief channel through which Englishmen must necessarily derive their contemporary ideas on the subject, namely, the American press, is, by reason of qualities peculiar to itself, not to be trusted to correct the misapprehensions which exist. Finally, we have seen that there exist in certain American minds some mistaken notions, not much dissimilar in character to those which I am trying to point out are present in the minds of Englishmen, about the character of a considerable section of the people of Great Britain; and if Americans can be thus mistaken about England, there is no inherent improbability in the suggestion that Englishmen may be analogously mistaken about the United States.

The English people has had abundant justification in the past for arriving at the conclusion that in many of the qualities which go to make a great and manly race it stands first among the peoples of the earth. The belief of Englishmen in their own moral superiority as a people is justified by the course of history, and is proven every day afresh by the attitudes of other races,—especially by the behaviour in their choice of friends, when compelled to choose as between England and other European powers, of the peoples more or less unlike the Anglo-Saxon in their civilisations in the remoter corners of the world. It is to the eternal honour of England that in countless out-of-the-way places, peoples more or less savage have learned to accept the word of a British official or trader as a thing to be trusted, and have grown quick to distinguish between him and his rivals of other European nationalities. There has been abundant testimony to the respect which the British character has won from the world,—from the frank admiration of the Prince-Chancellor for the "Parole de Gentleman" to the unshakable confidence of the far red Indian in the faith of a "King George Man"; from the trust of an Indian native in the word of a Sahib to the dying injunction to his successor of one of the greatest of the Afghan Ameers: "Trust the English. Do not fight them. They are good friends and bad enemies."[349:1] And the most solemn oath, I believe, which an Arab can take is to swear that what he says is as "true as the word of an Englishman."

But, granting all that has happened in the past, and recognising that British honour and the sacredness of the British word have stood above those of any other peoples, the American nation of to-day is a new factor in the situation. It did not exist at the time when the old comparisons were made. I have suggested elsewhere that the popular American contempt for the English climate is only an inheritance of the opinions based on a comparison of that climate with the climates of Southern Europe. If the climate of certain parts—of the greater part—of the United States had then been a factor to be taken into consideration, English skies would have had at least one fellow to share with them the opprobrium of the world. So in the matter of commercial morality; we are thinking and speaking in terms of a day that has gone, when other standards governed.

Englishmen have been very willing, within the last year or two, to believe in the revolution which has taken place in the character of another people, less akin to them than the Americans and farther away. The promptitude with which the British masses have accepted the fact that, in certain of the virtues on which Englishmen have most peculiarly prided themselves in the past, the Japanese are their superiors, has been curiously un-British. There should be no greater difficulty in believing that another revolution, much more gradual and less picturesque, and by so much the more easily credible, has taken place in the American character. The evidence in favour of the one is, rightly viewed, no less strong than that in favour of the other. It would have been impossible for the Japanese to have carried on the recent war as they did had they not been possessed of the virtues of courage and patriotism in the highest degree. It would have been equally impossible for the Americans to have built up their immense trade in competition with the great commercial powers of the world, unless they had in an equally high degree possessed the virtue of commercial honesty. No one ought to know better than the English business man that a great national commercial fabric is not built up by fraud or trickery.

On this subject Professor Münsterberg,[35].[1] striving to eradicate from the minds of his German countrymen the same tendency to underestimate the honesty of American business men, says (and let me say that neither my opinion, nor the form in which it is expressed, was borrowed from him): "It is naïve to suppose that the economic strength of America has been built up through underhanded competition, without respect to law or justice, and impelled by nothing but a barbarous and purely material ambition. One might better suppose that the twenty-story office buildings on lower Broadway are supported by the flag-stones in the street.... The colossal fabric of American industry is able to tower so high only because it has its foundations on the hard rock of honest conviction."

"It has been well said," says the same author, "that the American has no talent for lying, and distrust of a man's word strikes the Yankee as specifically European." Now in England "an American lie" has stood almost as a proverb; yet the German writer is entirely in earnest, though personally I do not agree with him. He sees the symptoms, but the diagnosis is wrong. The American has an excellent talent for lying, but in business he has learned that falsehood and deception are poor commercial weapons. Business which is obtained by fraud, any American will tell you, "doesn't stick"; and as every American in his business is looking always to the future, he prefers, merely as a matter of prudence, that his foundations shall be sound.

All society is a struggle for the survival of the fittest; and in crude and early forms of society, it is the strongest who proves himself most fit. In savage communities—and Europe was savage until after the feudal days—it is the big man and brutal who comes to the top. In the savage days of American commerce, which, at least for the West, ended only a generation back, it was too often the man who could go out and subdue the wilderness and beat down opposition, who rode rough-shod over his competitors and used whatever weapons, whether of mere brute strength or fraud, with the greatest ferocity and unscrupulousness, who made his mark and his fortune. But in a settled and complex commercial community it is no longer the strongest who is most fit; it is the most honest. The American commercial community as a whole, in spite of occasional exceptions and in defiance of the cynicism of the press, has grasped this fact and has accepted the business standards of the world at large.

Let me not be interpreted as implying that there are any fewer Americans than there are Englishmen who live rightly from the fear of God or for the sake of their own self-respect. The conclusion of most observers has been that the American people is more religious than the English, that the temperament, more nervous and more emotional, is more susceptible to religious influence. It may be so. It is a subject on which the evidence is necessarily so intangible—on which an individual judgment is likely to be so entirely dependent on individual observation in a narrow field—that comparison becomes extremely difficult. My own opinion would be that there is at least as much real religious feeling in England as in the United States, and certainly more in Scotland than in either; but that the churches in America are more active as organisations and more efficient agents in behalf of morality.

But we are now speaking of the business community as a whole, and the force which ultimately keeps the ethics of every business community pure is, I imagine, the same, namely that without honesty the community itself cannot live or prosper and that, with normal ability, he who is most honest prospers most. American business was dishonest before society had settled down and knitted itself together.

The change which has come over the American business world can perhaps best be made clear to English readers by taking a single example; and it must necessarily be an example from a field with which I am familiar.

There is in my possession an interesting document, being one of the (I think) two original manuscript copies of the famous "Gentleman's Agreement," bearing the signatures of the parties thereto, which was entered into by the Presidents or Chairmen of a number of railway companies at Mr. Pierpont Morgan's house in New York in 1891. In the year following the signing of the Agreement, I was in London in connection with affairs which necessitated rather prolonged interviews with many of the Chairmen or General Managers of the British railways,—Sir George Findlay, Sir Edward Watkin, Mr. J. Staats Forbes, and others. With all of them the mutual relations existing between railway companies in the two countries respectively formed one of the chief topics of our conversations, and that at that time the good faith and loyalty of attitude of one company towards another were much greater in England than in America it is not possible to question. British companies are subject to a restraining influence which does not exist in the United States, in the parliamentary control which is exercised over them. Every company of any size has, with more or less frequency, to go to Parliament for new powers or privileges, and any Chairman or Board of Directors which established a reputation for untrustworthiness in dealings with other companies would probably be able to expect few favours from the next Parliamentary Committee. But (although the two last of the gentlemen whose names I have mentioned were notoriously parties to a peculiarly bitter railway war) I believe that the motives which have chiefly operated to make the managers of English companies observe faith with each other better than the American have ever succeeded in doing, are chiefly the traditional motives of a high sense of personal honour—the fact that they were gentlemen first and business men afterwards.

The circumstances which led up to the formation of the Gentlemen's Agreement were almost inconceivable to English railway operators. The railways, it must always be borne in mind, have been the chief civilisers of the American continent. It is by their instrumentality that the Great American Desert of half a century ago is to-day among the richest and most prosperous agricultural countries in the world. The railways have always thrust out ahead of the settler into whatever territory, by reason of the potential fertility of its soil or for other causes, has held out promise of some day becoming populated. Along the railway the population has then flowed. In forcing its way westward each company in its course has sought to tap with its lines the richest strips of territory: all alike endeavoured to obtain a share of the traffic originating from a point where a thriving town was already established or topographical conditions pointed out a promising site. As the American laws impose practically no restrictions on railway construction it necessarily followed that certain districts and certain favourable strategic points were invaded by more lines than could possibly be justified either by the traffic of the moment or the prospective traffic of many years to come. This was conspicuously the case in the region Northwestward from Chicago. Business which might have furnished a reasonable revenue to two companies was called upon to support six or seven and the competition for that business became intense,—all the more intense because, unlike English railway companies, few American railways in their early days have had any material reserve of capital to draw upon. They have had to earn their living as they went, out of current receipts, or submit to liquidation.

The officials in charge of the Traffic Departments of each company had to justify their retention in their positions by somehow getting more than their share of the business, and the temptations to offer whatever inducements were necessary to get that business amounted almost to compulsion. Without it, not the particular official only, but his company, would be extinguished. The situation was further aggravated by the fact that the goods that were to be carried were largely staples shipped in large quantities by individual shippers—millers, owners of packing houses, mining companies from the one end, and coal and oil companies from the other. One of these companies might be able to offer a railway more business in the course of a year than it could hope to get from all the small traders on its lines combined—enough to amount almost to affluence if it could be secured at the regularly authorised rates. The keenness of the competition to secure the patronage of these large shippers can be imagined; for it was, between the companies, a struggle for actual existence. All that the shipper had to do was to wait while the companies underbid each other, each in turn cutting off a slice from the margin of profit that would result from the carrying of the traffic until, not infrequently and in some notorious cases, not only was that margin entirely whittled away but the traffic was finally carried at a figure which meant a heavy loss to the carrier. The extent to which the Standard Oil Company has profited by this necessity on the part of the railways to get the business of a large shipping concern at almost any price, rather than allow its cars and motive power to remain idle, has been made sufficiently public.

In some measure the companies were able to protect themselves by the making of pooling (or joint-purse) arrangements between themselves; but the enactment of the Interstate Commerce Law in 1887 made pooling illegal. The companies endeavoured to frame agreements which would not be repugnant to the law but would take the place of the pools; but it was impossible to attach any penalties to infringements of such agreements and under pressure of the necessity of self-preservation, no agreement, however solemnly entered into, was strong enough to restrain the parties. The Passenger Agents framed agreements to control the passenger traffic and the Freight Agents made agreements to control the goods traffic, and both were equally futile. Then the Traffic Managers made agreements to cover both classes of business, which held no longer than the others. So the General Managers tried their hands. But the inexorable exigencies of the situation remained. Each official was still confronted with the same dilemma: he must either secure more business than he was entitled to or he—and his company—must starve. And the agreements made by General Managers bound no better than those which Passenger Agents or Traffic Managers had made before. Then it was that the Gentlemen stepped in.

The Gentlemen, it should be explained, were the Presidents and Chairmen of the Boards of the respective companies. They, it was hoped, would be able to reach an agreement which, if once their names were signed to it, would hold. The meeting, as has been said, was held at Mr. Pierpont Morgan's house[358:1] and an agreement was in fact arrived at and signed, as has been said, in duplicate. It is lamentable to have to record that that agreement—except in so far as it set a precedent for other meetings of the same gentlemen, which in turn led to others out of which finally grew large movements in the direction of joint ownerships and consolidations of interests which have helped materially to make the conditions more tolerable—except for that, the Gentlemen's Agreement did no more good, and it lasted not appreciably longer, than any of the others which had been made by mere officials.

Englishmen will all agree that it is unthinkable that the Chairmen of the great British railway companies could meet and give their words *as gentlemen* that each of their companies would observe certain rules in the conduct of its business and that a few weeks thereafter it should become evident that no single company was keeping the word so pledged. But it would be just as absurd to question the personal integrity or sense of honour of such men as Mr. Marvin Hughitt, Mr. E. W. Winter, Mr. W. H. Truesdale, and the others, as it would be to question that of the most upright man in England. The fact is that the conditions are almost unthinkable to Englishmen. No company, in becoming party to the agreement, had surrendered its right to retaliate when another violated the provisions. The actual conduct of the business of the companies—the quoting of the rates to secure the traffic—was in the hands of a host of subordinate officials, and when a rate is cut it is not cut openly, but in secret and by circuitous devices. It was, on subsequent investigation, always impossible to tell where the demoralisation had begun, amid the cloud of charges, counter-charges, and denials. There was not one of the subordinate officials but declared (and seemingly proved) that he had acted only in retaliation and self-defence. As there was no way of obtaining evidence from the shippers, in whose favour the concessions had been made, it was impossible to sift out the truth. Each Chairman or President could only say that he had entire confidence in his own staff. There was no visible remedy except to discharge the entire membership of the Traffic Departments of all the companies simultaneously and get new men, to the number of several hundreds, who would be no better able to accomplish the impossible than their predecessors.

My reason for going into this, I fear, somewhat tedious narration is that British distrust of American commercial honesty was originally created, perhaps, more than by anything else, by the scandals which were notoriously associated with the early history of railways in the United States. It is not desired here either to insist on the occurrence of those scandals or to palliate them. The point is that the conditions which made those scandals possible (of which the incapacity on the part of the North-western lines to keep faith with each other may be regarded as symptomatic) were concomitants of a particular stage only in the development of the country. Competition must always exist in any business community; but in the desperate form of a breathless, day-to-day struggle for bare existence it need only exist among railway companies where lines have been built in excess of the needs of the population. With the increase in population and the growth of trade the asperity of the conditions necessarily becomes mitigated, until at last, when the traffic has assumed proportions which will afford all competitors alike a reasonable profit on their shares, the management ceases to be exposed to any more temptation than besets the Boards of the great British companies. Not a few railway companies in the United States have arrived at that delectable condition—are indeed now more happily circumstanced than any English company—and among them are some the names of which, not many years ago, were mere synonyms for dishonesty. In the North-western territory of which I have spoken the fact that the current values of all railway shares had on the average increased (until the occurrence of the financial crisis of the close of 1907) by about three hundred per cent. in the last ten years is eloquent.

In the old days the wrong-doing which was rampant, through excess of opportunity and more than abundant temptation, in the higher circles, ran also through all grades of the service; and there was one case at least of a railway company which used in fact to have to discharge all its servants of a certain class at intervals of once a month or thereabouts. The Northern Pacific Railway line was opened across the continent in 1883, and during the next twelve months it was my fortune to have to travel over the western portion of the road somewhat frequently. The company had a regularly established tariff of charges, and tickets from any one station to another could be bought at the booking offices just as on any other railway line in America or England. But few people bought tickets. The line was divided, of course, into divisions, of so many hundreds of miles each, the train being in charge of one conductor (or guard) to the end of his division, where he turned it over to his successor for the next division. It was the business of the conductor to take up the tickets, or collect the fares, while the train was running, and it was well understood among regular passengers on the line that each conductor expected to receive one dollar to the end of his division, no matter at what point a passenger entered the train. The conductor merely walked through the cars collecting silver dollars, of which he subsequently apportioned to the treasury of the company as many as he saw fit. They were probably not many.

On one occasion I stood at a booking-office and, speaking through the small window, asked the clerk for a ticket to a certain place. The conductor of the train, already waiting in the station, had strolled into the office and heard my request.

"Don't you buy a ticket!" said he to me. "I can let you travel cheaper than he can, can't I, Bill?"—this last being addressed to the clerk behind the window; and Bill looked out through the hole and said he guessed that was so.

The company, as I have said, used to discharge its conductors with regularity, or they resigned, at intervals depending on the periods at which accounts were made up, but it was said in those days that there was not a town between the Mississippi and the Pacific Coast which did not contain a drinking saloon owned by an ex-Northern Pacific conductor, and established out of the profits that he had made during his brief term of service.

In the American railway carriages, the method of communication between passengers and the engine, in case of emergency, is by what is known as the "bell-cord" which runs from end to end of the train, suspended from the middle of the ceiling of each car in a series of swinging rings. The cord sways loosely in the air to each motion of the train like a slackened clothes-line in a gale. On the Atchison, Topeka, and Santa Fé Railway the story used to be told that at the end of the day the conductors would toss each coin received into the air to see if it would balance on the bell-cord. The coins which balanced went to the company; those which did not, the conductor took as his own.

That, be it noted, was the state of affairs some twenty-four years ago. I question if there is much more peculation on the part of the employees of the Atchison, Topeka, and Santa Fé to-day than there is on the part of the servants of the Great Western of England or any other British company.

The place where the conductor advised me not to buy a ticket had then a few yards of planking laid on the prairie for a platform and a small shed as a station building. The town consisted of three or four brick buildings and a huddle of wooden shanties. To-day it is one of the twenty most populous cities in the United States with tall office buildings, broad busy streets, and sumptuous private residences. I used to have excellent trout-fishing in what is now the centre of a great town. Where the air to-day is filled with the hum of wheels and the roar of machinery, then was only open prairie innocent of any evidence of human occupation beyond some three or four things like dog-kennels badly built of loose lattice-work on the river's bank. These were the red Indians' Turkish baths.

The old code of morality has vanished with the red Indian and the trout-fishing. In the early days of that town there used to be nobody to maintain public order but an efficient Vigilance Committee, which executed justice by the simple process of hanging persons whom the public disliked, and which was still in nominal existence when I was there. Now the city has the proper complement of courts, from the United States Court downwards, and a bar which has already furnished one or two members to the United States Senate.

Of course this has happened in the very far West but the change which has come over New York in the same length of time is no less astonishing if less picturesque. It is as unjust to compare the morals or manners of the American people of to-day with those of even three decades ago as it would be to compare the state of twentieth-century society in New Zealand with the old convict days. In one generation Japan has stepped from the days of feudalism to the twentieth century. America, in all that goes to constitute civilisation, has in the last twenty-five years jumped, according to European canons, at least a hundred.

Certain outward manifestations of the change which has been wrought, the peoples of Europe have been unable to ignore;—the immense growth in the power of the United States as a nation, her invasion of the markets of the world even in lines wherein, twenty years ago, the internal markets of America herself were at the mercy of British manufacturers, the splendid generosity which individual citizens of the United States are showing in buying wherever they can all that is most beautiful or precious among the treasures of the Old World for the enrichment of their museums and galleries at home—these things the people of Europe cannot help but see. It would be well if they would strive also to understand the development of the moral forces which underlies these things, which alone has made them possible.

What has been the course of events in England in the same period? I have already said that I believe that Englishmen justly earned the reputation of being the most upright of all peoples in their commercial dealings; and for the sake of the context perhaps Americans who have had little opportunity of gauging the opinions of the world will accept it as true. It is probable that the world has seen no finer set of men engaged in commerce than those who laid the foundations of England's commercial greatness; and I imagine that there are more honest men in England to-day than ever there were—more men of what is, it will be noticed, instructively called "old-fashioned" honesty. Yet no one will be quicker than just one of these "old-fashioned" honest men to declare that the standard of commercial morality in England is deteriorating.

The truth is that a vast new trading community has sprung up with new ideas which no longer accepts the old canons or submits to the old authority. The old maxims pass current; there is the same talk of honest goods and honest methods, but under stress of keener competition and the pressure of the more rapid movement of modern life, there is more temptation to allow products to deteriorate, greater difficulty in living always up to the old rigid standards. The words "English made" no longer carry, even to English minds, the old guarantee of excellence.

In no small measure it may be that it is the example and influence of America itself which is working the mischief; which by no means implies that American example and influence must in themselves be bad. American methods, both in the production and sale of goods, might be wholly good, but the attempt to graft them upon established English practice might have nothing but deplorable results. It is not necessarily the fault of the new wine if old bottles fail to hold it. One factory may have the capacity to turn out one thousand of a given article, all of the highest quality and workmanship, *per diem*. If a factory with one tenth the capacity strains itself to compete and turns out the same number of articles of the same kind in the same time, something will be wrong with the quality of those articles. I am not prepared to say that in any given line English manufacturers are overstraining the capacity of their plants to the sacrifice of the quality of their goods in their effort to keep pace with American rate of production; but I do most earnestly believe that something analogous to it is happening in the commercial field as a whole, and that neither English commercial morality nor the quality of English-made goods has been improved by the necessity of meeting the intense competition of the world-markets to-day, with an industrial organisation which grew up under other and more leisurely conditions.

POSTSCRIPT.—Not necessarily as a serious contribution to my argument but rather as a gloss on Professor Münsterberg's remark that the American has no talent for lying, I have often wondered how far the Americans reputation for veracity has been injured by their ability as story-tellers. "Story" it must be remembered is used in two senses. The American has the reputation of being the best narrator in the world; and he loves to narrate about his own country—especially the big things in it. In nine cases out of ten, when he is speaking of those big things, he is conscientiously truthful; but not seldom it happens that what may be a mere commonplace to the American seems incredible to the English listener unacquainted with the United States and unable to give the facts as narrated their due proportion in the landscape.

More than a quarter of a century ago, when electric light was still a very new thing to Londoners, an American casually told myself and three or four others that the small town from which he came in the far Northwest of America was lighted entirely by a coronal of electric lights of some prodigious candle-power on the top of a mast, erected in the centre of the town, of a, to us, incredible height. It was, at the time, quite unbelievable; but in less than a year chance took me all the way to that identical little town in the far Northwest, and what the American had said was strictly true—true, I doubt not, to a single candle-power and to a fraction of a foot of mast. And a costly and indifferent method of lighting, for a whole town, it may be remarked, it was.

In an earlier stage of my youth I lost all confidence in an elderly and eminently respectable friend of the family who had travelled much because he once informed me that the Japanese watered their horses out of spoons. Of course I knew that the old gentleman was a liar.

An American travelling in an English railway carriage fell into conversation with the other occupants, who were Englishmen. Among divers pieces of information about things in the United States which he gave them he told (it was at the time when the steel construction of high buildings was still a novelty) of a twenty-storey "sky-scraper" which he passed daily on his way to and from his office on which, to save time, the walls were being put up simultaneously at, perhaps, the second, eighth, and fifteenth floors, working upwards from each point, the intervening floors being in the meanwhile left untouched. He explained that, in the system of steel construction, the walls did not support the building; that being done by the skeleton framework of metal, on which the walls were subsequently hung as a screen. They might, theoretically, be of paper; though as a matter of fact the material used was generally terra-cotta or some fire-proof brick. The American said that it was queer to see a house being built at the eighth storey in midair, as it were, with nothing but the thin steel supports and open sky below.

"I should imagine it would look very queer," said the Englishman whom he was addressing, with obvious coolness; and the American was entirely aware that every person in that carriage regarded him as a typical American liar. Time passed and the carriage relapsed into silence, each of the occupants becoming immersed in such reading-matter as he had with him. Suddenly one of them aroused the others with the ejaculation:

"By Jove! If here isn't a picture of that very building you were talking of!"

It was a *Graphic* or *Illustrated London News*, or some other such undoubtedly trustworthy London paper which he was reading, and he passed it round for the inspection of the rest of the company. The American looked at it. It was not his particular building but it did as well, and there was the photograph before them, with the walls complete, to window casing and every detail of ornament, on the eighth and ninth floors, while not a brick had been laid from the second storey to the seventh. A god from the machine had intervened to save the American's reputation. Often have I seen incredulity steal over the faces of a well-bred company in England at some statement from an American of a fact in itself commonplace enough, when no such providential corroboration was forthcoming.

Curiously enough, the true Yankee in America, especially of the rural districts, has the same distrust of the veracity of the Western American as the Englishman generally has of the Yankee himself (in which he includes all Americans). I had been living for some years in Minnesota when, standing one day on the platform of the railway station at, I think, Schenectady, in New York State, I was addressed by one who was evidently a farmer in the neighbourhood. Learning that I had just come from Minnesota he referred to the two towns of St. Paul and Minneapolis. "Right lively towns," he had heard them to be. "And how many people might there be in the two together?" he asked. "About a quarter of a million," I replied—the number being some few thousand less than the figure given by the last census. The farmer, perhaps, had not heard anything of the two towns for ten or a dozen years, when their population had been not much more than a third of what it had grown to at that time; and he looked at me. He did not say anything; he merely looked at me, long and fixedly. Then he deliberately turned his back and walked to the other end of the platform as far as possible from my contaminating influence. I was never so explicitly and categorically called a liar in my life; and he doubtless went home and told his family of the magnificent Western exaggerator whom he had met "down to the depot." I fear the American reputation often suffers no less unjustly in England.

FOOTNOTES:

[349:1] Even up to a quarter of a century ago, there was at least one corner of the United States, near to the Canadian border, where among Indians not yet rounded up or blanketed the old feeling still existed, so that an Englishman, proclaiming himself a "King George Man," could go and hunt and fish safely, sure of the friendship and protection of the red man, while an American would not have been safe for a night. The subject of the relations between the British and the Indian tribes in Revolutionary times has, of course, been provocative of much bitterness in the hearts of Americans; but happily their own historians of a later day have shown that this bitterness has only been partially justified. There was not much to choose between Patriots and Loyalists. Those who know the Indian know also that the universal liking for the Englishman cannot have rested only on motives of political expediency or from temporary alliances made in Revolutionary times. They must have had abundant proof of the loyalty and trustworthiness of Englishmen before so deep-rooted a sentiment could have been created. The contrast, of course, was not with the American colonist, but with the French. The colonists, too, were King George Men once.

[351:1] Yes; I am aware that elsewhere I quote Professor Münsterberg without enthusiasm, but on another class of subject. Except for the limitations which his national characteristics and upbringing impose upon him (and for the fact that he seems to be unacquainted with the West) the Professor has written a just and clear-sighted estimate of the American character. We do not look to a German for a proper understanding of the sporting instinct, as British and Americans understand it, nor perhaps for views that will coincide with ours on the subject of morality in the youth of either sex. But the laws of common honesty are the same in all countries. A German is as well able to estimate the commercial morality of a people as an Englishman, however little he may be qualified to talk about their games or about the *nuances* in the masculine attitude towards women.

[358:1] That meeting has an incidental historical interest from the fact that it was then that Mr. Morgan first stepped into the public view as a financial power. Up to that time, his name was not particularly well known outside of New York or the financial circles immediately connected with New York. Most Western papers found it necessary to explain to their readers (if they could) who the Mr. Morgan was at whose house the meeting was being held.

CHAPTER XIV

A Contrast in Principles

The Commercial Power of the United States—British Workmanship—Tintacks and Conservatism—A Prophetic Frenchman—Imperialism in Trade—The Anglo-Saxon Spirit—About Chaperons—"Insist upon Thyself"—English and American Banks—Dealing in Futures—Dog Eat Dog—Two Letters—Commercial Octopods—Trusts in America and England—The Standard Oil Company—And Solicitors—Legal Chaperons—The Sanctity of Stamped Paper—Conclusions—American Courts of Justice—Do "Honest" Traders Exist?

The Englishman, even the Englishman with industrial experience and commercial training, generally, when he makes a short visit to the United States, comes away with a certain distrust of the stability of the American commercial fabric—a distrust which he cannot altogether explain to himself. The rapidity of movement, the vastness of the results, these things are before his eyes; but there insists on obtruding itself a sense of unsubstantiality. Habituated to English surroundings, with their ages-old traditions, the rugged deep-rooted institutions, the deliberate revolutions of all the flywheels of a long-constituted society, he cannot believe that the mushroom establishments, thrust up as it were from the soil of a continent which is yet one half but partially broken wilderness, have permanence. He cannot deny the magnitude or the excellence of the work that is being done now, at this moment, under his eyes; but it all has too much the seeming of unreality, as though suspended in midair, unsupported. He misses the foundations of centuries of civilisation below and the lines of shafting running back into the past. Often, it is to be feared, having all his life been accustomed to see power exerted only in cumbersome processes and through old-fashioned channels, he has come to regard the cumbersomeness and the antiquity as necessary conditions of such exertion—nay, even to confuse them with the sources of the power themselves. It will be remembered that the first pig that was roasted in China was roasted by the accidental burning down of a house; and for a long time the Chinese supposed that only by burning down a house was it possible to come at roast pig. Finally arose a great philosopher ("like our Locke") who discovered that it was not necessary to burn houses, but that pigs might be cooked by much less costly and more rapid methods. Unquestionably many of those who had been accustomed to house-burning must have looked at the new and summary culinary processes with profound distrust. It may even be asserted with confidence that many of the older generation died unconverted, though pig-roasting over all sorts of makeshift fires had been going on around them for some years.

After a more or less prolonged residence in the United States, the Englishman finds his distrust lessening. He in turn becomes accustomed to doing without those traditions, those foundations, those lines of shafting, which once he considered so essential to all sound workmanship. When in due time he returns to England he is not seldom amazed to see how many of the things which he was wont to regard as effective links in the machinery are really no more than waste parts which do but retard the motion and cause loss of power. It is not difficult to make machinery so complicated that the power exhausts itself in overcoming the resistance of belts and pulleys and cogs.

I had lived in the United States for many years before I ceased to cling to the notion—which I never hesitated to impart cheerfully to Americans when occasion offered—that though American workmen turned out goods that served their purpose well enough, for really sound and honest workmanship you had, after all, to come to England. It was only after I had been back in England and had experience of the ways of English workmen once more that doubts began to accumulate. English furniture makers told me that England nowadays did not produce such well-made or solid furniture as pieces that I showed them from America, and which are made in America in wholesale quantities. English picture-frame makers marvelled at the costliness of material and the excellence of the work in American frames. A Sackville Street tailor begged me to leave in his hands for a few days longer some clothes which he was pressing for me, made in a far Western State, in order that he might keep them—where they then were—hanging in his work-room as an object-lesson to his men in how work ought to be done. These are but isolated instances out of many which have bred misgiving in one who for many years cherished the conviction that a British-made article was always the best. That English workmen should be slower, less quick-minded, more loth to take up new ideas, or to make things as you wanted them and not as they had always made them—these things I had expected to find, and found less often than I had expected. But that the English workman did ultimately produce a better and more trustworthy article—that I never doubted, till I found it, from the confessions of the workmen and manufacturers themselves, far from necessarily true.

Few Englishmen returning to England after many years of residence in the United States (unless perchance they have lived on a ranch where their contact with the industrial or commercial life of the people has been slight) do not find themselves more or less frequently appealed to for opinions, in giving which they are compelled, however reluctantly, to pose as prophets, warning their countrymen to flee from the wrath to come, telling them that they underestimate the commercial power of the United States. Sometimes it may be that there will be some one in the company who has spent some few weeks, perhaps, in the United States. "Now, I don't agree with you there," this traveller will say. "When I was in the States, I saw .." He saw, in fact, pigs being roasted at a commonplace sort of fire, made for the purpose, of logs and sticks and coal and things, whereas everybody knows that no pig can be duly roasted unless chimney stacks and window-casings and front-door handles be mixed up with the combustibles. And the others present take comfort and are convinced that the Old Country is a long way from going to the dogs as yet. Of course she is, bless her! But it is not many years since an eminently distinguished authority on iron and steel (was he not President of the Iron and Steel Association?), after having made a tour of the United States, assured British manufacturers that they had nothing to fear from American competition in the steel trade. It was some years earlier that Chatham declared that he would not allow the American colonies to manufacture even one hobnail for themselves.

I have no desire now to join the band of those who are urging England so insistently to "wake up." This is not the place for such evangelism, for that is not the gospel which this book is intended to spread. None the less one story I must tell, told to me many years ago in America by one who claimed to have had some part in the transactions; a story that has to do with (let us say, to avoid hurting any susceptibilities) the sale of tin-tacks to Japan. And whether the story is true or not, it is at least well found.

England, then, had had for years a monopoly of the sale of tin-tacks to the Japanese, when a trader in Japan became impressed with the fact that the traffic was badly handled. The tacks came out from England in packages made to suit the needs of the English market. They were labelled, quite truthfully of course, "Best English Tacks," and each package contained an ounce, two ounces, or four ounces in weight, and was priced in plain figures at so much in English money. The trader had continual trouble with those packages. His customers were always wanting them to be split up. They wanted two or three *sen* worth—not four pennyworth; also they did not care about ounces. So the trader, starting for a visit to England, had some labels written in Japanese characters, and when he arrived in England he went to the manufacturers and explained matters. He showed them the labels that he had had written and said:

"The Japanese trade is worth considering and worth taking some little trouble to retain; but the people dislike your present packages and I have to spend most of my time splitting up packages and counting tacks. If you will make your packages into two thirds of an ounce each and put a label like that on them, you will be giving the people what they want and can understand, and it will save a lot of trouble all around."

But the manufacturers, one after another, shook their heads. They could not read the label. They never had put any such outlandish stuff on anything going out of their works, nor had their fathers before them. The Japanese ought to be satisfied with the fact that they were getting the Best English Tacks and not be unreasonable about it. And the trader exhausted himself with argument and became discouraged.

He returned to Japan *via* the United States, and stopped to see the nearest tack-manufacturer. He showed him the label and told his story.

"Looks blamed queer!" said the manufacturer, "but you say that's what they want out there? Let's catch a Jap and see if he can read the thing."

So a clerk was sent out to fetch a Japanese, which he did.

"How' do, John?" said the manufacturer to the new arrival. (Chinese and Japanese alike were all "John" to the American until a few years ago.) "You can read that, eh?"

The Japanese smiled, looked at the label and read it aloud.

"All straight goods, eh, John?" asked the manufacturer. The Japanese answered in the affirmative and retired.

Then the manufacturer called for his manager.

"Mr. Smith," he said, as the manager came in, "this is Mr. Brown of Tokio, Japan. He tells me that if we do up tacks in two third of an ounce lots and stick that label on each package, we might do some good business out there. That label—it don't matter which is the top of the thing—calls for a price that figures out to us at about two cents a pound more than our regular export rates. I want this gentleman to have a trial lot shipped out to him and he'll see what he can do. Just go ahead will you and see to it?"

"Yes, sir," said the manager; and when the trader sailed from San Francisco a couple of weeks later the same vessel carried out a trial order of tacks consigned to him at Tokio, made up in two thirds of an ounce packages with mysterious hieroglyphics on the labels. It only took the trader a few days, after his return, to satisfy himself that the sooner he cabled the American manufacturer to duplicate the order the better. There never has been anybody in the American works who has been able to read what is on that label; but when instructions were given for printing new labels after six months of trial the order was for a quarter of a million, and British manufacturers were astonished to discover that by some unexplainable chicanery they had lost the Japanese market for tacks.

I have said that I do not know whether the story is true or not; but fifty similar stories are. And in the aggregate they explain a good deal.

But let me say again that the conservatism of British manufacturers is not now my theme. But I do most earnestly believe that Englishmen as a whole— even English traders and manufacturers—unwisely underestimate the commercial power of the United States. What the United States has accomplished in the invasion of the world's markets in the last ten years (since the trade revival of 1896-97) is only a foretaste of what is to come. So far from there being anything unsubstantial—any danger of lack of staying power, any want of reserve force—the power has hardly yet begun to exert itself. Of Europeans who have recently written upon the subject, it seems to me that none has shown a truer appreciation of the situation than M. Gabriel Hanotaux, the former French Minister for Foreign Affairs.[378:1] He sees the shadow of America's commercial domination already falling across Europe; and, so far as France is concerned, he discerns only two directions from which help can come. He pleads with young Frenchmen to travel more, so that the rising generation may be less ignorant of the commercial conditions of the modern world and may see more clearly what it is that they have to fight, and, second, he points to the Colonial Empire of France, with an area not much inferior to that of the United States, and believes that therein may be laid the foundations of a commercial power which will be not unable to cope even with that of America.

It may be only the arrogance and superciliousness of the Anglo-Saxon that prevent one sharing the sanguineness of M. Hanotaux as to any relief coming to the help of France from these two sources, for British hopes can only lie in analogous directions. Englishmen also need to understand better the conditions which have to be met and the power of their competitors; and it is the young men who must learn. Also, if it be impossible that the British Isles should hold their own against the United States, there appears no reason why the British Empire should not be abundantly able to do so.

It is not easy for one who has not lived all his life in England to share the satisfaction with which the English papers commonly welcome the intelligence that some great American manufacturing concern is establishing branch works in Canada. It is well for Canada that such works should be established; but it is pitiable for the Empire that it should be left to the United States to establish them. British capital was the chief instrumentality with which the United States was enabled to build its own railways and conduct the other great enterprises for the development of the resources of its mighty West, and it is, from the point of view of a British Imperialist, deplorable that British capitalists should not now be ready to take those risks for the sake of the Empire which American capital is willing to take with no other incentive than the probable trade profits.

His conservatism, it should be noticed, has a tendency to fall away from the Englishman when he goes out from the environment and atmosphere of the British Isles. The Canadian, or the Englishman who has gone to Canada young enough to imbibe the colonial spirit, is not easily to be distinguished from the citizen of the United States in his ways of doing business. Even the Anglo-Indian refuses to subject himself, in India, to all the cumbersome formalities with which he is compelled to conduct any business transaction when at home. Mr. Kipling in one of his latest stories has given us a delightful picture of the bafflement of the Australasian Minister struggling to bring his Great Idea for the Good of his Colony and the Empire to the attention of the officials in Whitehall.

The encumbering conservatism which now hangs upon the wheels of British commerce is no part of—no legitimate offshoot of—the English genius. It is a fungoid and quite alien growth, which has fastened upon that genius, taking advantage of its frailties. Englishmen, we hear, are slow to change and to move; yet they have always moved more quickly than other European peoples as the Empire stands to prove. And if the people of Great Britain had the remodelling of their society to do over again to-day, they, following their native instincts, would hardly rebuild it on its present lines. With the same "elbow room" they would, it may be suspected, produce something but little dissimilar (except in the monarchical form of government) from that which has been evolved in the United States.

When Englishmen, looking at the progress of the United States, doubt its permanence—when they distrust the substantiality or the honesty in the workmanship in the American commercial fabric—it might be well if they would say to themselves that the men who are doing these things are only Englishmen with other larger opportunities. Behind all this that meets the eye is the same old Anglo-Saxon spirit of pluck and energy which made Great Britain great when she was younger and had in turn her larger opportunities. Above all, that pluck and energy are unhampered by tradition and precedent in exerting themselves in whatever direction may be most advantageous; and to be unhampered does not necessarily mean freedom only to go wrong.

An American girl once explained why it was much pleasanter to have a chaperon than to be without one:

"If I am allowed about alone," she explained, "I feel that I am on my honour and can never do a thing that I would not like mama to see; but when a chaperon is with me, the responsibility for my behaviour is shifted to her. It is her duty to keep me straight. I have a right to be just as bad as I can without her catching me."

The tendency of American business life is first to develop the individuality and initiative of a man and, second, to put him, as it were, on his honour. It is, of course, of the essence of a democracy that each man should be encouraged to develop whatever good may be in him and to receive recognition therefor; but there have been other factors at work in the shaping of the American character besides the form of government. Chief among these factors have been the work which Americans have had to do in subduing their own continent and that they have had to do it unaided and in isolation. Washington Irving has a delightful sentence somewhere (in *Astoria* I think) about the frontiersman hewing his way through the back woods and developing his character by "bickering with bears." "The frontiersmen, by their conquest of nature, had come to despise the strength of all enemies," says Dr. Sparks in his *History of the United States*. It was only to be expected, it was indeed inevitable, that the first of American thinkers—the man whose philosophy caught the national fancy and has done more towards the moulding of a national temperament than, perhaps, any man who ever wrote, should have been before all things the Apostle of the Individual. "Insist upon Thyself!" Emerson says—not once, but it runs as a refrain through everything he wrote or thought. "Always do what you are afraid to do!" "The Lord will not make his works manifest by a coward." "God hates a coward." "America is only another name for Opportunity." My quotations come from random memory, but the spirit is right. It is the spirit which Americans have been obliged to have since the days when the Fathers walked to meeting in fear of Indian arrows. And they need it yet. It has become an inheritance with them and it, more than anything else, shapes the form and method of their politics and above all of their business conduct.

I have said elsewhere that in society (except only in certain circles in certain cities of the East) it is the individual character and achievements of the man himself that count; neither his father nor his grandfather matters—nor do his brothers and sisters. And it is the same in business. I am not saying that good credentials and strong friends are not of use to any man; but without friends or credentials, the man who has an idea which is commercially valuable will find a market in which to sell it. If he has the ability to exploit it himself and the power to convince others of his integrity, he will find capital ready to back him. It is difficult to explain in words to those accustomed to the traditions of English business how this principle underlies and permeates American business in all its modes.

One example of it—trivial enough, but it will serve for illustration—which visiting Englishmen are likely to be confronted with, perhaps to their great inconvenience, is in the bank practice in the matter of cheques. There is, as is well known, no "crossing" of cheques in America, but all cheques are "open"; and many an Englishman has gone confidently to the bank on which it was drawn with a cheque, the signature to which he knew to be good, and has expected to have the money paid over the counter to him without a word. All that the English paying teller needs to be satisfied of is that the signature of the drawer is genuine and that there is money enough to the credit of the account to meet the cheque. But the Englishman in the strange American bank finds that the document in his hands is practically useless, no matter how good the signature or how large the account on which it is drawn, unless he himself—the person who presents the cheque—is known to the bank officials. "Can you identify yourself, sir?" The Englishman usually feels inclined to take the question as an impertinence; but he produces cards and envelopes from his pocket—the name on his handkerchief—anything to show that he is the person in whose favour the cheque is drawn. Perhaps in this way he can satisfy the bank official. Perhaps he will have to go away and bring back somebody who will identify him. It is the *personality of the individual with whom the business is done* that the American system takes into account.[384:1]

It is, as I have said, a trivial point, but it suffices. Vastly more important is the whole banking practice in America. This is no place to go into the details at the controversy which has raged around the merits and demerits of the American banking system. In the financial panic of 1893 something over 700 banks suspended payment in the United States. At such seasons, especially, but more or less at all times, a great proportion of the best authorities in the United States believe that it would be better for the country if the Scotch— or the Canadian adaptation of the Scotch—system were to take the place of that now in vogue. Possibly they are right. The gain of having the small local banks in out-of-the-way places possess all the stability of branches of a great central house is obvious, both in the increase of security to depositors in time of financial stress and also in the ability of such a house to lend money at lower rates of interest than is possible to the poorer institution with its smaller capital which has no connections and no resources beyond what are locally in evidence. It may be questioned, however, whether the country as a whole would not lose much more than it would gain by the less complete identification of the bank with local interests. It would be inevitable that in many cases the local manager would be restrained by the greater conservatism of the authorities of the central house from lending support to local enterprises, which he would extend if acting only by and for himself as an independent member of the local business community. It is difficult to see how the country as a whole could have developed in the measure that it has under any system differing much from that which it has had.

In theory it may be that the functions of a bank are precisely the same in Great Britain and in America. In practice different functions have become dominant in the two. In England a bank's chief business is to furnish a safe depository for the funds of its clients. In America its chief business is to assist—of course with an eye to its own profit and only within limits to which it can safely go—the local business community in extending and developing its business. The American business man looks upon the bank as his best friend. If his business be sound and he be sensible, he gives the proper bank official an insight into his affairs far more intimate and confidential than the Englishman usually thinks of doing. He invites the bank's confidence and in turn the bank helps him beyond the limits of his established credit line in whatever may be considered a legitimate emergency. In any small town whenever a new enterprise of any public importance is to be started, the bank is expected to take shares and otherwise assist in promoting a movement which is for the common good. The credits which American banks—especially in the West—give to their customers are astoundingly liberal according to an English banker's standards. Sometimes of course they make mistakes and have to pocket losses. When a storm breaks, moreover (as in the case already quoted of the panic of 1893), they may be unable to call in their loans in time to take care of their liabilities. But that they have been a tremendous—an incalculable—factor in the general advancement of the country cannot be questioned.

The difference between the parts played by the banks in the two countries rests of course on two fundamental differences in the condition of the countries themselves. The first of these is the fact that while England is a country of accumulated wealth and large fortunes which need safeguarding, America has until recently been a country of small realised wealth but immense natural resources which needed developing. The policy of the banks has been shaped to meet the demands of the situation.

In the second place (and too much stress cannot be laid upon this in any comparison of the business-life of the two peoples) the American is always trading on a rising market. This is true of the individual and true of the nation. Temporary fluctuations there are of course, but after every setback the country has only gone ahead faster than before. The man with faith in the future, provided only that he looked far enough ahead to be protected against temporary times of depression, has always won. Just as the railway companies push their lines out into the wilderness, confident of the population that will follow, and are never disappointed, so in all other lines the man who is always in advance, who does not wait for the demand to be there before he enlarges his plant to meet it, but who sees it coming and is ready for it when it comes—the man who has always acted in the belief that the future will be bigger than the present,—that man has never failed to reap his reward. Of course the necessary danger in such a condition is that of over-speculation. But nearly every man who amasses wealth or wins large commercial success in the United States habitually takes risks which would be folly in England. They are not folly in him, because the universal growth of the country, dragging with it and buoying up all industries and all values, as it goes, is on his side. It is inevitable that there should result a national temperament more buoyant, more enterprising, more alert.

What is important, too, is that whereas in England the field is already more or less full and was handed down to the present generation well occupied, so that new industries can, as it were, only be erected on the ruins of old, and a site has to be cleared of one factory before another can be built (all of which is, in a measure, only relative and metaphorical), in the United States there is always room for the newcomers. New population is pouring in to create new markets: new resources are being developed to provide the raw material for new industries; there is abundance of new land, new cities, new sites whereon the new factories can be built. This is why "America" and "opportunity" are interchangeable terms; why young men need never lack friends or backing or the chance to be the architects of their own fortunes. Society can afford to encourage the individual to assert himself, because there is space for and need of him.

From this flow certain corollaries from which we may draw direct comparison between the respective spirits in which business in the two countries is carried on. In the first place, in consequence of the more crowded condition of the field and the greater intensity of competition, the business community in England is much more ruthless, much less helpful, in the behaviour of its members one towards the other. It is not a mere matter of the more exacting scrutiny of credits, of the more rigid insistence on the exact fulfilment of a bond (provided that bond be stamped), but it colours unconsciously the whole tone of thought and language of the people. There are two principles on which business may be conducted, known in America respectively as the "Live and let live" principle, and the "Dog eat dog" principle. There was until recently in existence in the United States one guild, or association, representing a purely parasitical trade—that of ticket-scalping—which was fortunately practically peculiar to the United States. This concern had deliberately adopted the legend "Dog eat dog" as its motto and two bull-dogs fighting as its crest; but in doing so its purpose was to proclaim that the guild was an Ishmaelite among business men and lived avowedly in defiance of the accepted canons of trade. On the other hand one meets in America with the words "Live and let live" as a trademark, or motto, on every hand and on the lips of the people. Few men in America but could cite cases which they know wherein men have gone out of their way to help their bitterest competitor when they knew that he needed help. The belief in co-operation, on which follows a certain comradeship, as a business principle is ingrained in the people.

I was once given two letters to read, of which one was a copy and the other an original. The circumstances which led up to the writing of them were as follows: Two rich men, A. and B., had been engaged in a business duel. It was desperate—*à outrance*,—dealing in large figures; and each man had to call up all his reserves and put out all his strength. At last the end came and A. was beaten—beaten and ruined. Then the letters passed which I quote from memory:

"DEAR MR. B.:

"I know when I'm beaten and if I was quite sure you wouldn't kick a man when he's down, I would come round to see you and grovel. As perhaps you can guess, I am in a bad way.

"Yours truly, A."

DEAR A.:

"There's no need to grovel. Come around to my house after supper to-morrow night and let us see what we can do together to put you straight.

"Yours truly, B."

I need hardly say that it was the second letter of which I saw the original, or that it was A. who showed them to me, when they were already several years old but still treasured, and A. was a wealthy man again as a result of that meeting after dinner. A. told me briefly what passed at that meeting. "He gave me a little more than half a million," he said. "Of course he has had it back long ago; but he did not know that he would get it at the time and he took no note or other security from me. At the time it was practically a gift of five hundred thousand dollars."

And as I write I can almost hear the English reader saying, "Pooh! the same things are done times without number in England." And I can hear the American, still smarting under the recollection of some needlessly cruel and unfair thrust from the hands of a competitor, smile cynically and say that he would like to tell me certain things that he knows. Of course there are exceptions on either side. It takes, as the American is so fond of saying, "all kinds of men to make a world." It is the same old difficulty of generalising about a nation or drawing up an indictment against a whole people. But I do not think that any man who has engaged for any length of time in business in both countries, who has lived in each sufficiently to absorb the spirit of the respective communities, will dissent from what I have said. Many Englishmen, without knowledge of business in England, go to America and find the atmosphere harder and less friendly than they were accustomed to at home, and come to quite another conclusion. But they are comparing American business life with the social club-and-country-house life of home.

Let them acquire the same experience of business circles in England, and then compare the tone with that of business circles in America, and they will change their opinions.

Let me recall again what was said above as to the difference in the motives which may impel a man to go into business or trade in the two countries. An Englishman cannot well pretend that he does it with any other purpose than to make money. The American hopes to make money too, but he takes up business as an honourable career and for the sake of winning standing and reputation among his fellows. This being so, business in America has a tendency to become more of a game or a pastime—to be followed with the whole heart certainly—but in a measure for itself, and not alone for the stakes to be won. It is not difficult to see how, in this spirit, it may be easier to forego those stakes—to let the actual money slip—when once you have won the game.

It is necessary to refer briefly again to the subject of trusts. In England a great corporation which was able to demonstrate beyond dispute that it had materially cheapened the cost of any staple article to the public, and further showed that when, in the process of extending its operations, it of necessity wiped out any smaller business concerns, it never failed to provide the owners or partners of those concerns with managerial positions which secured to them a larger income than they could have hoped to earn as individual traders, and moreover took into their service the employees of the disbanded concerns at equal salaries,—such a corporation would generally be regarded by the English people as a public benefactor and as a philanthropically and charitably disposed institution. In America the former consideration has some weight, though not much; the latter none at all.

When a trust takes into its service those men whom it has destroyed as individual traders, the fact remains that their industrial independence has been crushed. The individual can no longer "insist upon himself." He is subordinate and no longer free. One of the first principles of American business life, the encouragement of individual initiative, has been violated, and nothing will atone for it.

The Standard Oil Company can, I believe, prove beyond possibility of contradiction that the result of its operations has been to reduce immensely the cost of oil to the public, as well as to give facilities in the way of distribution of the product which unassociated enterprise could never have furnished. It can also show that in many, and, I imagine, in the majority, of cases, it has endeavoured to repair by offers of employment of various sorts whatever injuries it has done to individuals by ruining their business. But these things constitute no defence in the eyes of the American people.

There is the additional ground of public hostility that the weapons employed to crush competitors have often been illegal weapons. Without the assistance of the railway companies (which was given in violation of the law) the Standard Oil Company might have been unable to win more than one of its battles; but this fact, while it furnishes a handle against the company and exposes a side of it which may prove to be vulnerable, and is therefore kept to the front in any public indictment of the company's methods, is an immaterial factor in the popular feeling. Few Americans (or Englishmen) will not accept a reduced rate from a railway company when they can get it. Whatever actual bitterness may be felt by the average man against the Standard Oil Company because it procured rebates on its freight bills is rather the bitterness of jealousy than of an outraged sense of morality. The real bitterness—and very bitter it is—is caused by the fact that the company has crushed out so many individuals. On similar ground nothing approaching the same intensity of feeling could be engendered in the British public.

Let us now recur for a moment to the views of the young woman quoted above on the interesting topic of chaperons. We have seen that insistence on the individuality is a conspicuous—perhaps it is the most conspicuous—trait of the American character. Encouraged by the wider horizon and more ample elbow-room and assisted by the something more than tolerant good-will of his business associates, colleagues, or competitors, the individual, once insisted on, has every chance to develop and become prosperous and rich. Everything helps a man in America to strike out for himself, to walk alone, and to dispense with a chaperon. The Englishman is chaperoned at almost every step of his business career; and I am not speaking now of the chaperonage of his colleagues, of his fellows in the community, or of his elders among whom he grows up and, generally, in spite of whom the young man must make his way to the top. There is another much more significant form of chaperonage in English business circles, of which it is difficult to speak without provoking hostility.

The English business world is solicitor-cursed. I mean by this no reflection on solicitors either individually or in the mass. I am making no reference to such cases as there have been of misappropriation by solicitors here and there of funds entrusted to their charge, nor to their methods of making charges, which are preposterous but not of their choosing. Let us grant that, given the necessity of solicitors at all, Great Britain is blessed in that she has so capable and upright and in all ways admirable a set of men to fill the offices and do the work. What I am attacking is solicitordom as an institution.

It is not merely that there are no solicitors, as such, in the United States, for it might well be that the general practising lawyers who fill their places, so far as their places have to be filled, might be just as serious an incubus on business as solicitordom is on the business of London to-day. Names are immaterial. The essential fact is that the spirit and the conditions which make solicitors a necessity in England do not exist in America. I do not propose to go into any comparison in the differences in legal procedure in the two countries; not being a lawyer, I should undoubtedly make blunders if I did. What is important is that a man who is accustomed to walking alone does not think of turning to his legal adviser at every step. Great corporations and large business concerns have of course their counsel, their attorneys, and even their "general solicitors." But the ordinary American engaged in trade or business in a small or moderate way gets along from year's end to year's end, perhaps for his lifetime, without legal services. I am speaking only on conjecture when I say that, taking the country as a whole, outside of the large corporations or among rich men, over ninety per cent. of the legal documents—leases, agreements, contracts, articles of partnership, articles of incorporation, bills of sale, and deeds of transfer—are executed by the individuals concerned without reference to a lawyer. Probably not less than three fourths of the actual transactions in the purchase of land, houses, businesses, or other property are similarly concluded without assistance. "What do we need of a lawyer?" one man will ask the other and the other will immediately agree that they need one not at all.

Of course troubles often arise which would have been prevented had the documents been drawn up by a competent hand. The constitutional reluctance to go to a lawyer is sometimes carried to lengths that are absurd. But I do not believe that the amount of litigation which arises from that cause is in any way comparable to that which is avoided by the mere fact that legal aid is outside the mental horizon. The men who conduct most of the affairs of life directly without legal help are most likely to adjust differences when they arise in the same way. That is a matter of opinion, however, based only on reasonable analogy, which I can advance no figures to support; but what is not matter of opinion, but matter of certainty, is, first, that the general gain in the rapidity of business movement is incalculable, and, second, that business as a whole is relieved of the vast burden of solicitors' charges.

The American, accustomed to the ways of his own people, on becoming engaged in business in London is astounded, first, at the disposition of the Englishman to turn for legal guidance in almost every step he takes, second, at the stupendous sums of money which are paid for services which in his opinion are entirely superfluous, and, finally, at the terrible loss of time incurred in the conclusion of any transaction by the waiting for the drafting and redrafting and amending and engrossing and recording of interminable documents which are a bewilderment and an annoyance to him.

The Englishman often says that American business methods are slip-shod; and possibly that is the right word. But Englishmen should not for a moment deceive themselves into thinking that the American envies the Englishman the superior niceties of his ways or would think himself or his condition likely to be improved by an exchange. An example of difference in the practice of the two countries which has so often been used as to be fairly hackneyed (and therefore perhaps stands the better chance of carrying conviction than a more original, if better, illustration) is drawn from the theory which governs the building of locomotive engines in the two countries.

The American usually builds his engine to do a certain specified service and to last a reasonable length of time. During that time he proposes to get all the work out of it that he can—to wear it out in fact—feeling well assured that, when that time expires, either the character of the service to be performed will have altered or such improvements will have been introduced into the science of locomotive construction as will make it cheaper to replace the old engine with one of later build. The Englishman commonly builds his engines as if they were to last for all time. There are many engines working on English railways now, the American contemporaries of which were scrapped twenty years ago. The Englishman takes pride in their antiquity, as showing the excellence of the workmanship which was put into them. The American thinks it would have been incomparably better to have thrown the old things away long ago and replaced them with others of recent building which would be more efficient.

The same principle runs through most things in American life, where they rarely build for posterity, preferring to adapt the article to the work it has to perform, expecting to supersede it when the time comes with something better. If a thing suffices, it suffices; whether it be a locomotive or a contract. "What is the use," the American asks, "when you can come to an agreement with a fellow in ten minutes and draw up your contract with him that afternoon,—what is the use of calling in your solicitors to negotiate and then paying them heavily to keep you waiting for weeks while they draft documents? We shall have had the contract running a month and be making money out of it before the lawyers would get through talking."

Out of this divergence in point of view and practice have of course grown other differences. One thing is that the American courts have necessarily come to adopt more liberal views in the interpretation of contracts than the English; they are to a greater extent inclined to look more to the intent than to the letter and to attach more weight to verbal evidence in eliciting what the intent was. No stamping of documents being necessary in America, the documents calling themselves contracts, and which are upheld as such, which appear in American courts are frequently of a remarkable description; but I have a suspicion that on the whole the American, in this particular, comes as near to getting justice on the average as does the Englishman.

And the point is that I believe it to be inevitable that the habit of doing without lawyers in the daily conduct of business, the habit of relying on oneself and dealing with another man direct, must in the long run breed a higher standard of individual business integrity. Englishmen, relying always on their solicitors' advice, are too tempted to consider that so long as they are on the right side of the law they are honest. It is a shifting of the responsibility to the chaperon; whereas, if alone, you would be compelled to act on your honour.

What I think and hope is the last word that I have to say on this rather difficult subject has to do with the matter already mentioned, namely the absence of the necessity of stamping documents in America. Englishmen will remember that the Americans always have evinced a dislike of stamps and stamp duties and acts relating thereto. Of late years the necessity of meeting the expenses of the Spanish war did for a while compel the raising of additional internal revenue by means of documentary and other stamps. The people submitted to it, but they hated it; and hated it afresh as often as they drew or saw a cheque with the two-cent stamp upon it. The act was repealed as speedily as possible and the stamping of papers has for six years now been unknown.

I think—and I am not now stating any acknowledged fact, but only appealing to the reader's common-sense—that it is again inevitable that where a superior sanctity attaches to stamped paper a people must in the long run come to think too lightly of that which is unstamped. I do not say that the individual Englishman has as yet come to think too lightly of his word or bond because it is informal, but I do think there is danger of it. The words "Can we hold him?" or (what is infinitely worse) "Can he hold us?" spring somewhat readily to the lips of the business man of this generation in England.

Continual dependence on the law and the man of law, and an extra respect for paper because it is legal, have—they surely cannot fail to have—a tendency to breed in the mind a disregard for what is not of a strictly legal or actionable character. It is Utopian to dream of a state of society where no law will be needed but every man's written and spoken word will be a law to him; but it is not difficult to imagine a state of society in which there is such universal dependence on the law in all emergencies that the individual conscience will become weakened—pauperised—atrophied—and unable to stand alone.

That is, as I have said, the last point that I wish to make on this subject; and the reader will please notice that I have nowhere said that I consider American commercial morality at the present day to be higher than English. Nor do I think that it is. Incontestably it is but a little while since the English standard was appreciably the higher of the two. I have cited from my own memory instances of conditions which existed in America only twenty years ago in support of the fact—though no proof is needed—that this is so. I by no means underestimate the fineness of the traditions of British commerce or the number of men still living who hold to those traditions. On the other hand, better judges than I believe that the standard of morality in English business circles is declining. In America it is certainly and rapidly improving.

Present English ideas about American commercial ethics are founded on a knowledge of facts, correct enough at the time, which existed before the improvement had made anything like the headway that it has, which facts no longer exist. I have roughly compared in outline some of the essential qualities of the atmosphere in which, and some of the conditions under which, the business men in the two countries live and do their business, showing that in the United States there is a much more marked tendency to insist on the character of the individual and a much larger opportunity for the individuality to develop itself; and that in certain particulars there are in England inherited social conditions and institutions which it would appear cannot fail to hamper the spirit of self-reliance, on which self-respect is ultimately dependent.

And the conclusion? For the most part my readers must draw it for themselves. My own opinion is that, whatever the relative standing of the two countries may be to-day, it is hardly conceivable that, by the course on which each is travelling, in another generation American commercial integrity will not stand the higher of the two. The conditions in America are making for the shaping of a sterner type of man.

Postscript.—The opinion has been expressed in the foregoing pages that in one particular the American on the average comes as near to getting justice in his courts as does the Englishman. I have also given expression to my great respect, which I think is shared by everyone who knows anything of it, for the United States Supreme Court. Also I have spoken disparagingly of the English institution of solicitordom. But these isolated expressions of opinion on particular points must not be interpreted as a statement that American laws and procedure are on the whole comparable to the English. I do not believe that they are. None the less Englishmen have as a rule such vague notions upon this subject that some explanatory comment seems to be desirable.

Especially do few Englishmen (not lawyers or students of the subject) recognise that the abuses in the administration of justice in America, of which they hear so much, do not occur in the United States courts, but in the local courts of the several States. So far as the United States (*i. e.*, the Federal) Courts are concerned I believe that the character and capacity of the judges (all of whom are appointed and not elected) compare favourably with those of English judges. It is in the State courts, the judges of which are generally elected, that the shortcomings appear; and while it might be reasonable to expect that a great State like New York or Massachusetts should have a code of laws and an administration of justice not inferior to those of Great Britain, it is perhaps scarcely fair to expect as much of each of the 46 States, many of which are as yet young and thinly populated.

The chief vice of the State courts arises, of course, from the fact that the judges are elected by a partisan vote; from which it follows almost of necessity that there will be among them not a few who in their official actions will be amenable to the influence of party pressure. It is perhaps also inevitable that under such a system there will not seldom find their way to the bench men of such inferior character that they will be directly reachable by private bribes; though this, I believe, seldom occurs. The State courts, however, labour under other disadvantages.

We have seen how Congressmen are hampered in the execution of their duties by the constant calls upon their time made by the leaders of their party, or other influential interests, in their constituencies. The same is true on a smaller scale of members of the State legislatures. Congress and the legislatures of the several States alike are moreover limited by the restrictions of written constitutions. The British Parliament is paramount; but the United States legislatures are always operating under fear of conflict with the Constitution. Their spheres are limited, so that they can only legislate on certain subjects and within certain lines; while finally the country has grown so fast, the conditions of society have changed with such rapidity, that it has been inherently difficult for lawmaking bodies to keep pace with the increasing complexity of the social and industrial fabric.

If the limitations of space did not forbid, it would be interesting to show how this fact, more than any other (and not any willingness to leave loopholes for dishonesty) makes possible such offences as those which, committed by certain financial institutions in New York, were the immediate precipitating cause of the recent panic. Growth has been so rapid that, with the best will in the world to erect safeguards against malfeasance, weak spots in the barricades are, as it were, only discovered after they have been taken advantage of. With the preoccupation of the legislators stable doors are only found to be open by the fact that the horses are already in the street.

But, after all has been said in extenuation, there remain many things in American State laws for which one may find explanation but not much excuse.

Reference has already been made to the entirely immoral attitude of many of the State legislatures towards corporations, especially towards railway companies; and in some of the Western States prejudice against accumulated wealth is so strong that it is practically impossible for a rich man or corporation to get a verdict against a poor man. It would be easy to cite cases from one's personal experience wherein jurors have frankly explained their rendering of a verdict in obvious contradiction of the weight of evidence, by the mere statement that the losing party "could stand it" while the other could not. Of a piece with this is a class of legislation which has been abundant in Western States, where the legislators as well as most of the residents of the States have been poor, giving extraordinary advantages to debtors and making the collection of debts practically impossible. In some cases such legislation has defeated itself by compelling capitalists to refuse to invest, and wholesale traders to refuse to give credit, inside the State.

Yet another source of corruption in legislation is to be found in the mere numerousness of the States themselves. It may obviously inure to the advantage of the revenues of a particular State to be especially lenient in matters which involve the payment of fees. It is evidently desirable that a check should be put on the reckless incorporation of companies with unlimited share capital, the usual form of such a check being, of course, the graduation of the fee for incorporation in proportion to such capital. One State which has laws more generous than any of its neighbours in this particular is likely to attract to it the incorporation of all the companies of any magnitude from those States, the formal compliance with the requirements of having a statutory office, and of holding an annual meeting, in that State being a matter of small moment. Similar considerations may govern one State in enacting laws facilitating the obtaining of divorce.

There are, then, obviously many causes which make the attainment of either an uniform or a satisfactory code of jurisprudence in all States alike extremely difficult of attainment. It will only be arrived at by, on the one hand, the extension of the Federal authority and, on the other the increase in population and wealth (and, consequently, a sense of responsibility) in those States which at present are less forward than their neighbours. But, again, it is worth insisting on the fact that the faults are faults of the several States and not of the United States. They do not imply either a lack of a sense of justice in the people as a whole or any willingness to make wrong-doing easy. But it is extremely difficult for the public opinion of the rest of the country to bring any pressure to bear on the legislature of one recalcitrant State. The desire to insist on its own independence is indeed so strong in every State that any attempt at outside interference must almost inevitably result only in developing resistance.

And again I find myself regretfully in direct conflict with Mr. Wells. But it is not easy to take his meditations on American commercial morality in entire seriousness.

"In the highly imaginative theory that underlies the reality of an individualistic society," he says (*The Future in America*, p. 168), "there is such a thing as honest trading. In practice I don't believe there is. Exchangeable things are supposed to have a fixed quality called their value, and honest trading is I am told the exchange of things of equal value. Nobody gains or loses by honest trading and therefore nobody can grow rich by it." And more to the same effect.

A trader buys one thousand of a given article per month from the manufacturer at ninepence an article and sells them to his customers at tenpence. The extra penny is his payment for acting as purveyor, and the customers recognise that it is an equitable charge which they pay contentedly. That is honest trading; and the trader makes a profit of a trifle over four pounds a month, or fifty pounds a year.

Another trader purveys the same article, buying it from the same manufacturer, but owing to the possession of larger capital, better talent for organisation, and more enterprise, he sells, not one thousand, but one million per month. Instead of selling them at tenpence, however, he sells them at ninepence half-penny; thereby making his customers a present of one halfpenny, taking to himself only one half of the sum to which they have already consented as a just charge for the services which he renders. Supposing that he pays the same price as the other trader for his goods (which, buying by the million, he would not do), he makes a profit of some £2083 a month, or £25,000 a year. Evidently he grows rich.

This is the rudimentary principle of modern business; but because one man becomes rich, though he gives the public the same service for less charge than honest men, Mr. Wells says that he cannot be honest.

If two men discover simultaneously gold mines of equal value, and one, being timid and conservative, puts twenty men to work while the other puts a thousand, and each makes a profit of one shilling a day on each man's labour, it is evident that while one enjoys an income of a pound a day for himself the other makes fifty times as much. It is not only obvious that the latter is just as honest as the former, but he can well afford to pay his men a shilling or two a week more in wages. He can afford to build them model homes and give them reading-rooms and recreation grounds, which the other cannot.

Others, besides Mr. Wells, lose their heads when they contemplate large fortunes made in business; but the elementary lesson to be learned is not merely that such large fortunes are likely to be as "honestly" acquired as the smaller ones, but also that the man who trades on the larger scale is—or has the potentiality of being—the greater benefactor to the community, not merely by being able to furnish the people with goods at a lower price but also by his ability to employ more labour and to surround his workmen with better material conditions.

The tendency of modern business industry to agglutinate into large units is, as has been said, inevitable; but, what is better worth noting, like all natural developments from healthy conditions, it is a thing inherently beneficent. That the larger power is capable of greater abuse than the smaller is also evident; and against that abuse it is that the American people is now struggling to safeguard itself. But to assail all trading on a scale which produces great wealth as "dishonest" is both impertinent (it is Mr. Wells's own word, applied to himself) and absurd.

The aggregate effect of the great consolidations in America and in England alike (of the "trusts" in fact) has so far been to cheapen immensely the price of most of the staples of life to the people; and that will always be the tendency of all consolidations which stop at any point short of monopoly. And that an artificial monopoly (not based on a natural monopoly) can ever be made effective in any staple for more than the briefest space of time has yet to be demonstrated.

The other consideration, of the destruction of the independence of the individual, remains; but that lies outside Mr. Wells' range.

FOOTNOTES:

[378:1] Preface to the *Encyclopædia of Trade between the United States and France*, prepared by the Société du Repertoire Général du Commerce.

[384:1] I do not know whether the story is true or not that Signor Caruso was compelled, in default of other means of identification in a New York bank, to lift up his voice and sing to the satisfaction of the bank officials. As has been remarked, this is not the first time that gold has been given in exchange for notes.

CHAPTER XV

The Peoples at Play

American Sport Twenty-five Years Ago—The Power of Golf—A Look Ahead—Britain, Mother of Sports—Buffalo in New York—And Pheasants on Clapham Common—Shooting Foxes and the "Sport" of Wild-fowling—The Amateur in American Sport—At Henley—And at Large—Teutonic Poppycock.

In "An Error in the Fourth Dimension," Kipling tells how one Wilton Sargent, an American, came to live in England and earnestly laboured to make himself more English than the English. He learned diligently to do many things most un-American:—"Last mystery of all he learned to golf—well; and when an American knows the innermost meaning of '*Don't press, slow back and keep your eye on the ball,*' he is, for practical purposes, de-nationalised." Some six years after that was written an American golfer became Amateur Champion of Great Britain. Yes; I know that Mr. Travis was not born in the United States, but *qua* golfer he is American pure and simple. Which shows the danger of too hasty generalisation, even on the part of a genius. And it shows more. When he wrote those words Kipling was fully justified by the facts as they stood. It is the fault of the character of the American people, which frustrates prophecy.

Twenty-five years ago there was no amateur sport in America—none. Men, it is true, went off and shot ("hunted" as Americans call it) and fished and yachted for a few days, or weeks, in summer or autumn, in a rather rough-and-ready sort of way. Also, when at college they played baseball and football and, perhaps, they rowed. After leaving college there was probably not one young American in a hundred who entered a boat or played a game of either football or baseball on an average of once in a year. The people as a whole had no open-air games. Baseball was chiefly professional. Cricket had a certain foothold in Philadelphia and on Staten Island, but it was an exotic sport, as it remains to-day, failing entirely to enlist the sympathies of the multitude. Polo was not played. Lawn tennis had been introduced, but had made little headway. In all America there were, I think, three racquet courts, which were used chiefly by visiting Englishmen, and not one tennis court. Lacrosse was quite unknown, and as for the "winter sports" of snow-shoeing, ski-ing, ice-boating, curling, and tobogganing, they were practised only here and there by a few (except for the "coasting" of children) as rather a curious fad.

It was a strange experience for an Englishman in those days, fond of his games, to go from his clubs and the society of his fellows at home, to mix in the same class of society in America. As in the circles that he had left behind him, so there, the conversation was still largely on sporting topics, but while in England men talked of the games in which they played themselves and of the feats and experiences of their friends, in the leading young men's clubs of New York—the Union, the Knickerbocker, and the Calumet—the talk was solely of professional sport: of the paid baseball nines, of prize fighters (Sullivan was then just rising to his glory), and professional scullers (those were the days of Hanlan), and the like. No man talked of his own doings or of those of his friends, for he and his friends did nothing, except perhaps to spar for an hour or so once or twice a week, or go through perfunctory gymnastics for their figures' sakes.

Until a dozen years ago the situation had not materially changed. Lawn tennis had made some headway, but the thing that wrought the revolution was the coming of golf. It may be doubted if ever in history has any single sport, pastime, or pursuit so modified the habits, and even the character, of a people in an equal space of time as golf has modified those of the people of the United States.

Enough has already been written of the enthusiasm with which the Americans took up the game itself, of the social prestige which it at once obtained, of the colossal sums of money that have been lavished on the making of courses, of the sumptuousness of the club-houses that have sprung up all over the land. That golf is in itself a fascinating game, is sufficiently proved in England, where it has drawn so many thousands of devotees away from cricket, football, lawn tennis, and other sports. But can we imagine what the result might have been if there had been in Great Britain no cricket, or football, or other sports, so that all the game-loving enthusiasm of the nation had been free to turn itself loose into that one channel? And this is just what did happen in America. Golf had a clear field and a strenuous sport-loving nation, devoid of open-air games, at its mercy.

The result was not merely that people took to playing golf and that young men neglected their offices and millionaires stretched unwonted muscles in scrambling over bunkers. Golf taught the American people to play games. It took them out from their great office-buildings and from their five-o'clock cocktails at the club, into the open air; and they found that the open air was good. So around nearly every golf club other sports grew up. Polo grounds were laid out by the side of the links, croquet lawns appeared on one side of the club-house and lawn-tennis nets arose on the other, while traps for the clay-pigeon shooters were placed safely off in a corner.

Golf came precisely at the moment when the people were ready for it. Just as America, having in a measure completed the exploitation of her own continent and developed a manufacturing power beyond the resources of consumption in her people, was commercially ripe for the invasion of the markets of the world; just as she came, in her overflowing wealth and power, to a recognition of her greatness as a nation, and was politically ripe for an Imperial policy of colonial expansion; just as, tired of the loose code of ethics of the scrambling days, when the country was still one half wilderness and none had time to care for the public conscience, she was morally ripe for the wonderful revival which has set in in the ethics of politics and commerce and of which Mr. Roosevelt has been and is the chief apostle: so, by the individual richness of her citizens, giving larger leisure in which to cultivate other pleasures than those which their offices or homes could afford, she was ripe for the coming of the day of open-air games. And having turned to them, she threw herself into their pursuit with the ardour and singleness of purpose which are characteristic of the people and which, as applied to games, seem to English eyes to savour almost of professionalism. As a matter of fact they are only the manifestations of an essential trait of the American character.

The result was that almost at the same time as an American player was winning the British Amateur Golf Championship, an American polo team was putting All England on her mettle at Hurlingham, and it was not with any wider margin than was necessary for comfort that Great Britain retained the honours in lawn tennis, which she has since lost to one of her own colonies.

It is curious that this awakening of the amateur sporting spirit in the United States should have come just at the time when many excellent judges were bewailing the growing popularity of professional sport in England. Any day now, one may hear complaints that the British youth is giving up playing games himself for the purpose of watching professional wrestlers or football games or county cricket matches. My personal opinion is that there is no need to worry. The growing interest in exhibition games reacts in producing a larger number of youths who strive to become players. Not only in spite of, but largely because of, the greater spectacular attraction of both football and cricket than in years gone by, there is an immensely larger number of players of both—and of all other—games than there ever was before. It is little more than a score of years since Association football, at least, was practically the monopoly of a few public schools and of the members of the two Universities—of "gentlemen" in fact. Any loss which the nation can have suffered from the tendency to sit on benches and applaud professional players must have been made up a thousand times over in the benefit to the national physique from the spreading of the game into wide classes which formerly regarded it, much as they might fox-hunting, as a pastime reserved only for their "betters."

It is none the less interesting and instructive that in this field as in so many others the directly opposite tendencies should be at work in the two countries: that just when America is beginning to learn the delight of being a game-loving nation and amateur sport is thriving, not yet to the detriment of, but in proportions at least which stand fair comparison with, professional, the cry should be raised in England that Englishmen are forgetting to play games themselves in their eagerness to watch others do them better. Here, as in other things, the gap between the habits of the two peoples is narrowing rapidly. They have not yet met; for in England the time and attention given to games and sports by amateurs is still incomparably greater than on the other side. But that the advancing lines will meet—and even cross—seems probable. And when they have crossed, what then? Will America ever oust Great Britain from the position which she holds as the Mother of Sports and the athletic centre of the world?

Some things, it appears, one can predict with certainty. America has already taken to herself a disagreeable number of the records in track athletics; and she will take more. On the links the performance of Mr. Travis, isolated as yet, is only a warning of many similar experiences in the future. In a few years it will be very hard for any visiting golf team of less than All England or All Scotland strength to win many matches against American clubs on their home courses; and the United States will be able to send a team over here that will be beaten only by All England—or perhaps will not be beaten by All Britain. At polo the Americans will go on hammering away till they produce a team that can stand unconquered at Hurlingham. It will be very long before they can turn out a dozen teams to match the best English dozen; but by mere force of concentration and by the practice of that quality which, as has already been said, looks so like professionalism to English eyes, one team to rival the English best they will send over. In lawn tennis it cannot be long before a pair of Americans will do what an Australian pair did in 1907, just as the United States already holds the Ladies' Championship; and England is going to have some difficulty in recovering her honours at court tennis. In rifle shooting America must be expected to beat England oftener than England beats America; but the edge will be taken off any humiliation that there might be by the fact that Britain will have Colonial teams as good as either.

And when all this has happened, will England's position be shaken? Not one whit! Not though the *America's* cup never crosses the Atlantic and though sooner or later an American college crew succeeds—as surely, for their pluck, they deserve to succeed—in imitating the Belgians and carrying off the Grand at Henley. There remain games and sports enough which the United States will never take up seriously, at which if she did she would be debarred by climatic conditions or other causes from ever threatening British supremacy.

The glory of England lies in the fact that she "takes on" the best of all the nations of the world at their own games. It is not the United States only, but all her Colonies and every country of Europe that turn to Great Britain as to their best antagonist in whatever sport they find themselves proficient. Just now England's brow is somewhat bare of laurels, but year in and year out Britain will continue to win the majority of contests in her meetings with all the world; and if she lose at times, is it not better to have rivals good enough to make her extend herself? And is it not sufficient for her pride that she, one people, should win—if it be only—half of all the world's honours?

Meanwhile Englishmen can afford to rejoice ungrudgingly at the new spirit which has been born in the United States. Each year the number of "events" in which an international contest is possible increases. The time may not be far away when there will be almost as long a list of Anglo-American annual contests as there is now between Oxford and Cambridge. But it will be a very long time before the United States can displace Great Britain from the pre-eminence which she holds—and the wonderful character of which, I think, few Englishmen appreciate. Before that time comes such other sweeping changes will probably have come over the map of the world and the relations of the peoples that Britain's displacement will have lost all significance.

And Englishmen can always remember that, whatever triumphs the Americans may win in the domain of sport, they win them by virtue of the English blood that is in them.

It is, of course, inevitable that in many particulars the American and English ideas of sport should be widely different. There is an old, old story in America of the Englishman who arrived in New York and, on the day after his arrival, got out his rifle and proceeded to make enquiries of the hotel people as to the best direction in which to start out to find buffalo—the nearest buffalo at the time being, perhaps, two thousand miles away. It is a story which has contributed not a little to contempt of the Britisher in many an innocent American mind. It happens that in my own experience I have known precisely that same blunder made by an American in England.

I had met an American friend, with whom I have shot in America, at his hotel on the evening of his arrival in London one day in November. In the course of conversation I mentioned that the shooting season was in full swing.

"Good," he said. "Let me hire a gun somewhere to-morrow and let's go out, if you've nothing to do, and have some shooting."

Nothing, he opined, would be simpler, or more agreeable, than to drive out—or possibly take a train—to some wild spot in the vicinity of London—Clapham Common perhaps—and spend a day among the pheasants. It was precisely the Englishman and his buffalo—the prehistoric instinct of the race ("What a beautiful day! Let us go and kill something!") blossoming amid unfamiliar conditions. My American friend wanted to kill an English pheasant. He had heard much of them as the best of game-birds. He had eaten them, much refrigerated, in New York and found them good. And he knew nothing of preserving and of a land that is all parcelled out into parks and gardens and spinneys. Why not then go out and enjoy ourselves? Before he left England he had some pheasant shooting, and it is rarely that a man on his first day at those conspicuous but evasive fowl renders as good an account of himself as did he. Similarly every American with a sound sporting instinct must hope that that traditional Englishman ultimately got his buffalo.

Many times in the United States in the old days have I done exactly what that American then wished to do in London. Finding myself compelled to spend a night at some crude and unfamiliar Western town, I have made enquiries at the hotel as to the shooting—duck or prairie chicken—in the neighbourhood. Hiring a gun of the local gunsmith and buying a hundred cartridges, one then secured a trap with a driver, who probably brought his own gun and shot also (probably better than oneself), but who certainly knew the ground. The best ground might be three or five or ten miles out—open prairie where chicken were plentiful, or a string of prairie lakes or "sloughs" (pronounced "sloo") with duck-passes between. That evening one came home, hungry and happy as a hunter ought to be, with perhaps half a dozen brace of spike-tailed grouse (the common "chicken" of the Northwestern States) or ten or a dozen duck—mallard, widgeon, pintail, two kinds of teal, with, it might be, a couple of red-heads or canvas-backs,—or, not improbably, a magnificent Canada goose as the spoils.

With the settlement of the country, the multiplication of shooters, and the increase in the number of "gun-clubs," which have now included most of the easily accessible duck-grounds in the country in their private preserves, the possibilities of those delightful days are growing fewer, but even now there are many parts of the West where the stranger can still do as I have done many times.

Though the people had so few outdoor games, the great majority of Americans, except the less well-to-do of the city-dwellers of the Eastern States, have been accustomed to handle gun and rod from their childhood. The gun may at first have been a rusty old muzzle-loader, and the rod a "pole" cut from the bank of the stream with a live grasshopper for bait; and there are few better weapons to teach a boy to be a keen sportsman. The birds that he shot were game—duck or geese, turkeys, quail, grouse, or snipe—and the fish that he caught were mostly game fish—trout and bass. It is true that the American generally shoots foxes; so does the Englishman when he goes to the Colonies where there are no hounds and too many foxes, with game birds which he wishes kept for his own shooting, and domestic chickens which he destines for his own table. On the other hand the American does not mount a miniature cannon in a punt and shoot waterfowl by wholesale when sitting on the water. It is only the gunner for the market, the man who makes his living by it, who does that, and the laws do their best to stop even him. The American sportsman who cannot get his duck fairly on the wing with a 12- or 16-bore prefers not to get them at all. "But," objects the English wildfowl shooter, "suppose the birds are not get-at-able in any other way?" "So much," the American would retort, "the better for the birds. They have earned their lives; get them like a sportsman or let them go."

The time may not be far away—and many Englishmen will be glad when it comes—when to kill waterfowl at rest with a duck gun will no longer be considered a "sport" that a gentleman can engage in in England. Perhaps fox-hunting will become so popular in the United States that foxes will be generally preserved. The sportsmen of each country will then think better of those of the other. Meanwhile it would be pleasanter if each would believe that such little seemingly unsportsmanlike peculiarities that the other may have developed are only the accidents of his environment, and that under the same circumstances there is not a pin to choose between their sportsmanship.

Reference has more than once been made to the quality which looks to English eyes so much like semi-professionalism in American sport. It is a delicate subject, in handling which susceptibilities on one side or the other may easily be hurt.

The intense earnestness and concentration of the American on his one sport—for most Americans are specialists in one only—does not commend itself to English amateurs. The exclusiveness, which seems to be suspicious of foul play, and the stringent training system of certain American crews at Henley have been out of harmony with all the traditions of the great Regatta and have caused much ill feeling, some of which has occasionally come to the surface. Some of the proceedings of American polo teams have not coincided with what is ordinarily considered, in England, the behaviour of gentlemen in matters of amateur sport. On the other hand, Americans universally believe that Lord Dunraven acted in a most unsportsmanlike manner in the unfortunate cup scandal; and in one case they are—or were at the time—convinced that one of their crews was unfairly treated at Henley. Honours therefore on the surface are fairly easy; and, while every

Englishman knows that both the American charges quoted are absurd, every American is no less of the opinion that the English grounds of complaint are altogether unreasonable.

We must remember that after all a good many of the best English golfers and lawn-tennis players do nothing else in life but golf or play lawn-tennis. And this tendency to specialise is undoubtedly increasing. Meanwhile it will never be rooted out of the American character and in departments of sport where it, and it alone, will bring pre-eminence, Englishmen will either have to do as Americans do or, sooner or later, consent to be defeated. There is nothing in the practice at which the Englishman can fairly cavil. Americans have still much the fewer sports; and it is the national habit to take up one and concentrate on it with all one's might.[420:1]

A more difficult aspect of the situation has to do with the question of the definition of "gentleman-amateur"; the fact being, of course, that the same definition has not the same significance in the two countries. The radical difficulty lies in the fact that the word "gentleman" in its English sense of a man of gentle birth has no application to America. Let this not be understood as a statement that there are any fewer gentlemen in America or that the word is not used. But its usage is not re-inforced, its limits are not defined, as in England, by any line of cleavage in the social system. A large number of the gentlemen of America are farmers' sons; more than half are the sons of men who commenced life in very humble positions, and nearly all are the sons of men who are engaged in trade or in business, the majority of them being destined to go into trade or business (and to begin at the beginning) themselves. In England, of course, the process of the obliteration of the old line is going on with great rapidity. In America, on the other hand, there is a tendency towards the drawing of a somewhat corresponding line. But the fact remains that at present there exists this fundamental distinction and the consequence is that Englishmen continue to find among American "amateurs" and in teams of American "gentlemen," individuals who would not be accepted into the same categories in England.

But what Englishmen should endeavour to understand is that the man who on the surface seems to belong to a class which in England would be objectionable in the company of gentlemen probably has none of those characteristics which would make him objectionable were he English. He has far more of the characteristics of a gentleman than of the other qualities. The qualities which go to make a "gentleman," even in the English sense, are many and complex; but the assumption is that they are all present in the man who bears the public school and university stamp. The Englishman is accustomed to accept the presence or absence of one or a few of those qualities in an individual as evidence of the presence or absence of them all. In judging other Englishmen, the rule works satisfactorily. But in America, with its different social system, the qualities are not tied up in the same bundles, so that the same inference fails. The same, or a similar, peculiarity of voice or speech or manner or dress or birth does not denote—much less does it connote—the same or similar things in representatives of the two peoples. Particular Englishmen have learned this often enough in individual cases. How often has it not happened that an Englishman, meeting an American first as a stranger, not even being informed that he is an American, has, judging from some one external characteristic, turned from him as being an Undesirable, only to be introduced to him later, or meet him under other conditions, and find in him one of the best fellows that he ever met? The thing is happening every day. Very often, with a little more knowledge or a little clearer understanding, Englishmen would know that their judgment of some American amateur athlete is shockingly unjust. To bar him out would be incomparably more unjust to him than his inclusion is unjust to any antagonist.

This of course does not touch the fact—which is a fact—that in America what answers to the gentleman-amateur in England is drawn from a much larger proportion of the people. This does not however mean, when rightly viewed, what Englishmen generally think it means, that Americans go down into other—and presumably not legitimate—classes for their recruits. It only means that a very much larger proportion of the people belong to one class. There is no point at which an arbitrary line can be drawn. This is in truth only another way of saying what has been said already more than once, that the American people is really more homogeneous than the English, or rather is homogeneous over a larger part of its area, so that the type-American represents a greater proportion of the people of the United States than the type-Briton represents of the people of the British Isles.

This is obviously in the realm of sport so much to America's advantage. It is not a condition against which the Englishman has any right to protest, any more than he has to move amendments to the Constitution of the United States. When better comprehended, Englishmen will accept it without either resentment or regret. The United States has a larger population than Great Britain: so much the better for the United States. Also a larger proportion of that population must be admitted into the category of gentleman-amateur in sport; so much the more the better for them.

But, curiously enough, this condition has its inherent drawback, which not impossibly more than compensates for its advantages. The fact that young Americans grow up so much of a class involves the essential fact that the enormous majority of them are educated at the Public Schools, that is at the Board Schools or Government Schools or whatever they would be called if their precise counterpart existed in England. The United States has not (the fact has been touched on before) any group of institutions comparable to the great schools of England. A few excellent schools there are which bear some resemblance to the English models, but they are not numerous enough to go any way towards leavening the nation. It is to the Public Schools that, in the mass, the English gentleman-amateur owes his training, not only in sports but in many other things besides: especially in those things which stamp on him the mark by which he is recognised as belonging to his right class through life. The American, as has been said, is not so stamped; but in missing that stamp—or in failing to receive it—he necessarily missed also all that discipline and training in games which the Public School gave to the Englishman. The very same cause as gives America an advantage in the numbers from which she can draw her amateur athletes, also forbids that these recruits should have had the same advantages of early training as fall to the Englishman.

The thing is about as broad as it is long. It is not difficult to imagine that the great schools might never have come into existence in England, so that a larger proportion of the population than is now the case would be educated at some intermediate institutions, at the Grammar Schools let us say, when the English gentleman-amateur athletes—the polo, golf, and tennis teams and the crews that row at Henley—would be drawn from a larger circle of the population, and the individuals would not bear as close a superficial resemblance, one to the other, as they do to-day. They would in fact be more like the members of American athletic teams as Englishmen know them. The question is whether England would gain or lose in athletic efficiency. When Englishmen find something to cavil at in an individual American amateur or in an American amateur team or crew, would it not be better to stop and consider whether the disadvantages which compel America to be represented by such an individual or team or crew, do not outweigh the advantages which enable her to use him or them? If the United States were to develop the same educational machinery as exists in England, which would stamp practically all their gentlemen-amateurs with the same hall-mark, as they are so stamped in England, and would at the same time give them the English public-school boy's training in games, would not England, as a mere matter of athletic rivalry, be worse off instead of better?

For the purpose of pointing the moral of the essential likeness of the American and English characters, as contrasted with those of other peoples, reference has already been made to Professor Münsterberg and his book. It is an excellent book; but what English writer would think it necessary to inform English readers that "the American student recreates himself on the athletic field rather than in the ale-house"? We know something of the life of a German student; but it is only when a German himself says a thing like that that he illuminates in a flash the abyss which yawns between the moral qualities of the youth of his country and the young American or young Englishman.

Again the same author speaks on the subject of the Anglo-Saxon love of fair play (the sporting instinct, I have called it) as follows:

"The demand for 'fair play' dominates the whole American people, and shapes public opinion in all matters whether large or small. And with this finally goes the belief in the self-respect and integrity of one's neighbour. The American cannot understand how Europeans" (Continental Europeans, if you please, Mr. Münsterberg!) "so often reinforce their statements with explicit mention of their honour which is at stake, as if the hearer was likely to feel a doubt of it; and even American children are often apt to wonder at young people abroad who quarrel at play and at once suspect one another of some unfairness. The American system does not wait for years of discretion to come before exerting its influence; it makes itself felt in the nursery, where already the word of one child is never doubted by his playmates."

There is an excellent American slang word, which is "poppycock." The Century Dictionary speaks disrespectfully of it as a "United States vulgarism," but personally I consider it a first-class word. The Century Dictionary defines it as meaning, "Trivial talk; nonsense; stuff and rubbish," which is about as near as a dictionary can get to the elusive meaning of any slang word. English readers will understand the exact shade of meaning of the word when I say that the paragraph above quoted is most excellent and precise poppycock. Every American who read that paragraph when the book was published must have chuckled inwardly, just as every Englishman would chuckle. But the point which I wish to emphasise is that it is not at all poppycock from the author's point of view. I doubt not that his countrymen have been most edified by that excellent dictum, and the trouble is that one could never make a typical German understand wherein it is wrong. No, Mr. Münsterberg, it is not that the sentence is untrue—far be it from me to suggest such a thing. It is merely absurd; and you, sir, will never, never, never comprehend why it is so.

It is in the presence of such a remark, seriously made by so excellently capable a foreigner, that the Englishman and American ought to be able to shake hands and realise how much of a kin they are and how far removed from some other peoples.

I have dwelt on this subject of the games of the two peoples at what may seem to many an unnecessary length, because I do not think its importance can well be exaggerated. It is not only desirable, but it is necessary, for a thorough mutual liking between them that there should be no friction in matters of sport. No incident has, I believe, occurred of late years which did so much harm to the relations between the peoples as did the Dunraven episode in connection with the *America's* cup races. I should be inclined to say that it did more harm (I am not blaming Lord Dunraven) than the Venezuelan incident.

On the other hand, it is doubtful whether the more recent attempts to recover the cup, and the spirit in which they have been conducted, have not contributed as much as, say, the attitude of England in the Spanish War to the increased liking for Great Britain which has made itself manifest in the United States of recent years. Few Englishmen, probably, understand how much is made of such matters in the American press. The love of sport is in the blood of both peoples and neither can altogether like the other until it believes it to have the same generous sporting instincts and the same clean methods as itself. As a matter of fact, they do—as in so many other traits—stand out conspicuously alike from among all other peoples, but neither will give the other full credit for this, till each learns to see below such slight surface appearances as at present provoke occasional ill-will in one party or the other. Fuller understanding will come with time and with it entire cordiality.

FOOTNOTES:

[420:1] Though immaterial to the argument, it may be as well to state that my personal sympathies are entirely with the English practice. In the matter of college athletics especially the spirit in which certain sports (especially football and, in not much less degree, rowing and baseball) are followed at some of the American universities, is entirely distasteful to me. On the other hand, I know nothing more creditable to the English temperament than the spirit in which the contests in the corresponding sports are conducted between the great English universities. And this feeling is shared, I know, by some (and I believe by most) of those Americans who, as Rhodes scholars or otherwise, have had an opportunity of coming to understand at first hand the difference between the practice in the two countries. But this is an individual prepossession only; against which stands the fact that my experience of Americans who have won notoriety in athletics at one or other of the American universities, is that they are unspoiled by the system through which they have passed and possess just as sensitive and generous a sporting instinct as the best men turned out by Oxford or Cambridge.

CHAPTER XVI

SUMMARY AND CONCLUSION

A New Way of Making Friends—The Desirability of an Alliance—For the Sake of Both Peoples—And of All the World—The Family Resemblance—Mutual Misunderstandings—American Conception of the British Character—English Misapprehension of Americans—Foreign Influences in the United States—Why Politicians Hesitate—An Appeal to the People—And to Cæsar.

At first sight it may not seem the likeliest way to make two people care for each other to go laboriously about to tell each how the other underestimates his virtues. Don Pedro's wile would appear to be the more direct—to tell Benedick how Beatrice doted on him, and Beatrice how Benedick was dying for her love. I have always had my doubts, however, about the success of that alliance.

In the case of two peoples so much alike as the English and the American, between whom friendship and alliance would be so entirely in accord with eternal fitness, who are yet held apart by misunderstanding on the part of each of the other's character, there seems no better way than to face the misunderstandings frankly and to endeavour to make each see how unjustly it undervalues the other's good qualities or overestimates its faults. At present neither Americans nor Englishmen understand what good fellows the others are. Least of all do they understand how essentially they are the same kind of good fellows.

In summarising the contents of the foregoing pages, there is no need here to rehearse, except in barest outline, the arguments in favour of alliance between the countries. The fact that war between them is an ever-present possibility ought in itself to suffice—war which could hardly fail to be more sanguinary and destructive than any war that the world has known. The danger of such a war is greater, perhaps, than the people of either country recognises, certainly greater than most Englishmen imagine. The people of England do not understand the warlike—though so peace-loving—character of the American nation. It is just as warlike as, though no less peace-loving than, the English, without the restraint of that good-will which the English feel for the United States; without, moreover, the check, to which every European country is always subjected, of the fear of complications with other Powers. The American people, as a whole, it cannot be too earnestly impressed on Englishmen, have no such good-will towards Great Britain as Englishmen feel for them; and not even English reluctance to draw the sword, nor the protests of the better informed and the more well-to-do people in the United States would be able to restrain what Mr. Cleveland calls "the plain people of the land" if they once made up their mind to fight.

Apart from the possibility of war between the two nations themselves, there is the constant peril, to which both are exposed, of conflict forced upon them by the aggressions of other Powers. That peril is always present to both, to the United States now no less—perhaps even more—than to Great Britain. The fact that neither need fear a trial of strength with any other Power or any union of Powers, is beside the question. Consciousness of its own strength is no guarantee to any nation that it will not be forced into conflict. Rather, by making it certain that it, at least, will not draw back, does it close up one possible avenue of escape from catastrophe when a crisis threatens.

But beyond all this—apart from, and vastly greater than, the considerations of the interest or the security of either Great Britain or the United States—is the claim of humanity. The two peoples have it in their hands to give to the whole world no less a gift than that of Universal and Perpetual Peace. It involves no self-sacrifice, the giving of this wonderful boon, for the two peoples themselves would share in the benefit no less than other peoples, and they would be the richer by the giving. It involves hardly any effort, for they have but to hold out their hands together and give. It matters not that the world has not appealed to them. The fact remains that they can do this thing and they alone; and it is for them to ask their own consciences whether any considerations of pride, any prejudice, any absorption in their own affairs—any consideration actual or conceivable—can justify them in holding back. Still more does it rest with the American people—usually so quick to respond to high ideals—to ask its conscience whether any consideration, actual or conceivable, can justify it in refusal when Great Britain is willing—anxious—to do her share.

That such an alliance must some day come is, I believe, not questionable. That it has not already come is due only to the misunderstanding by each people of the character of the other. Primarily, the two peoples do not understand how closely akin—how of one kind—they are, how alike they are in their virtues, and how their failings are but the defects of the same inherited qualities, even though shaped to somewhat diverse manifestations by differences of environment. Two brothers seldom recognise their likeness one to the other, until either looks at the other beside a stranger. Members of one family do not easily perceive the family resemblance which they share; rather are they aware only of the individual differences. But strangers see the likeness, and in their eyes the differences often disappear. So Englishmen and Americans only come to a realisation of their resemblance when either compares the other critically with a foreign people. Foreigners, however, see the likeness when they look at the two together. And those foreigners who know only one of the peoples will sketch the character of that people so that it might be taken for a portrait of the other. In all essentials the characters are the same; in minor attributes only, such as exist between the individual members of any family, do they differ.

Not only does neither people understand with any clearness how like it is to the other, but each is under many misapprehensions—some trivial, some vital—in regard to the other's temperament and ways of life. These misapprehensions are the result chiefly of the geographical remoteness of the lands, so that intimate contact between anything like an appreciable portion of the two peoples has been impossible; and, when thus separated by so wide a sea, Great Britain has been too consumedly engrossed in the affairs of the world to be able to give much time or thought to the United States, while America has been too isolated from that world, too absorbed in her own affairs, to be able to look at England in anything like true perspective.

Arising thus from different causes, the errors of the two peoples in regard to each other have taken different forms. Great Britain, always at passes with a more or less hostile Europe, has never lost her original feeling of kinship with, or good-will towards, the United States. There has been no time when she would not gladly have improved her knowledge of, and friendship with, the other, had she at any time been free from the anxieties of the peril of war with one Power or another, from the burden of concern for her Empire in India, from the weight of her responsibilities in regard to Australia, South Africa, Egypt, and the various other parts of Britain over seas. Engrossed as she has been with things of immediate moment to her existence, she has been perforce compelled to take the good-will of the remote United States for granted, and to assume that there was no need to voice her own. Until at last she was awakened with a rudeness of awakening that shocked and staggered her.

For the United States had had no such constant burden of anxiety, no perpetual friction with other peoples, to keep her occupied. Rather, sitting aloof in her isolation she had looked upon all the Powers of Europe as actors in a great drama with which she had no other than a spectacular concern. Only of all the Powers, by the very accident of common origin, by the mere circumstances of the joint occupation of the continent, Great Britain alone has been constantly near enough to the United States to impinge at times upon her sphere of development, to rub against her, to stand in her way. Great Britain herself has hardly known that this was so. But it has had the effect to make Great Britain in the mind of the United States the one foreign Power most potentially hostile.

In aloofness and silence, ignorant of the world, the American people nursed its wrath and brooded over the causes of offence which have seemed so large to it, though so trivial or so unintentional on the part of England, till the minds of the majority of the people held nothing but ill-feeling and contempt in response to England's good-will towards them. And always the United States has had those at her elbow who were willing—nay, for their own interests, eager—to play upon her wounded feelings and to exaggerate every wrong and every slight, however small or imaginary, placed upon her by Great Britain.

Thus the two peoples not only misunderstand each other but they misunderstand each other in different ways. They look at each other from widely sundered points of view and in diverse spirits. The people of the United States dislike and distrust Great Britain. They cannot believe that Great Britain's good-will for them is sincere. The expressions of that good-will, neglected while the American people was comparatively weak and finding expression now when it is strong, the majority of Americans imagine to be no more than the voice of fear. That alone shows their ignorance of England—their obliviousness of the kinship of the peoples. The two are of one origin and each may take it for granted that neither will ever be afraid of the other—or of any other earthly Power. That is not one of the failings of the stock.

The American people has thus never attained to any right view of the British Empire. By the accident of the war which gave the nation birth, the name "British" became a name of reproach in American ears. They have never since been able to look at Great Britain save through the cross-lights of their own interests, which have distorted their vision, while there have always been those at hand poisoning the national mind against the English. So they think of the British Empire as a bloody and brutal thing: of her rule of India in particular as a rule of barbarity and cruel force. Of late years American writers have come to tell Americans the truth; namely, that if the power of Great Britain were to be wiped out to-morrow and all her monuments were to perish except only those that she has built in India, the historians of future generations, looking only to those monuments in India, would pronounce Great Britain to have been, of all the Powers that have held great Empire since the beginning of time, the largest benefactor to the human race. But of this the American people as a whole knows nothing. It only knows that sepoys were blown from the mouths of British guns. So Englishmen, know that negroes in the South are lynched.

And as the American people has formed no comprehension of the British Empire as a whole and is without any understanding of its spirit, so it has drawn for itself a caricature of the British character. As the Empire is brutal and sanguinary, so is the individual bullying and overbearing and coarse. The idea was originally inherited from England's old enemies in Europe. It was a reflection of the opinion of the French; but it has been confirmed by the frankness of criticism of English travellers of all things in the United States.

Americans do not recognise that by their own sensitiveness and anxiety for the judgment of others—a necessary, if morbid, result of their isolation and self-absorption—they invited the criticism, even if they did not excuse its occasional ill-breeding; nor has it occurred to them that the habit of outspoken criticism of all foreign things is a common inheritance of the two peoples and that they themselves are even more garrulously, if less bluntly—even more vaingloriously, if less arrogantly—frank in their habit of comment even than the English.

The same isolation and self-absorption as bred in them their sensitiveness to the opinions of others, made the Americans also unduly proud of such traits or accomplishments as strangers found to praise in them. This in itself might be good for a nation; but, so far as their understanding of Englishmen is concerned, it has unfortunately led them to suppose that those characteristics which they possess in so eminent a degree are proportionately lacking in the English character, which thereby incurs their contempt. Having been over-complimented on their own humour, they have determined that the Englishman is slow-witted, with no sense of fun—an opinion in itself so lacking in appreciation of its own absurdity as to be self-confounding. Too well assured of their own chivalrousness (a foible which they share with all peoples) they know the Englishman to be a domestic tyrant, incapable of true reverence of womanhood. Proud, not without reason, of their own form of government, wherein there is no room for a titled aristocracy, they delight in holding the peerage of Great Britain up to contempt (withal that there is a curious unconfessed strain of jealousy mingling therewith), and piecing together, like a child playing with bricks, the not too infrequent appearances of individual peers in the divorce or bankruptcy courts, they have constructed a fantastic image of the British aristocracy as a whole, wherein every member appears as either a *roué* or a spendthrift. Because they are—and have been so much told that they are—so full of push and energy themselves, they believe Englishmen to be ponderous and without enterprise; whereas if, instead of keeping their eyes and minds permanently intent on their own achievements, they had looked more abroad, they would have seen that, magnificent as has been the work which they have done in the upbuilding of their own nation and wonderful as is the fabric of their greatness, there has simultaneously been evoked out of chaos a British Empire, vaster than their own estate, and which is only not so near completion as their own structure in proportion as it is on a larger ground plan, inspired by larger ideas and involving greater (as well as infinitely more diffused) labour in its uprearing.

The statement of these facts involves no impugnment of American urbanity, American wit, American chivalry, or American enterprise. Only they are not so unique as Americans, in their isolation, conceive them to be. There are, in fact, others. It might not even be worth saying so much, if it were not that the belief in their uniqueness has necessarily resulted in American minds in a depreciation of the English character, which by so much helps to keep the two peoples estranged. Americans will be vastly more ready to believe in their English kinship, to like the English people, and to welcome a British alliance if they once get it into their heads that the English, as a nation, are just as fearless, just as chivalrous, no less fond of a joke or more depraved, nor much less enterprising or more careless of the feelings of others than themselves. That they think of Englishmen as they do to-day is not to be wondered at, and no blame attaches to them; for it is but a necessary result of causes which are easily seen. But the time has come when some effort to correct the errors in their vision is possible and desirable—not merely because they are unfair to Englishmen, which might be immaterial, and is no more than a fair exchange of discourtesies, but because the misunderstandings obstruct that good-will which would be such an untellable blessing, not only to the two peoples themselves, but to all the human race.

I am well aware that many American readers will say: "What is the man talking of? I do not think of Englishmen like that!" Of course you do not, excellent and educated reader—especially if you have travelled much in Great Britain or if you are a member of those refined and cultured classes (what certain American democrats would call the "silk-stocking element") which constitute the select and entirely charming society of most of the older cities of the Atlantic seaboard as well as of some of the larger communities throughout the country. If, belonging to those classes, you do not happen to have made it your business, either as a politician or a newspaper man, to be in close touch with the real sentiments of the masses of the country as a whole, you scarcely believe that anybody in America—except a few Irishmen and Germans—does think like that. If, however, you happen to be a good "mixer" in politics or have enjoyed the austerities of an apprenticeship in journalism,—if in fact you know the sentiments of your countrymen, I need not argue with you. Nor perhaps are very many Americans of any class conscious of holding all these views at once. None the less, if a composite photograph could be made of the typical Englishman as he is figured in the minds of, let us say, twenty millions of the American people—excluding negroes, Indians, and foreigners—the resultant figure would be little dissimilar from the sketch which I have made.

And I have said that, in holding these ideas, the Americans do but make a fair exchange of discourtesies; for the Englishman has likewise queer notions of the typical American. There is always this vast difference, however, that the Englishman is predisposed to like the American. In spite of his ignorance he feels a great—and, in view of that ignorance, an almost inexplicable—good-will for him. But it is not inexplicable, for once more the causes of his misapprehensions are easily traced.

First, there has been the eternal pre-occupation of the English people with the affairs of other parts of the world. When Great Britain has been so inextricably involved with the policies of all the earth that almost any day news might come from Calcutta, from Berlin, from St. Petersburg, from Pekin, or Teheran, or from almost any point in Asia, Africa, or Australia, which would shake the Empire to its foundation, how could the people spare time to become intimately acquainted with the United States? Of coarse Englishmen talk of the "State of Chicago," and—as I heard an English peasant not long ago—of "Yankee earls."

During all these years individual Americans have come to England in large numbers and have been duly noted and observed; but what the people of any nation notices in the casually arriving representatives of any other is not the points wherein the visitors resemble themselves, but the points of difference. In the case of Americans coming to England the fundamental traits are all resemblances and therefore escape notice, while only the differences—which by that very fact stand proclaimed as non-essentials—attract attention. So it is that the English people, having had acquaintance with a number of typical New Englanders, have drawn their conclusion as to the universality of one strong nasal American accent; they think the American people garrulously outspoken in criticism, with a rather offensive boastfulness, without any consciousness that precisely that same trait in themselves, in a slightly different form, is one of the chief causes why Englishmen are not conspicuously popular in any European country. From peculiarities of dress and manner which are not familiar to him in the product of his own public schools and universities, the Englishman has been inclined to think that the American people is not, even in its "better classes," a population of gentlemen.

Moreover, many Englishmen go to the United States—the vast majority for a stay of a few days or weeks, or a month or two—and they tell their friends, or the public at large in print, all about America and its people. It is not given to every one to be able, in the course of a few weeks or a month or two, to see below the surface indications down to the root-traits of a people—a feat which becomes of necessity the more difficult when those root-traits are one's own root-traits and the fundamental traits of one's own people at home, while on the surface are all manner of queer, confusing dazzlements of local peculiarities which jump to the stranger's vision and set him blinking. Yet more difficult does the feat appear when it is realised that the American people is scattered over a continent some three thousand miles across—so that San Francisco is little nearer to New York than is Liverpool—and that the section of the people with whom the Englishman necessarily comes first and, unless he penetrates both far and deep into the people, most closely in contact is precisely that class from which it is least safe to draw conclusions as to the thoughts, manners, or politics of the people as a whole. Therefore it is that one of the most acute observers informed Europe that in America "a gentleman had only to take to politics to become immediately *déclassé*"—which, speaking of the politics of the country as a whole, is purely absurd. The visiting Englishman has generally found the whole sphere of municipal and local politics a novel field to him and has naturally been interested. Probing it, he comes upon all manner of tales of corruption and wickedness. He does not see that the body of American "politics," as the word is understood in England, is moderately free from these taints, but he tells the world of the corruption in that sphere of politics which he has studied merely because it does not exist at home and is new to him; and all the world knows that American politics are indescribably corrupt.

Similarly the visiting European goes into polite society and is amazed at the peculiar qualities of some of the persons whom he meets there. He tells stories about those peculiar people, but the background of the society, against which these people stood out so clearly, a background which is so much like his own at home, almost escapes his notice or is too uninteresting and familiar to talk about. There is no one to explain fully to the English people that while in England educated society keeps pretty well to itself, there are in America no hurdles—or none that a lively animal may not easily leap—to keep the black sheep away from the white, or the white from straying off anywhere among the black, so that a large part of the English people has imbibed the notion that there are really no refined or cultured circles in the United States.

Whenever a financial fraud of a large size is discovered in America, the world is told of it, just as certainly as it is told when an English peer finds his way to the divorce court; but nobody expounds to the nations the excellence of the honourable lives which are led by most American millionaires, any more than the world is kept informed of the drab virtue of the majority of the British aristocracy. Wherefore the English people have come to think of American business ethics as being too often of the shadiest; whereas they ought on reflection to be aware that only in most exceptional cases can great or permanent individual commercial success be won by fraud, and that nothing but fundamental honesty will serve as the basis for a great national trade such as the United States has built up.

Visiting Englishmen are bewildered by the strange types of peoples whom they see upon the streets and by the talk which they hear of "German elements" and "French elements" and "Scandinavian elements" in the population. But they do not as a rule see that these various "elements," when in the first generation of citizenship, are but a fringe upon the fabric of society, and when in the second or third generation they have a tendency to become entirely swallowed up and to merge all their national characteristics by absorption in the Anglo-Saxon stock; and that apart from and unheeding all these irrelevant appendages, the great American people goes on its way, homogeneous, unruffled, and English at bottom.

Finally Englishmen read American newspapers and, not understanding the different relation in which those newspapers stand to the people, they compare with them the normal English papers and draw inferences which are quite unjust. Similar inferences no less unjust may be drawn from hearing the speech of a certain number of well-to-do Americans, belonging, as Englishmen opine, to the class of "gentlemen."

These misunderstandings do less harm to the Englishman than to the American, inasmuch as the Englishman has that predisposition to national cordiality which the American has not. But, though the Englishman's mistakes do not influence his good-will to the United States, though he himself attaches no serious importance to them, his utterance of them is taken seriously by the Americans themselves and does not tend to the promotion of international good feeling. Therefore it is that it is no less desirable that English misconceptions of the United States should be corrected than it is that the American people should be brought to a juster appreciation of the British character and Empire.

It is in America, doubtless, that missionary work is most needed, inasmuch as all England would at any minute welcome an American alliance with enthusiasm; while in the United States any public suggestion of such an alliance never fails to provoke immediate and vehement protest. It is true that that protest issues primarily from the Irish and German elements; and it may seem absurd that the American people as a whole should suffer itself to be swayed in a matter of so national a character by a minority which is not only comparatively unimportant in numbers, but which the true American majority regards with some irritability as distinctly alien.

There are a large number of constituencies in the United States, however, where the Irish and German votes, individually or in combination, hold the balance of power in the electorate, and not only must many individual members of Congress hesitate to antagonise so influential a section of their constituents, but it is even questionable whether the united and harmonious action of those two elements might not, under certain conditions, be able to unseat a sufficient number of such individual members as to change the political complexion of one or both of the Houses of Congress, and even, in a close election, of the Administration itself. Nor is it necessary to repeat again that when the anti-British outcry is raised, though primarily by a minority and an alien minority, it finds a response in the breasts of a vast number of good Americans in whom the traditional dislike of England, though latent, still persists solely by reason of misapprehension and misunderstandings. Therefore it is that so many of the best Americans, who in their hearts know well how desirable an alliance with England would be, are content to deprecate its discussion and to say that things are well enough as they are; though again I say that things are never well enough so long as they might be better. However desirable such an alliance may be, however much to the benefit of the nation, it would, they say, be bad politics to bring it forward as a party question. And to bring it forward without its becoming from the outset a party question would be plainly impossible.

But would it be bad politics? Can it ever, in the long run, be bad politics to champion any cause which is great and good? It might be that it would be difficult for an individual member of Congress to come forward as the active advocate of a British alliance and not lose his seat; but in the end, the man who did it, or the party which did it, would surely win. When two peoples have a dislike of each other based on intimate knowledge by each of the other's character, to rise as the champion of their alliance might be hopeless; but when two peoples are held apart only by misunderstanding and by lack of perception of the boons that alliance between them would bring, it can need but courage and earnestness to carry conviction to the people and to bring success.

In such a cause there is one man in America to whom one's thoughts of necessity turn; and he is hampered by being President of the United States. Perhaps when his present term of office is over Mr. Roosevelt, instead of seeking the honourable seclusion which so often engulfs ex-Presidents, will find ready to his hand a task more than worthy of the man who was instrumental in bringing peace to Russia and Japan,—a task in the execution of which it would be far from being a disadvantage that he is as cordially regarded in Germany as he is in England and has himself great good-will towards the German Empire. Any movement on the part of Great Britain in company with any European nation could only be regarded by Germany as a conspiracy against herself: nothing that England or France or Japan—or any Englishman, Frenchman, or Japanese—could say or do would be received otherwise than with suspicion and resentment. But, after all, the good of humanity must come before any aspirations on the part of the German Empire, and it is the American people which must speak, though it speaks through the mouth of its President. If the American people makes up its mind that its interest and its duty alike dictate that it should join hands with England in the cause of peace, neither Germany nor any Power can do otherwise than acquiesce.

It is no novelty, either in the United States or in other countries, for considerations of temporary political expediency to stand in the way of the welfare of the people, nor is there any particular reason why an American politician should attach any importance to the desires of England. But we find ourselves again confronted with the same old question, whether the American people as a whole, who have often shown an ability to rise above party politics, can find any excuse for setting any consideration, either of individual or partisan interest, above the welfare of all the world. Yet once more: It is for Americans individually to ask their consciences whether any considerations whatever, actual or conceivable, justify them in withholding from all humanity the boon which it is in their power, and theirs alone, to give,—the blessing of Universal and Perpetual Peace.

And yet, when this much has been said, it seems that so little has been told. It was pointed out, in one of the earlier chapters, how the people of each country in looking at the people of the other are apt to see only the provoking little peculiarities of speech or manner on the surface, overlooking the strength of the characteristics which underlie them. So, in these pages, it seems that we, in analysing the individual traits, have failed to get any vision of the character of either people as a whole. It is the trees again which obscure the view of the forest.

We have arrived at no general impression of the British Empire or of the British people. We have shown nothing of the majesty of that Empire; of its dignity in the eyes of a vast variety of peoples; of the high ambitions (unspoken, after the way of the English, but none the less earnest), which have inspired and still inspire it; of its maintenance of the standards of justice and fair dealing; of its tolerance or the patience with which it strives to guide the darkened peoples towards the light. Nothing has been said of the splendid service which the Empire receives from the sons of the Sea Wife; yet certainly the world has seen nothing comparable to the Colonial services of Great Britain, of which the Indian Civil Service stands as the type.

Nor have we said anything of the British people, with its steadfastness, in spite of occasional frenzies, its sanity, and its silent acceptance, and almost automatic practice, of a high level of personal and political morality. Above all we have seen nothing of the sweetness of the home life of the English country people, whereof the more well-to-do lead lives of wide sympathies, much refinement, and great goodness; while the poor under difficult conditions, hold fast to a self-respecting decency, little changed since the days when from among them, there went out the early settlers to the New England over seas, which never fails, notwithstanding individual weaknesses, to win the regard of one who lives among them.

So of the American people; we have conveyed no adequate impression of the manly optimism, the courageous confidence in the ultimate virtue of goodness and sound principles, on which the belief in the destiny of their own country is based. The nation has prospered by its virtues. Every page of their history preaches to the people that it is honesty and faith and loyalty which succeed, and they believe in their future greatness because they believe themselves to possess, and hope to hold to, those virtues as in the past.

It may be that, living in the silences and solitudes of the frontier and the wilderness, they have found the greater need of ready speech when communication has offered. It may be that the mere necessity of planning together the framework of their society and of building up their State out of chaos has imposed on them the necessity of more outspokenness. Certainly they have discarded, or have not assumed, the reticence of the modern English of England; and much of this freedom of utterance Europeans misinterpret, much (because the fashion of it is strange to themselves) they believe to be insincere. In which judgments they are quite wrong. The American people are profoundly sincere and intensely in earnest.

Since the establishment of the Republic, in the necessity of civilizing a continent, in the breathless struggle of the Civil War, in the rapidity with which society has been compelled to organize itself, in the absorption and assimilation of the continuous stream of foreign immigrants, the people have always been at grips with problems of immediate, almost desperate urgency; and they have never lost, or come near to losing, heart or courage. They have learned above all things the lesson of the efficacy of work. They have acquired the habit of action. Self-reliance has been bred in them. They know that in the haste of the days of ferment abuses grew up and went unchecked; and they know that in that same haste they missed some of the elegancies which a more leisurely and easier life might have given opportunity to acquire. But for a generation back, they have been earnestly striving to eradicate those abuses and to lift themselves, their speech, their manners, their art and literature to, at least, a level with the highest. It has been impossible in these pages (it would perhaps be impossible in any pages) to give any unified picture of this national character with its activity, its self-reliance, its belief in the homely virtues and its earnest ambition to make the best of itself. But of the future of a people with such a character there need be no misgivings, and Americans are justified in the confidence in their destiny.

What is needed is that these two peoples holding, with similar steadfastness, to the same high ideals, pushing on such closely parallel lines in advance of all other peoples, should come to see more clearly how near of kin they are and how much the world loses by any lack of unison in their effort.

Once more let me ask readers to turn back and read again the paragraphs from other pens with which this book is introduced.

APPENDIX.
(See Chapter III., pp. 81, *sqq.*)

This book was almost ready for the press when Dr. Albert Shaw's collection of essays was published under the title of *The Outlook for the Average Man*. Dr. Shaw is one of America's most lucid thinkers and he contributes what I take to be a new (though once stated an obviously true) explanation of what I have spoken of as the homogeneousness of the American people. The West, as we all know, was largely settled from the East. That is to say that a family or a member of a family in New York moved westward to Illinois, thence in the next generation to Minnesota, thence again to Montana or Oregon. A similar movement went on down the whole depth of the United States, families established in North Carolina migrating first to Kentucky, then to Ohio, so to Texas, and finally on to California. All parts of the country therefore have, as the nucleus of their population, people of precisely the same stock, habits, and ways of thought. The West was settled "not by radiation of influence from the older centres, but by the actual transplantation of the men and women." Dr. Shaw proceeds:

"England is not large in area and the people are generally regarded as homogeneous in their insularity. But as a matter of fact the populations of the different parts of England are scarcely at all acquainted in any other part. Thus the Yorkshireman would only by the rarest chance have relatives living in Kent or Cornwall. The intimacy between North Carolina and Missouri, for example, is incomparably greater than that between one part of England and another part. In like manner, the people of the North of France know very little of those of the South of France, or even of those living in districts not at all remote. Exactly the same thing is true of Italy and Germany, and is characteristic of almost every other European land. As compared with other countries, we in America are literally a band of brothers."—*The Outlook for the Average Man*, pages 104, 105.